The Byrons
and Trevanions

The Byrons
and Trevanions

A.L. Rowse

Weidenfeld and Nicolson
London

First published in Great Britain by
Weidenfeld and Nicolson
91 Clapham High Street
London sw4

ISBN 0 297 77548 0

Printed in Great Britain by
Butler & Tanner Ltd, Frome and London

To
Rosalie Glyn Grylls (Lady Mander)
in constant affection and faithful Cornishry

Contents

Illustrations

Acknowledgements

I should like to thank the following for help of various kinds in the research for and writing of this book: the Morgan Library, New York, and its kindly officials: the Cornwall County Record Office and its archivist, Mr P.L. Hull; Mr Julian Williams of Caerhays Castle and Sir John Summerson, who enabled me to see that enchanted place anew with his instructed eyes; Mr Hugh Trevanion, whose ancestor built it; the Byron Society and, in particular, Mr Robin Byron for the portrait of Sophia Trevanion; the Vicar of Caerhays for permission to photograph the Trevanion aisle in his church, and Mr Charles Woolf who took the photographs; Mr I.C. Cook, and Mr Andrew Festing of Sotheby's, for the hitherto unknown portrait of Admiral Byron; Professor Jack Simmons for lending me books on my remote Cornish headland, and Miss Joyce Batty for help with research.

Trenarren,   A.L. ROWSE
St Austell.

Prelude

FAMILY, CLAN OR TRIBE is the living unit of society; the indivi-
dual, even an outstanding one, is a part of it and in part takes
his colouring from it. So family history, though a somewhat
neglected form, is of the first importance, as Gibbon saw; bio-
graphies, so much more popular and to the fore today – they
make easier writing – should be seen to rise properly out of the
family background.

It is all the more difficult to write a double family history,
to illustrate the mixing of stocks, their intricate cross-con-
nexions, their mutual fertilization, the subtleties of inheritance.
With the Byrons and Trevanions we are given a fascinating
example of the process. Living for centuries at opposite ends
of the country – North-West and eastern Midlands against
extreme South-West – with no common meeting-ground
(except occasionally in Parliament), in three generations in the
eighteenth and beginning of the nineteenth centuries there happened a whole series of Byron–Trevanion marriages, besides
their extra-matrimonial intermixings.

A spotlight is thrown on these affairs by the fabulous career
of the poet Byron, whose genius was the upshot of these hidden
genes. He was in love with his half-sister Augusta, who was
married to her cousin, Colonel Leigh: they were all three
grandchildren of Admiral Byron and Sophia Trevanion. Of their
children, Mad Jack – the poet's father – was in love with his
full sister Fanny, who responded. The Trevanions' part in all
this is rather overlaid by their having been mostly women, and
their name submerged in marriage. But no one today will

suppose that the women's part in family life is less important than
the men's. Yet people are as unaware of the Trevanion element
in the poet Byron's make-up as they are of the significant Pen-
rose inheritance in Matthew Arnold's.

On his mother's side Byron was a Scottish Gordon; on the
paternal side was his blue-stocking, scribbling grandmother,
Sophia Trevanion, with her marked Cornish temperament,
mercurial, abnormally sensitive, all up and down. In no sense
was Byron very English – only partly, by education and culture:
one might almost use the word 'brain-washed', if very hap-
hazardly, at Harrow and Cambridge. (He was bitterly disappointed at not going to Oxford: it is amusing to speculate
how things would have turned out if he had gone to Christ
Church, as he wished: the college hadn't a room for him!)

Anyone can understand the rational elements of education
and culture; it is a more subtle matter to appreciate the nature
and character, the *differentiae*, of temperament – evident
enough, visible enough to us all, yet hardly susceptible of analysis. A man's temperament arises from the deeper levels of his
nature, the sub-rational, the subconscious, the unconscious. He
is often unconscious of its operations himself – though its urges
are more powerful and demanding than those of reason. It is
not my business here to analyse the nature and meaning of 'temperament' – we can all recognize it – though we may claim
that to appreciate its importance is in keeping with the findings
of modern psychology.

The business of the historian is rather to describe and illustrate concretely – in any case, it is subtler and more satisfactory
than abstract, theoretical analysis, less liable to lead one astray.
An incisive writer of genius, Flannery O'Connor, brings home
to us that it is in moments of crisis, emergency or stress, that
the underlying character most authentically reveals itself and
comes to the surface. We can all recognize that to be true,
though it is given to few to express that truth so powerfully and
dramatically as in her stories.

Many such moments of illumination occur in the family his-
tories of Byrons and Trevanions, still more in their extremely
temperamental story when interwoven. With portrayal and
such revelation we may be well content.

I

The Byron Family

THOUGH THE WORLD associates the Byrons with Newstead
Abbey in Nottinghamshire – because of our overwhelming
memory of the poet – they were in Lancashire earlier and longer
than they were at Newstead. For centuries they were seated
at Clayton, now swallowed up in the sombre suburbs of Manchester, along the old main road thence to Ashton-under-Lyne.*
Unexpectedly, and mercifully, something of their ancient home
has survived, though overborne by Butterfield's Victorian
church of Holy Cross, and overwhelmed by the characteristic
cooling towers of a twentieth-century power-station.

A recognizable fragment of the old house within its moat
remains: a two-storey, timber-constructed range, relic of an
original quadrangle, for a chapel existed in the north-west
corner up to the reign of Queen Anne. A stone bridge carries
over the moat, crossed by so many generations of Byrons going
about their business in the hundred of Salford, on sheriff's tourn
(for they were often sheriffs of the county), on service to the
Crown or the duchy of Lancaster (for they were always loyal), or
on private forays (for they were usually energetic and aggressive).

The Byrons were a conquering Norman family, who
apparently go back to the Conquest itself: they appear in
Domesday Book as holding scattered lands in the North and
northern Midlands. Their name is said to be derived from
Buron in Fresnoy le Vieux, and is evidently cognate with Biron,

* Pevsner's guide to *South Lancashire*, for example, mentions Humphrey
Chetham's brief tenure of Clayton, but nothing of the Byrons who were there
for so long.

as it is often spelt (Berowne in Shakespeare's *Love's Labour's Lost*). Prolific, demographically vigorous, they came by Clayton in the usual way, through marriage to an heiress of the Claytons. Here they settled.

Through the Middle Ages we find them adding field to field, manor to manor, building up their inheritance mainly in Lancashire, though they had lands elsewhere. Shortly after their coming into Clayton we find them acquiring the neighbouring townships of Droylesden and Failsworth. In the reign of Edward I they got lands in Butterworth through marriage to a well-heeled widow. The Byron Cartulary, or 'Black Book of Clayton', in the Bodleian records their progress. In 1230 Richard de Byron had the king's protection on going overseas to serve under the earl of Chester. In 1250 Sir John de Byron acquired, with a wife, lands in Royton and in the enormous parish of Rochdale, which opened still more promising prospects to the future.

Two generations later, in poor Edward II's reign, a Sir Richard de Byron got the grant of free warren (i.e. licence to preserve game), over all his demesne lands in Clayton, Butterworth and Royton. He also acquired various lands in Oldham, Huddersfield, and more in Rochdale. This man's son, a Sir John, fought under Edward III at famous Crécy (1346), and the hardly less renowned Siege of Calais, and in later life was granted a convenient licence for divine service to be held in his own oratory at Clayton. His brother, Sir Richard, notably increased the estate by his marriage to the heiress of Colwick, on the River Trent, which effectively brought them south to Nottinghamshire, for in the next generation or two they resided at Colwick rather than at Clayton. However, in 1415 – early in Henry V's reign – this Lady Byron complained to the lord chancellor that her son, Sir John, had forcibly carried her from Colwick to Lancashire, where he made her promise not to alienate her lands.

This son, Sir John, married a Booth, of that Lancashire family, and had three sons and five daughters. He made a grant of his lands to his grandson, son of his son Nicholas, sheriff till 1460 and knighted in 1461, during the readeption of Henry VI – evidently a supporter of the royal house of Lancaster, as most of the country was. This grandson, another John, was the ultimate heir to all the Byron lands, but, dying without issue, was succeeded by his brother Nicholas, who was made a knight of the Bath at the marriage of Prince Arthur in 1501. He would not have been old when he died in 1504. It was his son, yet another Sir John who succeeded, and whose personality is the first to come into the light of day, with the Reformation and Henry VIII's Reformation Parliament. He is usually described as 'of Colwick', where he chiefly resided; and he it was who made the most of the chances offered to a member of the Reformation Parliament to buy Newstead Abbey. Thereafter the Byron interests came to be concentrated in Nottinghamshire; they left their old home at Clayton, which was purchased by the successful and philanthropic Manchester merchant, Humphrey Chetham, founder of his hospital and library.

In the next generation, the reign of Elizabeth, a bastard son became head of the family, 'Little Sir John with the Great Beard'. Encumbered with debts and many children, he sold most of the Lancashire estate to concentrate on Newstead and the delights of Sherwood Forest.

So much for the building-up, and dispersal, of lands, the chops and changes of estate – let us turn back now to the evidence that remains of service, the snail-tracks in the records that throw even a glimmer of light on the activities of these people out of the surrounding dark.

In 1253 Geoffrey de Byron was granted protection (i.e. from suits and processes against him) in the following of the king, Henry III, going to Gascony, for as long as he was in his service. Four years later he received similar protection in the king's service, serving in Wales. Meanwhile Richard de Byron had killed a man, by misadventure as it was reported. Inquisition followed, to know whether it really was 'a sudden chance, which human diligence could not have foreseen, or of malice aforethought'. We see the conscience of remote medievals at work, and the sense of responsibility in the difficulties even of their administration of justice.

In the last years of Edward I's reign, darkened by his overambitious campaigns to reduce Scotland, we find John de Byron busily employed. In 1303 Byron and two others were to select 1,600 footmen from the West Riding and conduct them to Roxburgh: the invasion of Scotland was on. From the Court at Stirling Castle the following year an appeal touching someone's death in Lancashire was committed to Byron and one other to hear and decide (*oyer* and *terminer*). In 1306 he and another were made keepers of the temporalities of the see of York, until William Grenville was made archbishop, when they were to be restored. The expenses of this grievous war had to be met. Byron was one of the four for Yorkshire to collect the 30th and 20th granted by the counties and towns, and to deliver to the exchequer 'on the morrow of the Purification, a week after Holy Trinity, and the morrow of All Souls', according to the endearing phrases of the Middle Ages.

Meanwhile, the dying king and his Court had moved back over the border to rose-red Lanercost, whence another commission of *oyer* and *terminer* was issued to John and others to try a case at York. In 1307, as sheriff, he was to pardon a fellow who had killed in self-defence. Next, he was on the commission, for Lancashire, to keep the Merchant Statutes, the currency of the same value, etc., during the king's absence, evidently in Scotland. Two years later followed a commission touching prises, and various other commissions recorded for 1313 and 1315 – all in Lancashire: evidently he was based in Clayton in his last years. For before Easter 1318 he was dead; his widow married a Strickland. He had been a trusted servant of the Crown in the North.

We find his son, Sir Richard – the one who got free warren over all his lands – serving on various commissions in the West Riding and Lincolnshire, where the Byrons had interests. In 1380, early in Richard II's reign, complaint was made against Sir John of assaulting the sheriff of Lincolnshire and hunting within his warren. Next year we find the Sir Richard who had married the heiress of Colwick in the commissions of the peace for Nottinghamshire for the first time, as thereafter the Byrons continued to be for some time, along with Lancashire. This year, 1381, was that of the Peasants' Revolt: the commission enjoined that the justices were to 'arrest unlawful assemblies throughout the country'. Evidently Sir Richard and his wife resided at Colwick, for complaint was made that he had closed off pools and mills along the Trent, to the hindrance of navigation to Nottingham and damage to people there. In June 1397 he died; John, his son and heir, was aged only ten: his wardship and marriage were granted to a Lancashire neighbour, Ralph Radcliffe.

This son John, who carried off his mother to make sure that she did not alienate her lands, is however known as 'of Clayton'. He served as knight of the shire for Lancashire in the Parliaments of 1421 and 1429. His son, Sir Nicholas, also made a marriage within the county. They were both sheriffs of it over many years, the first from 1437 to 1449, the second until 1460. Like all the gentry of Lancashire they were supporters of Henry VI and the royal house of Lancaster. It is an indication of the movement of the family interests south that he served as MP for Nottinghamshire in the Parliament of 1477–8. And he received his reward there from Henry VII, being made constable of Nottingham Castle and warden of Sherwood Forest. Knighted by the king in 1486 'as he came from York', Sir John died in 1484.

His brother, Sir Nicholas, who succeeded and is known as 'of Colwick and Clayton', made a Lincolnshire marriage. The son, the Henrician character who bought Newstead, it is therefore convenient to call the first Sir John of Newstead. Many snail-tracks in State papers remain to bring this vigorous fellow alive. In 1512 he supplies ten soldiers for Henry VIII's first French war, and sails on the *Gabriel Royal* (captain: Sir William Trevelyan). He serves on many of the royal commissions for Nottinghamshire, on that of the peace, of array (i.e. to muster men for war), and to seize the goods of Scots, the allies of France. (In a Lancashire church, at Middleton, we find mementoes of Flodden in a stained-glass window, with the names of those from the parish who fought there.) Sir John was rewarded for service with a long lease of the manor of Parlethorp.

In 1519 he was made an esquire of the body – Henry VIII's large body – and chief steward of the lordship of Stoke Bardolph, Notts, one of the four foresters of Sherwood. Next year he was at the Field of the Cloth of Gold, in attendance upon Henry at his interview with the French king. In 1523 and 1524 he had two unpopular assignments as collector of the subsidy for his county, and the loan for the second of Henry's wars with France. He was rewarded with a lease of the manor of Bolsover, eight coal pits, a clay pit, and the site of the castle and park, on favourable terms. Two years later he was further rewarded by a grant of the manor and castle of Clipstone. The following year he was returned, with Sir John Markham, as knight of the shire to the historic Reformation Parliament, which broke with Rome and ended monasticism.

In 1530 he was appointed to the commission to inquire into the fallen Wolsey's possessions in Nottinghamshire, where the see of York owned a great deal, including Southwell. Three years later Sir John appears in Cromwell's minatory *Memoranda*, for misdemeanours in hunting in Sherwood Forest. Nothing deleterious happened; in the same year Sir John was one of the attendants on pregnant Anne Boleyn at her coronation banquet in Westminster Hall. After Henry VIII's various matrimonial misadventures we find Sir John one of a similar retinue to receive Anne of Cleves, Henry's 'Flanders mare'.

Let us retrace our steps from these public appointments to watch the Byrons' personal affairs as they are set down, from the time of the family's removal south, in the records of the borough of Nottingham. We learn more about the Sir Richard who married heiress Joan, of Colwick, and of his obstruction of the River Trent there. He had diverted the water into a trench to work his mill at Over Colwick; he had filled the former course with earth, fixed piles, planted willows and made a weir. At the octave of Holy Trinity, in the summer of 1392, Sir Richard and his wife were cited before Richard II at Nottingham, and pleaded the right of Joan's Colwick ancestors by grant from Edward I. Sir Richard pleaded that only part of the water from the Trent had been diverted. It was ordered that impediments be removed and the weir cast down.

A century later, in mid-August 1485, Richard III was concentrating his army at Nottingham to meet the challenge of Henry Tudor and his followers, who were gathering against the king who had made away with his nephews in the Tower. On 20 August Richard reached Leicester, to march forth on the 21st, and receive his come-uppance at Bosworth on the 22nd. The day was soon over – only Richard's cronies would fight for him; he felt himself betrayed, as indeed he was. Most of his large army stood on their arms and would not fight for the man who had turned the people's stomachs – for even in the

Wars of the Roses one did not kill children in their beds – and the Lancashire forces under the Stanleys decided the issue against the king. On the day of Bosworth, 22 August 1485, the corporation of Nottingham treated John Byron to a gallon of red wine and a gallon of claret: he and his companions must have been thirsty after a hot day. On 26 January the following year he was received with a pottle of sweet wine and a pottle of red (cost 12d); and on 10 April with three pottles (cost 15d).

This John did not live long to enjoy his knighthood, dying in 1489. In 1501 a gold signet ring of Byron's brother was ordered to be destroyed, brother Nicholas being present; *his* son John required the mayor to have it recorded: the arms stood the contrary way in wax. This son John, the heir, along with Master Pierrepont, was greeted with a gallon of red wine in 1503; while on 10 January 1504, a jolly breakfast – provided by Goodwife Ridgely – was eaten in the chapel on the south side of St Mary's church by the mayor, Byron, Pierrepont and others. That year John succeeded to his inheritance and had a long run for his money.

In 1521 Byron, with Henry Willoughby, John Markham and other Nottinghamshire neighbours, was granted the benefit of a papal indulgence – not long before such things were put out of use by Parliament. Willoughby appears again, consuming ale at Nottingham 'as he came home from my Lady Byron's', on a November day in 1523. In 1530 the corporation treated her ladyship to a pottle of wine at the castle and later provided a gallon for her and 'Mistress Mayoress and her sisters', i.e. aldermen's wives, which they drank at Dalderbury's. On Michaelmas day 1539 Sir John's minstrel received the goodly reward of 12d, doubtless for the entertainment he gave. St Anne's Well in the vicinity had been the property of Newstead Abbey (really a priory), which Sir John purchased in 1540. There were traditional jollifications there on Black Monday, i.e. Easter Monday; in 1541 his keepers there received 3s 4d, in 1558, 5s (inflation had progressed).

Sir John was on friendly terms with the Rutland family at Belvoir Castle – as he was with other neighbours who have left no such rewarding papers. In 1539 his servant carried a hake over as a present; a couple of years later Lady Byron was visiting at Belvoir, with Lady Westmorland and the local bishop. At

Christmas Sir John sent a doe from Sherwood Forest over for their festivities. Next month a servant 'rode all night to bring my Lady a fat doe that was sent to Austen Porter's daughter's marriage'. (A mark, 3s 4d, was the reward, or tip, on each occasion.) We find the earl next year considering Sir John's queasy stomach: 5d paid Roger Hall's wife for ale, 'bought for Sir John Byron because he could drink no beer'. In September 1552 'my Lord rode a-hunting to Sir John Byron', as no doubt on other occasions which have left no trace. At New Year 1553 Sir John's man brought over two does, and received 5s.

The Dissolution of the Monasteries and the overdue reform of the Church opened up marvellous opportunities for the governing class, and many were those all over the country who took advantage of it. In the backward North there was a reaction against the dynamic drive from London and the progressive South and East. In Lincolnshire and Yorkshire the peasantry, led by reactionary gentry and clergy, broke into rebellion, the Pilgrimage of Grace, which had its repercussions in Lancashire. When the peasantry rose to support the monasteries, Henry Byron was among those who did not rally to the earl of Derby to support law and order. Sir John Byron, head of the family, did so. Derby sent him and others on from Whalley, where there was resistance, to Furness to take the abbey into charge and see that nothing was embezzled until the king's orders arrived. Henry's personal instructions were to string up the abbot and the ringleaders who had opposed the nation's decision in Parliament, but spare ordinary folk who had been misled, while enforcing the lesson on them. It seems that Byron and his companions took the surrender of Furness. The monastic receiver of Whalley became vicar of Blackburn; he resigned that in Queen Mary's reign to become chaplain to Sir John Byron, who remained a Catholic.

Sir John took his opportunity, however, to buy delectable Newstead, the priory of Augustinian canons founded by Henry II in the shady depths of Sherwood. To raise the purchase price, some £810, he needed to sell some of his lands in Lancashire. In return, the grant recites what he got: the church, steeple and churchyard of Newstead; lands and a water-mill in Papplewick; the common at Ravenshead and Gighill in the forest. In addition, the manor and priory possessions in Papplewick, with

the rectory (i.e. the greater tithes) and advowson (i.e. presentation to the living); also the grange of Normanton, of the late
priory of Haverholme. Byron had to provide a chaplain, a mere
vicar, for Papplewick, a pittance of 53s 4d a year, and pay a
Crown rent of £4 10s. Sir John had a pretty good bargain, but
perhaps his manifold service was taken into account.

The church would be already unroofed, since the king was
seizing all the lead he could to arm, equip and fortify the
country with all the castles and forts he was constructing around
the coasts. 'From prayer to power' might have been his motto:
the country was doubled and trebled in strength, militarily and
navally, when Henry faced France alone – with its size three
times and its population four times that of England – in his
third French war, 1543–6.

Many monasteries – which for the most part had outlived
their usefulness, let alone their vocation – became the seats of
the expanding gentry, which was strongly reinforced thereby.
On scores of sites which had once housed communities of passive
monks, active families now took their place, sometimes new
men, or younger sons, cultivating the soil, pushing ahead, making the most of their opportunities. The Byrons were an old
family, making the most of theirs. They followed the usual plan
of allowing the monastic church to fall into ruin and settled
themselves comfortably in the prior's lodgings and such
adjacent buildings as could be conveniently converted.

Thus based, in that beautiful countryside, commons and
warrens around him for game, Sherwood Forest with its
delights surrounding him, Sir John was well placed to pursue
an active and busy life. He was a trusted servant of the Crown,
and from this time forth we find him a leading figure in Nottinghamshire. He regularly serves on the commissions of the
peace, on commissions of assize for the Midland circuit, and
is much relied on in military matters, recruiting men and super-
vising musters. For 1542–3 he was sheriff of Nottinghamshire
and Derby. In September 1542 he was appointed one of the
captains, with six more, who went under the king – evidently
with the Scottish war in view, which culminated in the rout
of Solway Moss. Next month he was paid coat-and-conduct
money for himself, two captains, three petty captains and fifty
men he had raised, from Colwick to Newcastle – a distance of

120 miles. Larger payments followed for a contingent of 270 foot and 30 archers on horseback, serving for twenty days, and for leading 300 men back from Ridingburn in Scotland to Colwick.

In March 1544 he wrote to Hertford, Queen Jane Seymour's brother, commanding and laying waste in Scotland for the irate king, baulked of his sensible desire to unite the countries by marrying the infant Mary Stuart to his son Edward. Byron reported that he had sent 200 to serve under Hertford's command, including ten men of Richard Lee, 'who is of my learned counsel', and five of another servant of his – both from Cheshire. Next year Byron was appointed to go into France with the king, ageing, swollen, obese, but indomitable as ever.

In 1551, during the inflation that afflicted Edward VI's reign, Sir John served on the county commission investigating the enhancing of corn prices and victuals, with power to apprehend and punish offenders. Two years later he was a commissioner to inquire into church goods, to compare them with the inventories – a considerable leakage took place in every county at this time when the going (for the gentry) was good. In the same year he got the keepership of Clipstone Park from the Crown, the fee £3 10s – little enough, but every little helps.

Sir John had no children by his first wife; so he lived openly with the wife of one George Haugh, by whom he had several children, and afterwards married her. He must have regarded this, in the religious confusion of the time, as legitimizing the previous issue in the old Church manner, made legal in our time. For in 1547 he arranged to settle his estates on his bastard son, John, 'Little Sir John with the Great Beard'. Anyone who knows the history of the northern counties in Tudor times will know how loosely the gentry of Lancashire and the area up to the Borders regarded the institution of marriage; in many cases little distinction was made between legitimate and illegitimate, in others complexities were such that it was hard to tell which was which. The Byrons, like many others, got the benefit of the doubt.

At the Reformation Henry VIII reasonably annexed a large number of fat ecclesiastical manors from the archbishop of Canterbury in exchange for spiritualties, i.e. rectorial tithes the monasteries had appropriated. Rochdale rectory was one of these, and in 1561 Archbishop Parker suggested building a school there. The Protestant vicar he had collated to the living was very keen and granted a site out of his glebe for the school. The tithes had been leased to Sir John, who for several years refused to pay the stipulated £26 13s 4d for the poor vicar's income, as well as the stipends to the vicars of Whalley and Blackburn, the tithes of which he garnered on condition of paying the vicars. His Catholic faith corroborated his selfish interests – in the usual human fashion. Archbishop Parker brought him to earth with a series of injunctions and suits, until in 1564 Sir John threw himself on the mercy of the Protestant archbishop. He was compelled to pay the vicars' stipends, as stipulated, as well as rents of £17 a year to the archbishop for his grammar school of 50 to 150 scholars: a great boon to the area. A prosperous yeoman, Thomas Roughley, acquired the property of Sherdley Hall from the Byrons, to establish a grammar school for Windle, Sutton and Eccleston in the huge parish of Prescot – far more than the knightly family of Byron ever did for education.

Sir John's thoughts were elsewhere. Though now handsomely established on monastic land, like a good many others similarly endowed, he remained a Catholic. When he came to die in 1567, in Elizabeth I's reign, his will affirms the faith, which, since it

now of late hath sore decayed, I think it good to open and declare my faith that others out of the right faith may (if it please God) return by my confession into the same again.... Item, I believe in all the other blessed sacraments of Christ's Church, and that the Mass is a pure and clean sacrifice pleasing God, and a sacrifice propitiatory for the quick and dead. I firmly and steadfastly believe in all and every the articles abovesaid, and in all and every other point and article of our faith as the holy and Catholic and known Church doth believe, out of the which Church there is no salvation [whatever that means]. And I utterly detest and abhor the Manichees, the Arians, the Anabaptists and the Sacramentaries, and all other heretics with their damnable sects and opinions, praying and beseeching Almighty God to revocate and call home again all them that have severed and divided themselves from the said Catholic Church.

Almighty God did not. We do not have to take seriously what this man supposed himself to think, for there is no nonsense that humans will not believe; it serves rather to bring him alive for us at the last. I suspect that this rather rhetorical statement was written for him by his chaplain, the ex-monk of Whalley – clerics often wrote men's wills for them in those days. He left £10 per annum for founding a chantry at Colwick, where the family tombs were, 'if the laws should be revised to permit of such a foundation', and to pray for his soul. No doubt he felt he needed it. But the laws were not revised: the endowment went more usefully to the poor, with £5 for the prisoners at Lancaster, Nottingham, York and Lincoln, where he had been so active in his vigorous life. For the family succession he devised his manor to his base son, John, with trustees to make the inheritance secure as if he were legitimate. The succession was accepted by all concerned, and so it passed.

II

The Trevanions Emerge

THE TREVANIONS were an indigenous, autochthonous Cornish family, springing out of the soil. The grander families in the county – like the Byrons in the North – were of Norman origin : Arundells, Grenvilles, St Aubyns, Bassets, Edgcumbes (through the Valletorts). The native Cornish gentry were on a smaller scale – Trevelyans, Tremaynes, Treffrys, Killigrews. The name Trevanion came from an eponymous Celtic owner, Einion – *Tref-einion*, the homestead of Einion, the place itself swallowed up today in the park and grounds of Caerhays Castle. These have now been made, by several generations of the Williams family, famous gardeners, into a paradise of rhododendrons, camellias, azaleas, magnolias and splendid New Zealand tree-ferns. The site of the ancient Trevanion is forgotten; even in the eighteenth century the antiquary Tonkin says that 'it would be hard to guess where it stood, had not the footsteps of two or three ways leading towards it pointed out the former situation'.

This refers to vanished Trevanion itself. The house the Trevanions built when they succeeded to Caerhays may have been on the present site of Nash's romantic Regency castle, with its view of cliffs and sea. From higher up still, at the wind-swept church of St Michael Caerhays – St Michael, we know, made his appearances on the tops of hills – one has a wonderful view of that exquisite combe: woods and fields, stream running down to the porth – indeed of the whole parish, the historic manor comprising nearly all of it. The church would seem, as is often the case in Cornwall, to occupy the original *caer*, or prehistoric round-camp; the word '*hays*' refers to the hedges which abound. Contrary to what most books say, the church was originally a chapelry dependent on the larger church of St Stephen-in-Brannel (i.e. crows' land, or arable). The little church was dedicated by Bishop Bronescombe in 1259, on his busy tour of church dedications that year. It still has its mementoes of the vanished Trevanions in their aisle, monuments and relics, a funeral hatchment and pieces of armour (folk tradition says going back to Bosworth, but more likely to the Civil War).

The Trevanions got Caerhays in the reign of Edward III, by a marriage to an Arundell heiress, Joan, daughter of Ralph Arundell of that numerous clan, most important of Cornish families throughout the Middle Ages and into the seventeenth century. Before this lucky marriage we find traces of them in the episcopal registers at Exeter; it is interesting that the name Stephen occurs several times, for St Stephen was the patron saint of the parish as a whole. In 1303, towards the end of Edward I's reign – when the Byrons were cavorting in Scotland – Stephen Trevanion, rector of St Ladock, complains that miners have entered his churchyard and upheaved trees and turf. It was a frequent complaint in Cornwall – there were minerals underneath.

Ten years later John de Trevanion, clerk, obtained a grant of the farm of the chapelry of St Michael Caerhays (i.e. the rectorial, or greater, tithes), 'within the mother church of St Stephen-in-Brannel', for five years. William de Trevanion, who already enjoyed the rectory of Lapford in North Devon, was ordained subdeacon by Archbishop Walter Reynolds in Lambeth chapel in December 1317. Two years later he was priested on becoming rector of Grade, to which the family had the presentation. Thus he was provided for. In 1409 Richard and Thomas Trevanion presented Michael Lercedekne (archdeacon) to Grade, the church of the Holy Cross; a few days later he resigned, and the patrons presented John Polglase. When this man resigned in 1451, the right to present was disputed. A chapter of the surrounding clergy testified on oath that the right belonged to Thomas Trevanion, whose father Richard had presented last, by reason of his lordship in the vill of Landewennec.

A century before, on a May day in 1350, a Master Stephen

de Trevanion had been ordained subdeacon by the bishop of
Winchester in his chapel at Southwark. As rector of St Ladock
– in which the family seems to have had an interest – he was
given a dispensation from residing for one year, to study, and
this was renewed a year later. Once more there is a complaint
about mining in the churchyard there. In 1357 the rector complained that, since the Black Prince's passage to Gascony, tin-
miners had dug and mined within the churchyard. The order
was sent down to inquire on the spot and certify to the prince's
council in London.

Meanwhile a member of the family, John Trevanion, was
achieving prominence in the law as a king's serjeant, later promoted judge of the king's bench. In 1331, early in the reign
of Edward III, he had to investigate who had murdered John
de Salisbury at Southampton, and a complaint of the abbot
of Beaulieu about depredations on his cattle; he was placed on
a commission to inquire into oppressions in Devon and Cornwall by officers of the late king and queen, Edward II and
Isabella. Next year Trevanion and his wife Joan had grounds of
complaint against John de Trejago and others, who attacked
the manor of Guthvos Meor, while he was away on the king's
service, and handed over his wife to the tithing men as a hostage.
They had forced the house, trampled his crops and imprisoned
his servants at Brannel so that they absconded. Such were
medieval amenities; one never knows how much to believe in
these complaints – no doubt there was an element of retaliation
among the offenders for what the king's serjeant had previously
done to them.

In 1334 Richard Trevanion was among those who broke into
houses at Tregorrick, just over the hill from where I write these
words six centuries and a half later. He was also accused of
entering Redewry moor, 'with a huge multitude of evil-doers,
carrying away Duchy tin to the value of £1000', and assaulting
the stannary* men working there. Medieval exaggeration, no
doubt; probably much to be said on both sides.

In this same year John Trevanion was appointed judge of
the king's bench, along with Simon de Trewythosa, who moved

---

* Tin-mining in Devon and Cornwall came under the jurisdiction of the
stannary courts of the duchy of Cornwall, part of the appanage of the prince
of Wales.

on shortly to the common pleas and died in 1339. During a decade Sir John, as he would now rank, has left traces of his manifold activities, this year on commissions touching the carrying away of a ship, the taking of beasts for the king's amercements (fines), housebreak and assault; also as judge of assize in Cornwall. In the next year he has to inquire into the complaint of a Cork merchant that his ship, *La Rudecoque* of Howth, with a cargo of wool and hides for Normandy, had been driven ashore at Porth Wynhely (Gunwalloe?) where a large number of folk wrecked the goods. No doubt they did!

In 1343 came up the complaint of the Black Prince, to whom Edward III had lately granted by charter all wrecks, prizes, stannary and coignage* rights, that a large number of persons, including Joan and John Trevanion, were taking advantage of wrecks around the coasts of Cornwall, carrying tin in vessels and in blocks out of the county, fishing in the River Fowey and others, breaking into the duchy parks, etc., etc. Everybody who was anybody in the West, from the bishop of Exeter downwards, was cited. Evidently the object of the exercise was to test the rights of the duchy of Cornwall, newly constituted by Edward III in 1336 as an appanage to provide for the sovereign's eldest son – as it remains to this day.

It would appear that this same Trevanion was summoned in 1365 before the king's bench at Westminster to answer a plea regarding assizes and gaol delivery at Exeter. He had acquitted two Hamblys, Ralph Archdekne and Michael Gross of various felonies. Trevanion submitted his commission, presumably of *oyer* and *terminer*, and his calendar; the question was the validity of the commission – the chancery clerks denied that it was in their hand. The council at Westminster decided that these men's release was without warrant and that they should be arrested. But they could not be found. It was much easier to go into hiding in those days, the country so much larger and emptier. John Trevanion was brought up to Westminster as late as 1377, and fined £20; he was to give bail of £100 (on the security of a Mohun, a Trewinnard, and others) to appear if

---

* Coignage is nothing to do with coinage, but is the right of clipping the corner (*coign*) of a block of tin, for revenue purposes, which accrued to the duchy.

in future he were accused of the principal charge of falsity, i.e. in regard to the commission upon which he had operated.

The head of the family in the reigns of Henry IV and Henry V was Richard Trevanion of Caerhays; a good deal of evidence remains as to his activity, clearly a leading figure in the county. In 1402 the lieutenant of the castle of Cherbourg petitioned that two ships of his town, *La Trinité* and *La George*, with goods also in *La Catherine*, had been taken at sea by privateers; the goods were now in the possession of Richard Trevanion, Arnold Boscaswith of St Just-in-Roseland, John Killigrew of Penryn and others, to the value of 1,500 francs. They refused to give them up, though captured contrary to the truce between the two countries. The petition was backed by Henry IV's French queen, Joan of Navarre, widow of the duke of Brittany. These medieval cogs, with their endearing names – one sees an example of one of them sculpted on a bench-end in St Winnow church, up the river from Fowey, whence the privateers and venturers went forth into the Channel.

In 1404 Richard Trevanion with others gave surety of £100 in chancery, on behalf of John Tregadock, that he 'shall do no harm to Robert Saperton or his servants' – one observes the medieval background of frequent aggression, assault and battery. Trevanion was chosen knight of the shire, with John Chenduit, for the Parliament which met at Gloucester from 20 October to 2 December 1407. This assembly had its importance in affirming the right of the Commons to originate money grants. Having done so, it provided the king with the means for ending Glendower's resistance in Wales. For fifty-two days' service the two knights of the shire received £20 16s. Two years later John Polmorva petitioned that Thomas Tregorra and others had laid an ambush to kill him at Trevanion, broken into his house there and carried off his rents – evidently Polmorva had taken over the old house on the Trevanions' removal to Caerhays.

In 1412 Richard Trevanion and Robert Hull laid a complaint against the abbot of Beaulieu (this Hampshire monastery owned the large and valuable manor of St Keverne near the Lizard). The abbot, they claimed, had dispossessed them of ten messuages, two mills, and half one Cornish acre (about five English acres) in Tregonan, in St Ewe. The abbot had agreed to pay them 200 marks in compensation, but had refused payment.

That same year the king removed Trevanion from the office of coroner, as too sick and infirm; the sheriff was to act in his place, and again in 1424 and 1426. Well or not, he continued to be placed on commissions of the peace and of array; in 1418 and 1419 he served with the Botreaux on one to inquire into treasons, felonies, escapes from prison and wrecks of the sea. This comprehensive assignment was during Henry v's absence on his campaigns in France.

In 1424 John Fursdon of Fursdon in Devon, between Exeter and Tiverton, laid a complaint that Richard and John Trevanion of Caerhays, gentlemen, Thomas Trevanion of Tregony, bastard, with a following of husbandmen and servants, had broken his gates, entered his house and taken away goods and chattels to the value of £40, his charters and deeds, and assaulted his wife then pregnant so that she had a miscarriage. Divers times they had lain in wait so that he dared not go about his business. The mention of charters and deeds indicates that this was a dispute over property; no doubt Fursdon had done something. It was the regular thing to whistle up sympathy with pregnant wives, miscarriages, etc. In 1426 Richard Trevanion was still one of the 'quorum', the leading JPS of the county; then he was gathered to his fathers.

Two years later an order from above throws some light on the obscure early stages of the Trevanion pedigree.* The judge's wife, Joan, was the daughter and heir of Otho Bodrugan, of that family which owned a large house and park on the headland between Mevagissey and Goran. Joan held the manor of Grogoth, near Creed, in right of dower from Sir John, with reversion to his great-nephew, John Trevanion of Trevanion. If this is the new head of the family, then Sir John would have been a younger brother of John's grandfather. This young John served in the Parliament of 1433 – Henry vi was not yet twelve – as member for Lostwithiel, a duchy coignage town. That year he was serving on a commission to inquire into a long suit over the *St Guillaume* of Brittany: a Plymouth ship, the *Magdalen*, had taken her, bound for London with wines and goods, which had been brought into Falmouth and sold.

* J. L. Vivian's *The Visitations of Cornwall* is not reliable in these.

From 1455 politics were dominated by the Yorkist campaign to capture power from the feeble hands of Henry VI, not fully in his right senses, and this led to the Wars of the Roses. Most of the country and the Church were with the Lancastrian house, which had been called to the throne by the misgovernment of Richard II and recognized – as even Henry VI affirmed – as the rightful ruling family by Parliament and nation in three generations, Henry IV, Henry V, and Henry VI himself. The feebleness of government at the centre, distracted by feuds, was reflected in party conflict in every county. When Edward IV won the crown for the Yorkists by sheer military ability, the party leadership in Cornwall was exercised by the Bodrugans, who came to the fore. Henry Bodrugan was on all the commissions of the peace from 1477 to 1484.*

In 1475 the sheriff was sent a writ to attach Henry Bodrugan and John Beaumont, his illegitimate son, and John Trevanion of Caerhays on a recognizance of £100 made to a London alderman, but not yet paid. In the following year Sir Henry Bodrugan and Ralph Cavell were bound in £200, payable in Cornwall, to the alderman, on condition of paying 100 marks at Michaelmas, and £100 which they, with Trevanion and others admitted owing, at the rate of £25 a quarter. On 23 May 1483 – amid all the excitement of Richard III's *coup d'état* – a commission was directed to Sir Henry Bodrugan, his son John Beaumont and John Trevanion to inquire into the complaint of a Breton ship of Lantrégar (Tréguier). A ship of Fowey had seized her with a cargo of Gascon and Rochelle wines, paper and some gold crowns, and carried her into Fowey. Two other ships at Fowey were also to be restored, *La Madeleine* and the *Croissant* of Spain. Next year Bodrugan and Trevanion served on the commission of array by which Richard III was raising forces against his enemies who were gathering against the usurper.

As early as the autumn of 1483 there were movements against him in every county town throughout the south of England. At Exeter, Henry of Richmond – the last sprig of the house of Lancaster (the Yorkists having killed both Henry VI and his son, as well as Richard's own brother, Clarence, and Edward IV's sons!) – was proclaimed king by the bishop, Edward Courtenay of Boconnoc, now head of the family after the Yorkists had

* For his career, *v.* my *Tudor Cornwall*, 102–7.

killed off the main line, and Sir Walter Courtenay of Powder-
ham. Richard's own brother-in-law, Sir Thomas St Leger,
who had married his sister Anne, joined in against him:
Richard had him executed. The sympathies of the Cornish
gentry, Arundells, Trevelyans, Treffrys, were Lancastrian; the
leadership fell to the very able (and respectable) Sir Richard
Edgcumbe, who was with Henry at Bosworth. He had had a
narrow escape when pursued to the Tamar by Bodrugan, cast-
ing his cap to float in the river, while he hid in the woods and
got away to Brittany. After Bosworth, Bodrugan was tracked
down but made his escape from Edgcumbe and Trevanion by
leaping down his cliffs to a boat waiting for him. The place
was long known in Cornish folklore as 'Bodrugan's Leap'.

Edgcumbe, who was much trusted by Henry VII, got the
lion's share of the Bodrugan estates, including Bodrugan itself.
Trevanion's son and heir, William, received promotion at
Court – no doubt through Edgcumbe's influence – as esquire
for the body to the king. It was not until 1504 that the careful,
prudent king rewarded him with the manors of Restronguet
and Newham, down the river from Truro, and Trethulla
(Trethowel) in St Austell parish. The alliance was confirmed
by William's marriage to Edgcumbe's daughter, Anne.

Service at Court may have prevented Sir William, as he
became, from being as active in the county as his father had
been, though we find him on all the commissions of the peace
in Henry VII's reign. In 1504 he was to inquire into escapes
and felons in Cornwall; in 1505 and 1506 into concealed lands,
i.e. of the Crown, from which rents were detained, wards,
reliefs, treasure-trove, goods of outlaws – all sources of revenue
the provident Henry VII wanted examining. In 1506 Sir Piers
Edgcumbe and he were rewarded with the wardship and marriage of the daughters and co-heirs of Thomas Tregarthen –
a source of profit.

Sir William made his will in 1512. He was to be buried, in
accordance with the endearing tradition of those vanished days
and their ancestral beliefs, 'in St Michael's church in Caerhays,
within Our Lady's chapel in the south side thereof, where I
have appointed my place to lie in. And I will that there be made
a tomb of marble with a picture upon for myself, the picture
to be made armed with a shield of mine arms thereupon.' For

his wife, Edgcumbe's daughter, 'if her mind be to lie there as I do and with me, then I will she have a picture made for her with her arms upon her mantlet in such manner'. A priest was to sing Mass for him for three years at the altar; he left 20s to the store of St Michael, 6s 8d to that of Our Lady, 6s 8d to that of All Hallows, and 10s to the parson for tithes he had forgotten. To his son and successor he bequeathed his best pair of vestments, 'a Mass book and a pair of altar cloths and curtains of silk for a chapel' – presumably at the house. This brings him alive for us for a moment, though nothing remains of his monument in the Trevanion aisle today.

In 1518 Sir William died and was succeeded by his son Hugh, who carried on the family tradition of being a leading figure in the public life of the county, more notably than any of his predecessors. In 1519 he received his expenses, £13 9s 8d for bringing up prisoners who had escaped out of the Tower of London. He was on all the commissions of the peace and had to collect the subsidies granted by Parliament, as also the benevolences inflicted to pay for Henry VIII's expensive foreign policy, competing with and fighting France. In 1527 he was in bond for the marriage settlement of his cousin, Sir Piers Edgcumbe, knight of the body, with Lady Catherine Griffith ap Rhys. The same year he was sheriff, a burdensome office, and again in 1532. In the next year, on Trinity Sunday, he was one of the knights at the festivities of Queen Anne's coronation, already pregnant with the Elizabeth that was to be. That October he wrote to Cromwell, 'When I was last in London, at the Queen's coronation, I asked you to excuse me this term as Sheriff of Cornwall.' Pain in his kneebone made the job impossible: 'I have sent money due into the Exchequer by my attorney in that court.'

Meanwhile a John Trevanion was mayor of Dartmouth in 1521 and MP for the borough in the Parliament of 1529–36 that carried through Henry's onslaught on the Church and the Reformation settlement. Later, this John, comptroller of the ports of Plymouth and Fowey, was exempt from war service, having compounded with the king's commissioners. In the critical second half of Henry VIII's reign, with all the crises, rebellions and wars which the new deal brought on the country, Sir Hugh Trevanion and Sir William Godolphin were the leaders in the county's military affairs. During the Pilgrimage of Grace, Sir Hugh and Sir William were named to attend on the king, each with a hundred men, as were John Arundell of Trerice and John Reskymer (of Merthen, near Helford) with forty men each.

In 1539, when Henry feared a combination of France and the Emperor Charles v against him, Trevanion was one of the commissioners to survey the coastal defences. He was rewarded with the office of escheator and feodary of the duchy (i.e. not the county) – the officer receiving forfeitures and escheats, and the rents of lands in wardship. With this went the office of constable of Launceston Castle, the tall keep that overtowers all that neighbourhood as a duchy stronghold, where he could keep the cash and the papers securely. In 1542–3 he was sheriff again, and on the commission of *oyer* and *terminer* for the assizes held at Launceston.

In Henry's third war with France, cheated by the emperor, he fought the first of European countries alone and successfully: it was a tremendous proof of the great increase in military and naval strength resulting from the nationalization of the wealth of the moribund monasteries. Trevanion was to raise the forces from Cornwall, though exempt from service abroad by his duties in the county. Next year he was a commissioner to collect the benevolence to help to pay for the war (as Sir John Byron was for Nottinghamshire). At the end of it disturbed conditions still prevailed in the Channel. Sir Hugh was ordered to recall privateers, because of complaints from the emperor; to arrest pirates (as opposed to privateers: people rarely make the proper distinction)* who had seized a Lübeck ship with grain on the coast and set the master and mariners adrift in a boat. Another piratical exploit concerned spoil of velvets and other wares. In the last year of Henry's reign Sir Hugh was one of the commission to survey the chantries – another source of ecclesiastical revenue, uselessly employed on Masses for the dead, to be explored and exploited.

In the renewal of trouble with France early in Edward vi's reign, Trevanion, Godolphin and John Grenville were to commission privateers to take French ships and goods off the

---

* Privateers are armed vessels commissioned and authorized by governments to attack the enemy; pirates are mere sea-robbers.

coasts of Cornwall. He surrendered his patents as duchy escheator and feodary in both Cornwall and Devon, and constable
of Launceston Castle, to have these offices renewed for life and
in survivorship to his son Hugh. This year he was pricked sheriff
again, and had to collect the subsidy granted by Edward VI's
first Parliament. In the Edwardian inflation he was a commissioner to investigate the rise in the prices of corn and victuals,
with power to apprehend and punish. On Queen Mary's acces-
sion he was one of those to inquire into what had happened
to Church goods, and to compare the state of them with previous inventories.

It is interesting to observe how closely all this work in Cornwall parallels that of the Henrician Sir John Byron in Nottinghamshire. Each was one of the leading men in his county,
Trevanion dying in 1562, Byron in 1567; each of them was
tough and had a long tenure. The differences were that Trevanion was a respectable Protestant, who lived with his wife,
the daughter of Sir Lewis Pollard of Devon, and he did not
invest in or seat himself on Church lands. He remained where
his inheritance was, at delectable Caerhays, conveniently on
the coast midway between Fowey and Falmouth. Two years
before his death Sir Hugh wrote to the judge of admiralty excus-
ing himself from journeying up to testify in a case brought by
two foreigners against John Killigrew. He pleaded the queen's
command to keep watch on the ports from Fowey to Falmouth
in case of invasion, and that he was 'far stricken in years and
weak in body for so great and chargeable a journey'.

His son Hugh made a more interesting marriage, which had
fascinating consequences. His wife was the sister of Lady Hunsdon, wife of Queen Elizabeth's first cousin, Lord Chamberlain
Hunsdon, patron of the Burbages and Shakespeare's Company, whose dark and musical Italian mistress infatuated and
inspired the actor-dramatist during the years 1592–4, when she
had been discarded and married off, and the sonnets were being
written. Lady Hunsdon was able to promote the interests of
her niece, Elizabeth Trevanion, so that in the event she has
a place in the nation's history.

Hunsdon was the son of Henry VIII's discarded mistress,
Mary Boleyn, by William Carey, a gentleman of the chamber
to whom she was married off. The Careys got a footing in

Cornwall through being granted tenure of the estates of Francis
Tregian, a neighbour of the Trevanions, an obstinate Catholic
recusant who spent many years in the Fleet rather than go to
church.* The queen's relations, always in need of cash, got the
benefit of his folly, which ultimately extinguished his family.
Hunsdon, a military man, was for many years the leading
official on the Scottish borders, warden of the East Marches,
governor of Berwick. (One of his bastards, Valentine Carey,
became a blameless and celibate bishop of Exeter.)

It is this connexion that accounts for Elizabeth Trevanion's
marriage to a gentleman in far-away Northumberland, Sir
Henry Widdrington of Widdrington, near Morpeth. She was
married in July 1580; in April 1588 she was introduced at Court
by her aunt, Lady Hunsdon, along with Lady Hunsdon's
daughter, Philadelphia, Lady Scrope. This was the exciting
time when Hunsdon came south to take command of the
Queen's personal bodyguard, in expectation of the Armada,
and when he took up with the attractive orphaned girl, whose
father, Baptista Bassano, had been one of the Queen's musi-
cians. In the spring of 1593 – 'Unruly blasts wait on the tender
Spring' – Sir Henry Widdrington died; on 20 August Elizabeth
married her cousin, Robert Carey, at Berwick-on-Tweed,
where he was serving under his father.†

This happy and successful marriage led to a career of some
historic import, of which we learn from her husband's *Memoirs*,
when he became earl of Monmouth. Carey, as a good-looking
and fashionable young man, had attracted the attention and
promised favour of the susceptible King James on an earlier
visit across the border. He writes somewhat ungallantly of his
marriage to his cousin: 'I married a gentlewoman more for her
worth than her wealth, for her estate was but £500 a year
jointure, and she had between £500 and £600 in her purse.'
If this was so, most of it must have come with her from her
late husband and she was quite a good catch: it was not a bad
thing to marry a widow. Carey admits candidly, 'neither did
she marry me for any great wealth, for I had in all the world
but £100 a year pension out of the Exchequer, and that was
but during pleasure. And I was near £1000 in debt. Besides,

* *v.* my *Tudor Cornwall*, 351 foll.
† *The Memoirs of Robert Carey*, ed. F. H. Mares, 25.

the Queen was mightily offended with me for marrying, and most of my best friends; only my father was no ways displeased at it, which gave me great content'. Old Hunsdon was quite right: his youngest son could hardly have done better for himself; it led on unexpectedly to fortune.

'After I was married', wrote Carey, 'I brought my wife to Carlisle, where we were so nobly used by my Lord that myself, my wife and all my servants were lodged in the Castle; where we lived with him, and had our diet for ourselves, our servants and horses, provided for as his own were.' This would refer to the warden of the West Marches, apparently his brother-in-law, Lord Scrope, whom he was serving as deputy – well provided for, as we see. It was a promising beginning. Shortly afterwards he had a difference with Scrope, and 'resolved not to continue his deputy any longer. We parted on very good terms; and about six weeks after my daughter was born, my wife and I took our leaves of him and came to Widdrington, which was her jointure' – evidently marrying her had its uses. Carey sounds an ingenuous, not unappealing egoist.

There we stayed till towards the Spring the next year and, having no employment, I resolved to repair again to the Court.

My wife was by this time again with child. We set out from Widdrington, and by easy journeys we got to London. My father having the keeping of Somerset House, I got lodging in it for myself, my wife and my servants.* I went daily to Court and passed the time as merrily as before. . . . By this time my wife grew something big, and, by reason she could not well agree with the air of London, I went with her to a place called Denham, hard by Uxbridge, and there she stayed till she was brought to bed of a boy.

As the result of his visit to Court, Carey got the grant of the deputy wardenship of the East Marches; when his father died in July 1596 he carried on there, where a second son was born in the following year.

In 1598 he was promoted warden of the Middle March, and 'removed my wife, children and household to Alnwick Abbey . . . the house where Sir John Foster ever lived when he was Warden'. Carey was at Court during the Queen's last illness, and made his famous unlicensed get-away to be first to carry

* Carey says Arundel House, but this was a slip for Somerset House nearby, of which Hunsdon was keeper.

the news to James in Scotland. He was rewarded by being made gentleman of the bedchamber; but by the union of the two crowns his border office ceased, 'and I lost the pay of forty horse, which were not so little (both) as £1000 per annum'. He hung about the Court, being careful not to appear before the sensitive James with a discontented countenance. This went on until Queen Anne arrived next summer.

My wife waited on her, and at Windsor was sworn of her Privy Chamber and Mistress of her Sweet Coffers, and had a lodging allowed her in Court. This was some comfort to me, that I had my wife so near me. . . . I bestirred myself as well as I could and charged the King with his promise, but could do no good. They [i.e. James Hay and Philip Herbert, who were younger, better looking and un-married] were taken in and poor I refused, never after to hope for it [i.e. to become a favourite].

His whole future came to depend upon his wife.

The queen had brought with her her second son, Charles, duke of York. The elder son, Prince Henry, was a healthy, energetic boy; the younger was sickly and weakling, suffering from rickets, backward in speech, with a tongue too large for his mouth. Great ladies at Court were not anxious to take charge of him, for fear that he would die on their hands. 'The Queen made choice of my wife to have the care and keeping of the Duke. Those who wished me no good were glad of it, thinking that if the Duke should die in our charge – his weakness being such as gave them great cause to suspect it – then it would not be thought fit that we should remain in Court after.'

In fact, under Elizabeth's devoted care, the poor little fellow who was to be Charles I grew stronger. The clue to her treatment was to allow nature and diet to work the remedy. Anyone who knows the medical treatment and prescriptions of the time will recognize that the child would have been killed by them.

The Duke was past four years old when he was first delivered to my wife, he was not able to go, nor scant stand alone, he was so weak in his joints, and especially his ankles, insomuch as many feared they were out of joint. Many a battle my wife had with the King, but she still prevailed. The King was desirous that the string under his tongue should be cut, for he was so long in beginning to speak as he thought he would never have spoke. Then he would have him put in iron boots, to strengthen his sinews and joints; but my wife protested so much against them both as she got the victory, and the King was fain to yield.

Clarendon tells us that Cornish people 'are used to speak what they think', and we have an example of Elizabeth's straight talk to the King in a letter of hers that survives. Some three years later, in 1607, she asked for reforms to be made in the little Duke's household,

For as things now stand, his Grace oftentimes is not so well fed as were fit, the company ill pleased with their scant diet, and your Majesty nevertheless so far at this present charged as I dare undertake – within that expense – to have it performed more wholesomely for the Duke, more plentifully for his people, and more honourably for your Majesty. Wherein, if your Highness command my service and so deliver your pleasure unto the Council, I will, as becomes, obey your commandment.*

The king was so pleased, and ordered his lord chamberlain to make out a contract with her on her terms. The progress Prince Charles was making under her maternal care gave the king and queen absolute confidence in her wisdom, and of course the little boy grew attached to the Careys. 'My wife had charge of him from a little past four till he was almost eleven year old; in all which time he daily grew more and more in health and strength both of body and mind, to the amazement of many that knew his weakness when she first took charge of him.' At eleven the boy, in accordance with custom, was transferred to a household set up under the care of menfolk. 'Now was my wife to leave her charge . . . and so with great grief took leave of her dear master, the Duke.'

The rewards to the Careys were generous, and expressed the favour and esteem Elizabeth had won for them both.

My wife had £400 a year pension during her life, and admitted to the Queen's service in the place she was before. By her procurement, when I was from Court, she got me a suit [i.e. grant] of the King that was worth to me afterwards £4 or £5,000. I had the charge given me of the Duke's household, by which means I preferred to him a number of my own servants. In the meantime that my wife

* *Salisbury Mss.* H.M.C., xix, 412.

had the charge of him my daughter was brought up with the King's daughter and served her [this was the celebrated Elizabeth, queen of Bohemia, from whom the Hanoverian line is descended].

Carey sounds well pleased with himself; he had more reason to be pleased with his wife. 'My wife waited on the Queen, and myself on the Prince; so, for the time it lasted, we lived at no great charge, and most of the little means we had we employed, as it came in, to the bettering of our estate.' When the Prince became king as Charles I, 'he gave to me and my heirs for ever £500 per annum in fee farm, which was a very bountiful gift ... especially because I continued my place of Gentleman of the Privy Chamber'. At the coronation he was created earl of Monmouth, and with that apotheosis Carey ends his *Memoirs*.

Charles I had every reason to be grateful for Elizabeth's care of him: without it, in those formative years, he might not have lived to manhood. As the result of care and discipline he grew, though undersized and always with an impediment of speech, physically tough and strong. With that admirable rearing Charles grew to discipline himself, in marked contrast to his father: where James was self-indulgent and slovenly, apt to be drunken and unwashed, Charles was meticulous and controlled, a man who ate and drank sparingly, of regal dignity and distinction – not so clever a man as his father, he was an aesthete of exquisite taste.

When Elizabeth's father, Hugh Trevanion, succeeded to the old house and estate he was already over forty, and had only nine years to rule at lovely Caerhays as head of the family. Few traces of him remain in the State papers: in 1565, a reproof came down for lack of diligence in apprehending some ill-doer, who had escaped – apparently Trevanion was under-sheriff. In 1571, as sheriff, he was ordered by the privy council to deliver up merchandise hidden in the cliffs at Padstow, which were in his and some others' hands. In that year he died, leaving four sons to follow in rapid succession. Today, with our penal taxation this would have extinguished this interesting historic family, for the benefit of those of no interest, historic or otherwise – in Disraeli's words, 'without pride of ancestry or hope of posterity'.

Richard Carew, writing towards the end of Elizabeth I's reign, refers to the youngest son, Charles, who carried on the family: 'the present possessioner, by a long rank of ancestors, from Arundel's daughter and heir. His father married the daughter of Morgan and sister to the first Lord Hunsdon's wife, which brought him an honourable ally.' Indeed it did, as we have seen. 'Three of this gentleman's elder brethren – Edward, John, and Hugh – forewent him in succession to their father's inheritance, and passed to the better world in a single life.' Edward died at twenty-six in 1576. John, the second son, had matriculated from Jesus College, Oxford, in October 1583 at the age of thirteen. He was the scholar of the interesting John Case, who wrote about both music and medicine.* Young John died at Launceston in 1580, thus about twenty. Hugh, the next heir, died in 1588, Armada year.

We derive a little information about the family from Hugh's will,† made the last day of May 1588, when he was 'of perfect memory but weak of body. . . . All such goods, cattle and corn which I had of my mother by way, use and such corn as doth now grow or is in my mowhay do remain to my mother. . . . To my sister Elizabeth, if this summer she come into the country, any such one gelding as she shall best like of.' For his two unmarried sisters he made up the sum of 100 marks each, which his 'late brother John' had left them, to £100. This was not much – Elizabeth had done much better for herself by going so far afield. Another £100 to cousin Ann Shelton; 'to Hercules Killiow, my godson, my grey mare which I had for a heriot out of Lanreath; to Sybil Trelawny my young black mare colt; to cousin Richard Trevanion the colt which I bought of Smith'. His two new grist mills, now in his own occupation, he leased to his servant John Cardew. His executor was his brother Charles, survivor of the four brothers.

The women of the family were tougher: all married and had children. Elizabeth's son was the second earl of Monmouth; Anne married John Killiow, of the old family which took their name from that place (it means 'grove of trees') in Lansallos parish. Beatrice married John Trelawny, of the historic line which still survives, though no longer in their familiar home.

* v. my *The Elizabethan Renaissance: The Cultural Achievement*, 86 foll.
† Prob/11/72. f. 48.

Katherine married John Roscarrock, of that fascinating Tudor house which survives, dilapidated and unkempt, on the north coast looking over Padstow bay. Margaret became the wife of Sir John Trevor, who thus was returned to Parliament for Bodmin in 1621, East Looe in 1625, and Grampound during the Long Parliament. The Trevanions were ardent Royalists, but he became a prominent Parliamentarian and Cromwellian. The marriage carried on this political family, with its varied careers, and brought them into the peerage as viscounts Hampden.

During these rapid successions – perhaps the brothers were sickly and ailing – their uncle Richard, Elizabeth's brother, took on the public chores. In 1572 he and John Killigrew supervised the musters for the western hundreds of Penwith and Kerrier. During 1578–80 he and neighbour Robert Trencreek were engaged in sorting out a dispute concerning a lease between Sir John Killigrew and Henry Farnaby, of the family that produced the composer Giles Farnaby. In 1586 Richard sat in Parliament for Tregony; two years before, his young nephew Charles for Grampound.

Charles, the youngest brother, now takes his place as head of the family, marries a Devon wife and carries it on. In 1595 St Ives – where the family owned a few small parcels of land – paid 'Mr Trevanion of Caerhays', collector for the maimed soldiers for this year, 13s. In 1599 the tenants of the Mines Royal, operating in Cornwall, complain that their chiefest and best mine is withheld from them by Mr Trevanion – evidently in the course of some official duties – though they had followed the directions of the council and appealed to Sir Walter Ralegh, who was lord warden of the stannaries. Next year, Trevanion, with Sir John Trelawny, Sir Reginald Mohun and others, was to investigate the complaints of Lostwithiel people against the multitude of weirs, fish-gathers, stakes, kiddles and floodgates lately set up by the people at St Winnow and other places along the River Fowey. Lostwithiel complained that the passage of boats was thus stopped. Charles was vice-admiral of Cornwall and – the long war with Spain still continuing – in 1601 he was to imprest two hundred mariners and send them to Plymouth: an unpleasant job.

That year he died, and left a complicated will, from which

one can see some way into the family affairs.* He left to his brother-in-law, John Trelawny, the properties in Trenear and Pennalina, which he had recently purchased from him – this would seem to be sister Beatrice's dower. More intricate provisions followed regarding properties in Killiow and Fentonwoon, which Richard had also purchased from Trelawny, or got by mortgage – for Trelawny was to render £330 or these properties would come to Trevanion's heir, Charles. In default of heirs to him the bulk of the estate was to come to nephew Charles Roscarrock, though lands at Ardevora, in those wooded combes beside the Fal in the heart of Roseland,† would go to cousin Hugh Trevanion. To my 'loving and faithful servant, John Cardew', a house and home was left for life – he, apparently, was Richard's agent or 'steward', as the term was in Cornwall.

Charles can hardly have been forty when he died. His heir was under age, so the estate came to the widow to manage until the youth was twenty-one; if she meanwhile re-married, it was to be held in trust for the heir, by 'my cousin, Sir Reginald Mohun, my brother-in-law John Trevor, esquire, my cousin William Treffry, esquire, my cousin Hugh Trevanion and John Cardew'. This provision was a necessary insurance at the time against a second husband of a widow playing fast and loose with a young stepson's inheritance. Charles's mother was assured such land as his father had assigned to her.

Richard Carew, in his delightful *Survey of Cornwall*, with his Elizabethan fascination for curiosities, human or animal, fish and fowl, folklore, superstitions, dreams and tales, tells us that 'at Caerhays, Mr Trevanion's house, which bordereth on the cliff, an old gull did – with an extraordinary charity – accustom, for divers years together, to come and feed the young ones, though perhaps none of his alliance, in the court where they were kept'. Carew must have known the old house well: it throws a little shaft of light into those days and ways.

* P.C.C., I.P.M., C42, vol. 268, no. 141.
† Roseland has nothing to do with roses: it means 'heath-land'.

III

Elizabethans and Jacobeans

IN NOTTINGHAMSHIRE the reign of 'Little Sir John with the Great Beard' coincides roughly with that of the queen; he reigned there from 1567 to 1604. The second in possession, he is the first to come down in popular memory and folklore as a person, no doubt owing to his beard, perhaps to his bastardy or even to his extravagances, for the little man certainly had a good fling. Thoroton, the local antiquarian, refers to his father's living with another man's wife, 'on whom he begot (soon enough) Sir John Byron of Newstead to succeed him'.

In our time the little man has come back there on his tomb, brought from Colwick: as we go down into the crypt there he lies in armour, small bird-like face and the recognizable long beard, with plump, respectable wife beside him. He married a neighbour's daughter, Alice Strelley of Strelley. His father's altar-tomb has been brought here too, upon which he had hoped for Masses to be said for the good of his soul. So also a painted Jacobean monument to the two next heads of the family and their wives, husband and wife kneeling facing each other.

Little John's extravagance began early: we find him maintaining a troupe of players in 1569. In public affairs he was as busily employed as his father had been: during the Rebellion of the Northern Earls, Northumberland and Westmorland, that same year, Byron, with Sir Gervase Clifton and others, was responsible for the musters at Nottingham. Next year he made return of seven hundred footmen for the North – himself, as sheriff, responsible for the wapentake of Broxtowe. In 1574 he

was to report at Belvoir Castle before the earl of Rutland with
two light horsemen fully equipped, again for Broxtowe
hundred. Next Christmas Byron sent the earl 'as good a hind
as you are likely to have this year out of the Forest'. This is
followed shortly by a request for favour in a cause between him
and a neighbour. He and Robert Markham in 1577 were to certify
the Catholic recusants in the county, with the values of their
property – this was the year of the sensational round-up of the
first seminary priest at Francis Tregian's in Cornwall, next door
to Caerhays.

On Sunday, 24 January 1580, Little John was knighted at
Westminster. Now appointed sheriff of Lancashire, where he
was to keep household, he was in charge of musters there and
trusted that he would not be obliged to perform also for Nottinghamshire. He evidently moved between Newstead and the
old home at Clayton – in itself expensive, keeping two households; for in one year he is called on to arbitrate a Nottinghamshire dispute; in another the earl of Derby, who kept semi-royal
state, sends for him to attend as squire in his absence. Early
in Armada year Byron was taking the musters, with other
deputy lieutenants, at Nottingham; the borough accounts
record a gallon of Gascon wine and half a pound of sugar, consumed when they reviewed the men in the castle yard.

Sir John kept noble company. In September 1590 a Rutland
son made two journeys over to Newstead, and another the following July. That August the earl of Shrewsbury wrote to his
Manners uncles at Belvoir, 'I am just ready to go a-hunting
with Sir John Byron's hounds, if the rain will permit.' (The
English summer! We recall his descendant the poet's complaint
that it began on 31 July and ended on 1 August.) In Sherwood
Forest Sir John was keeper for Newstead, Blidworth and Papplewick, each with an underkeeper to do the keeping. In Papplewick there was a hollow rock traditionally known as Robin
Hood's Stable: a cave near the lodge to Papplewick Hall, with
hollows well contrived for holding fodder, where two horses
could feed together. From his lodging in Holborn in 1590 Sir
John writes a friendly letter to Shrewsbury; while next year
he apologizes for not attending the late earl's funeral at Shef-
field. He had been unable to come north, but offered the new
earl the use of his hawks and hounds for the hunting season.

The little man then goes on to complain that he is slighted at Court.

In the Christmas holidays of 1595 we find Roger Manners writing, from his lodgings in the Savoy, to his brother John: 'Sir John Byron sent me four pies of a dainty roe, but your fat hind will be welcome when it comes.'

Meanwhile, under the stress of the war with Spain and the campaign of Jesuits and seminary priests to subvert the religious establishment, the government was tightening up the laws. Shakespeare identified himself with the popular point of view, in downright fashion, referring to them as

> the fools of time,
> Which die for goodness, who have lived for crime.

Byron was placed in 1592 with the earl of Shrewsbury on the commission to administer the Oath of Supremacy to all in public place throughout Nottinghamshire. In 1595 he was appointed once more, with others, to supervise the musters in both Nottinghamshire and Lancashire. The government found him a willing maid-of-all-work, but again this implied house-keeping at Clayton as well as at Newstead.

He may have been unbusinesslike, or have bitten off more than he could chew, in his dealings over land. For in 1590 he leased the rectory of Rochdale, i.e. the larger tithes over that huge parish, with the chapelries of Saddleworth and Butter-worth, for twenty-one years, at the rent of £80 0s 7d a year. He was to pay besides £15 a year to the schoolmaster and £2 to the usher; £8 a year and £6 13s 4d increased rent to the vicar. One would need to be on the spot to make that pay. But in 1597 he was still acquiring land in Bulwell in Nottingham-shire. In this year his son and heir served as knight of the shire in the Parliament that laid the basis for the salutary Poor Law, which remained in essence until scrapped in our own eleemo-synary time for hand-outs all round.

The years 1592 and 1593 were plague years – we know now the extreme importance that had for the theatre folk with the closing of the theatres, in particular for William Shakespeare who was so fortunate as to find a patron, Southampton, to look after him. Hardship and want prevailed in all parts. At Nottingham collections were made 'for relief of the poor and the plague-stricken'. Everyone had to contribute: Sir John gave twenty strikes of rye and twenty of malt. (A 'strike' was a grain measure, usually about a bushel; but it varied in different localities from half a bushel to four in some places.) Later that year Sir John contributed 30s in cash, as did others of the gentry.

After the crisis of Essex's fatuous outbreak in 1601 – which the queen denominated *rebellio unius diei* – Byron reported to Robert Cecil some of the gossip of local wiseacres: all in favour of the irresponsible Essex, always a favourite with the mob, and against Cecil, the responsible statesman who was never popular. In the growing insecurity as the queen's death approached, Lady Arbella Stuart, whose proximity to the throne caused trouble, was under observation at nearby Hardwick. It was reported that 'Sir John Byron is very old, and his son at her devotion and not well reported of.' The port of Hull was only forty miles away – was she intending for Scotland?

However, Cecil managed the succession of Scots James to the English throne with supreme skill. He was proclaimed king at Nottingham, on 23 March 1603, by Roger, earl of Rutland, and the sheriffs, old Sir John, his son and heir, and John Stanhope. When James came south, in April 1603, Byron's son was knighted at Worksop among the extravagant number of creations which the old queen had been careful not to inflate. In June Queen Anne with Prince Henry passed through Nottingham on their way from Newstead (where they must have stayed – an expensive honour) to London. The borough turned out to receive the new sovereign in all their finery, scarlet gowns, etc., and presented her with a large silver cup and a purse of gold sovereigns.

Old Sir John remained active to the last. His neighbours, the Markhams, were Catholics, several of them engaged in conspiracies. Sir Griffin Markham was a conspiratorial soldier involved in supporting Lady Arbella Stuart, and was incriminated in the plots that nearly brought him and Ralegh to the block. Markham admitted that he had yielded to the persuasions of Father Watson, a busy but crazy intriguer. The proclamation for Markham's arrest described him, in the vivid language of the time, as 'a man with a large broad face, of a bleak complexion, a big nose, and one of his hands maimed by shot of a bullet'. Neighbour Byron was handed the unattractive job of reporting on Sir Griffin's absconding from Beskwood in the depths of the forest. Sir John made no entry, for the gates were locked and kept by keepers; the house was so seated in a large park, nine miles around, that it could not be spied until one was upon it.

Neighbourly disputes continued while there was breath in their bodies. At the last Sir John was wrangling with the Chaworths, with whom the Byrons were to be entangled later in marriage, manslaughter and romantic love. In 1603 Byron and Chaworth were in conflict over property, the lease of the prebend of Oxton, presumably belonging to Southwell minster. The new earl of Shrewsbury reported that Sir John had slandered Chaworth; the earl wished to wash his hands of the matter and refer it to the king.

Early in 1604 Little Sir John died, leaving a load of debt, for he had lived ostentatiously on a more than baronial scale. The earl sent his condolences to the heir, and added his advice: 'I know the estate of that which is left you is good and great; but, withal, I take it you are in great debts and have many children to provide for. I do therefore advise you that so soon as you have, in such sort as shall be fit, finished your father's funerals, to dispose and disperse that great household, reducing them to the number of forty or fifty at the most, of all sorts.' On what a scale the little fellow must have lived, if a household of fifty was to be the maximum! The son and heir was able to report an honourable funeral at Colwick to the earl, and the good conduct of the heralds at it. There remained to pay the piper.

This third Byron at Newstead did not succeed, owing to his father's longevity, until he was well over forty; for he matriculated from Queen's College, Cambridge, in 1573, and so would have been born about, or before, 1560. His father's debts hung a millstone round his neck. William Trinder, a husbandman of Snenton, had been bound for £85 on behalf of Little Sir John, who had given an extravagant bond in return for £200. In 1609 the son is writing to Trinder.

I thank you for your payment of £100 on the bond in which you have joined me. Sir Henry Pierrepont [a neighbour] is pleased to pleasure me with this sum for some further time, upon your bond and mine. I have already sealed a new bond, which I entreat you to join me in, and that you will come to Sir Henry's on Thursday next to perform the same. On Saturday you shall receive from me at Nottingham a new counter-bond.

One sees how complicated these transactions were, in primitive developments of credit, without banks or much currency circulating. Trinder must have been a prosperous yeoman – one hopes that he didn't lose in his dealings with the harassed knight.

There was no help for it but to part with the ancient Lancashire inheritance. In 1560 Little Sir John had enclosed and reclaimed 260 acres of Bersdall Moor; in 1606 his grandson had to sell nearly the whole of it. Humphrey Chetham bought the old home at Clayton, and in 1611 the lease of the rectory of Rochdale fell in. The heir was thus to concentrate on Nottinghamshire, where he succeeded to the duties, chores and pleasures of his position.

In 1606 he has to apprehend a recusant, one Richard Farmer, fairly certainly one of the Catholic Fermors. Amenities continue with the grandees at Belvoir Castle: in August 1608 half a buck was sent over from Newstead. In August a couple of years later Sir John's man 'brought victuals to his lordship hunting in the Forest'. Next year, a servant brought three carps and three tenches to Belvoir. That year it was reported that Sir John Byron and Sir John Ratcliffe 'were overseas long since' – probably for a duel; disallowed in England, fighting fools went abroad to do battle. This foolery continued right up to the threshold of the Victorian age.

Some years later a friend 'lately met old Sir John Byron', who had had orders from the king not to impark his grounds at Newstead until his pleasure was known. James was mad about hunting, and adverse to the forests – Crown demesnes – being diminished. This became a serious cause of trouble with the gentry against the Crown under Charles I. In 1612 the Crown claimed that Newstead Priory, Colwick, Bulwell Park and other lands of the Byrons were within the bounds of Sherwood as royal forest, and subject to forest jurisdiction. Sir John Byron, Sir Charles Morison and other local landowners refused to compound with the commissioners for titles thus claimed to be defective. Sir John, it appears, had given no directions for enclosure, but left the decision to his son. Young Sir John was then in Lancashire, but on his return had ordered the palings to go forward. The father did his duty as an acting magistrate regularly at Nottingham from 1604 to 1618, and was among the contributors to the building of the Shire Hall there. In that year, 1618, a joiner was sent to the house of correction for striking Sir John Byron, junior, a JP: the joiner threatened to have his blood – such was demotic freedom in the Midlands even then.

The Reformation, with the vast amount of Church property thrown on the market, obviously led to a great increase in the economic strength and wealth of the gentry. Here we have a case in point, among hundreds over the country: the Byrons taking the place of the monks at Newstead, the Chethams taking their place at Clayton – two families, where one had been before. Now the gentry were pushing for an increased share in political power at the centre: hence their keenness for a seat in the Commons, their own political institution, their prime instrument. Throughout the country the gentry came more and more to occupy the representation of the boroughs, ever keener to acquire seats and voice the demands of their class. Nottingham provided an example of this too. For the Parliament of 1624 there were no less than ten suitors for one of the burgesses' places, among them Sir Charles Cavendish, Sir George Chaworth, and the Byron son and heir. Young Byron got it; no doubt it cost something. He was also returned for the borough to the next Parliament of 1625–6. These restive Parliaments of the early seventeenth century sharpened the conflict with the Crown, which had always held executive power, and expressed the demand of the gentry all over the country to share in it. Out of the conflict came the Civil War.

Of this generation prior to the Civil War we have more intimate glimpses from Mrs Hutchinson's classic biography of her husband, Colonel Hutchinson, for though he was a Puritan Parliamentarian, he was a Byron on his mother's side. (He was infected with Puritanism at Cambridge.) 'He was the eldest surviving son of Sir Thomas Hutchinson and the lady Margaret, one of the daughters of Sir John Byron of Newstead: two persons so eminently virtuous and pious that to descend from them was to set up in the world upon a good stock of honour, which obliged their posterity to improve it as much as it was their privilege to inherit their parents' glories.' This improving couple had been married in April 1612. We learn that the lady was 'of as noble family as any in the country, of an incomparable shape and beauty', and embellished with the best education those days afforded and, above all, had such a generous virtue joined with attractive sweetness that she captivated the hearts of all that knew her. She was pious, liberal, courteous, patient, kind above an ordinary degree, ingenious in all things to which she would apply herself and – notwithstanding she had had her education at Court – delighted in her own country habitation and managed all her family affairs better than any of the homespun house-wives that had been brought up to nothing else.

She was a most observant and affectionate wife, a great lover of her father's house. She was a wise and bountiful mistress in her family, a blessing to her tenants and neighbourhood ... but death veiled all her mortal glories in the twenty-sixth year of her age. One that was present at her death told me that she had an admirable voice and skill to manage it, and that she went away singing a psalm, which this maid apprehended she sung with so much more than usual sweetness as if her soul had been already ascended into the celestial choir.

It is a charming, if somewhat unexpected, portrait of a Byron lady – perhaps Mrs Hutchinson was imputing to her some of her own moral perfection. She goes on to introduce us further into the affairs of the Byron family, in particular to Margaret Byron's father, the Sir John who married a Fitzwilliam. He was

not the eldest son of his father, Sir John Byron, but had an elder brother that had married a private gentleman's daughter in the country – and so displeased his father in that match that he intended an equal part of his estate to this Sir John Byron, his younger son. He thereupon married him to a young lady who was one of the daughters of my Lord [Fitzwilliam], that had been Deputy of Ireland in the reign of Queen Elizabeth and lived as a prince in that country.

This daughter of his, having an honourable aspiring to all things excellent and being assisted by the great education her father gave her, attained to a great degree of learning and languages, to such an excellency in music and poetry that she made rare compositions of both kinds.

It is pleasant to think of this courtly Jacobean Lady Byron fill-
ing the somewhat gloomy, monkish chambers of Newstead with
music and poetry, strumming the lute or tinkling on the virgi-
nals. 'Besides all these ornaments of soul she had a body of as
admirable frame and beauty, which justly made her husband
so infinitely enamoured of her as never man was more.'

There was, however, a snake in this paradise. 'She could not
set too high a value on herself if she compared herself with other
women of those times. Yet it was an alloy to her glories that
she was a little grieved that a less woman, the elder brother's
wife, was superior to her in regard of her husband, though inferior in regard of her birth and person. But that grief was soon
removed by a sad accident.' Mrs Hutchinson comments, with
some complacency, that

that marriage wherein the father had not been obeyed was fruitless.
And the young gentleman himself, being given to youthful vanity,
as he was one day to go out a-hunting with his father, had commanded
something should be put under the saddle of a young serving-man,
to make sport at his affright when his horse should prove unquiet.
The thing succeeded as it was designed and made them such sport
that the young gentleman, in the passion of laughter, died.

Censorious Mrs Hutchinson improves the occasion with a
moral. 'The younger brother by this means was heir of the
family, and father of a numerous and hopeful issue.' This Sir
John now reigned with his paragon of a Fitzwilliam wife in
great felicity at Newstead, until

God in one moment took it away and alienated her most excellent
understanding in a difficult childbirth.... All the art of the best physi-
cians in England could never restore her understanding. Yet she was
not frantick, but had such a pretty deliration that her ravings were
more delightful than other women's most rational conversations.

Upon this occasion her husband gave himself up to live retired with
her, and made haste to marry his son, which he did so young that
I have heard say, when the first child was born, the father, mother
and child could not make one and thirty years old.

They must have been married at fifteen. Margaret, who
became Colonel Hutchinson's mother, was the youngest
daughter:

at nine years old so taking and of such an amiable conversation that
the Lady Arbella would needs take her from her parents along with

her to the Court. Where she minded nothing but her Lady, and grew up so intimate in all her counsels that the princess was more delighted in her than in any of the women about her. But when she was carried away from them to prison...so constant was her friendship to the unfortunate princess, as I have heard her servants say, even after her marriage she would steal many melancholy hours to sit and weep in remembrance of her.

We have one or two external notices of the sympathy of the Byrons for the Lady Arbella Stuart: here is the inwardness of the matter.

Upon Lady Hutchinson's death, in her 'pretty deliration' of her wits, 'her brother, Sir John Byron, came over and found the most desolate afflicted widower that ever was beheld, and one of his sisters, the Lady Ratcliffe, who was the dear sister of the dead lady, scarce alive for sorrow'. Such was the lamentation in the house and neighbourhood that, to avoid its prolongation in the usual solemn ceremonies, Sir John Byron took the initiative and had his sister interred quickly in the church next door. On the next day, while taking the bereaved family away in his coach there was an accident, in which the young George Hutchinson had a narrow escape and 'was taken up unhurt and carried to Bulwell, where his aunt had such a motherly tenderness for him that he grew and prospered in her care. Every child of the family loved him much better than their own brothers and sisters, and Sir John Byron and my Lady were not half so fond of any of their own.'

Whether this spoiling of the infant so providentially saved was altogether a good thing may be doubted: he grew up to be the self-satisfied, uncompromising Puritan of history, who held Nottingham Castle against the king and all his Byron cousins, and ended, always conscious of his own rectitude, as a regicide.

Mrs Hutchinson, who was fond of death-bed scenes and moralizing upon them, tells us that this third Sir John died on the same day as his wife: they were buried at Colwick in the same grave. Their son went back to Lancashire for a wife, marrying a Molyneux of Sefton. They produced a brood of soldierly sons.

Of these the most celebrated is the eldest, the fifth Sir John to reign at Newstead and first lord, created so for his services to the king in the course of the war. Born in 1599 he matriculated from Trinity College, Cambridge, in Easter term 1615, and graduated master of arts in 1618. Like so many who fought in the war, including other Byrons, he had his military training abroad – perhaps, like his brother Gilbert, in their uncle Sir Nicholas's company, which served James i's daughter, Elizabeth, queen of Bohemia, in the Netherlands. He returned to take up the duties that went with his position at Newstead. He married, first, Cecily, daughter of Lord De la Warr; and second, Eleanor, daughter of Lord Kilmorey. There were no children by either marriage: he was more successful as a soldier. Clarendon gives him a good character: 'a person of a very ancient family, an honourable extraction, good fortune, and as unblemished a reputation as any gentleman in England'.

In the year of his succession he is at once made a commissioner to take the musters. In 1634 he has a dispute with Viscount Coke concerning hunting rights in Sherwood – we must remember how important the supply of deer was for provisioning great households in winter. We learn that 'old Sir John Byron with the Great Beard, when Lieutenant of the Forest, was taken up for hunting, yet was neither sued nor convicted for it, as is now the fashion'. Charles i was trying to exert his rights over the royal forests and put the Forest Laws into operation – anything to gather in supplies without depending upon Parliament, after his unfortunate experiences with those of 1625 to 1629. 'Lord Chaworth says he never shot at any deer in the Forest, which is more than Sir John Byron can say. A list of presentments against Lord Chaworth and his servants will be made good by a longer list against Sir John Byron and his.'

In 1637 we find brother Richard, who had married the widow of a Strelley and lived conveniently on her property there, as a justice of the peace judging a charge of deer-stealing brought against a Mr Innocent.

The Cornishman, Attorney-General Noy, suggested the expedient of extending Ship Money from the coastal counties to those inland – and this was only fair, since they profited as well as the sea-coasts from an efficient navy which the tax had been designed to provide. To begin with, it was accepted and paid, though with reluctance, for no one likes paying taxes. The job of collecting it fell to Byron, as sheriff in Nottinghamshire

in 1635–6. He reported progress to the privy council, but submitted that unless noblemen, such as Lord Chaworth, were
assessed, it was impossible to levy the expected amount on the
poor county, where noblemen were numerous and possessed a
large part of it. (This is the land that became known, with the
cornucopia of the Industrial Revolution, as 'the Dukeries': a
title now forgotten in the social revolution of our time, the great
houses mostly destroyed, their treasures dispersed.)

At New Year 1636 Byron reports that few will pay their
assessment without distraining, an excessive burden and charge
to himself as sheriff. Only Mr Markham is entirely refractory,
though 'he has £800 per annum in land, £40,000 in money
out at use, is miserly and has only two bastards to leave it to'.
Mr Markham speaks up for himself in reply against 'intolerable
oppression'. Byron has made the writer a separatist [note the
opprobrious overtones, from a Catholic, i.e. no better than a
Puritan] from all the rest of his rank of that county. Lord Chaworth is marked at £35, 'and the writer extolled to £50'. Many
others are put down at £35, himself at £50! 'Neither is the
vulture humour stayed here' – the sheriff of Yorkshire has taken
£10 forcibly from him by distraint, etc. Mr Markham certainly
had a way of expressing himself.

In the event Byron managed very well. By February he had
paid in £3,200 of the county assessment of £3,509. Nottingham
was rated at £200, Newark at £120, Retford at £30. They could
all well afford it. In August, when Byron ceased to be sheriff,
he reported £100 in collectors' hands; the remainder of the
money would not be in before the end of September. Of course
people said that he was partial to the neighbours where he lived.
Two years later he refused to pay £3 of his own assessment.

But he could raise thousands to buy the whole great manor
of Rochdale. In 1634 Sir Robert Heath mortgaged it to him;
in 1638 Byron was, for another £2,500, able to buy the property
outright, thus renewing the family stake in Lancashire.
Manorial rights, or former possession of rectorial tithes, made
him responsible for the chancel of the church. The bishop of
Chester reported to Archbishop Laud, straining every nerve to
restore order and decency in the churches, that the chancel had
been formerly neglected and out of order; he had caused it to
be paved and seated choir-wise, and decently repaired at the

cost of Sir John Byron, the archbishop's farmer – so he must have renewed his great-grandfather's lease of the rectory. The cost of the restoration was £40: it must have warmed the heart of poor Laud, amid so many discouragements and such uphill work.

Meanwhile, down in Cornwall, we see the same factors at work with similar consequences: the increasing competition for places in Parliament, dissatisfaction with royal government, the envy of the outs for the ins, the nasty dislike for Laud's endeavour to restore beauty in the churches, the growing conflict with the Crown and its ministers. The conflict in Cornwall is of particular significance because of the large number of members it returned to Parliament: two knights of the shire and forty-two burgesses for the towns. These minimal places – Bosinney, Mitchell, St Mawes, Grampound and suchlike – had been given seats by the Crown at the wish of the gentry, increasingly avid of place in Parliament. The bulk of these was collared by West Country gentry; even the egregious Peter Wentworth, who tirelessly (and tiresomely) kept up opposition to Elizabeth's government, until she very properly put him in the Tower, owed his seat for Tregony to his family connexion by marriage with the Seymours who owned the manor. (His brother Paul, MP for Liskeard, obtained Burnham Abbey, a neat convent of Benedictine nuns, by marriage, for his wife was the widow of the man who had gained it at the Dissolution. The gentry were indubitably rising.)

In the growing conflict between Crown and Parliament, Court and Country, between those in power and office and those who wanted to get their trotters into the trough – there was by no means room for all, and never enough to go round – Cornwall produced the most inflammable opponent of the Crown in Sir John Eliot, seated in what had been the priory of St Germans. An abler and more dangerous opponent was John Pym, who was brought up on the banks of the Tamar; for his widowed mother married Sir Anthony Rouse, and all these Rouses were distastefully Puritan. The conflict, heated by the intemperate oratory of Eliot, divided families. Charming young Bevil Grenville followed his friend Eliot, of whom his father, Sir Bernard Grenville, strongly disapproved. This led to a breach between father and son. Similarly the

Trevanions and Arundells were divided. Young Charles, head of the family at Caerhays, followed Eliot; while Richard, of the older generation, went with the Court party, a king's man at the impassioned election of 1628. Much had happened in the West Country to account for the bitterness with which it was contested.

Charles Trevanion was sixteen at his father's death in 1601. His family's standing in the county was recognized by his being chosen by the freeholders, i.e. holders of land, as knight of the shire for the Parliament of 1625, along with Sir Robert Killigrew. The West Country, in particular Plymouth, was much to the fore in the lamentable expedition to Cadiz in this year; and to the Isle de Rhé and La Rochelle in 1627 and 1628, which punctuated (and punctured) the rash and irresponsible chops and changes of youthful Charles I and Buckingham's foreign policy (if that is the word for it). They were young and inexperienced; these disastrous fiascos, with the repercussions they provoked in the country and in Parliament, undermined confidence in the king's government and created distrust from which it never recovered.

Eliot had begun as a follower of Buckingham – whom James I had promoted to his bedchamber and everything else – and owed both knighthood and office as vice-admiral of Devon to the favourite. His colleague as vice-admiral of Cornwall was James Bagg of Plymouth, a more solid and consistent agent for Buckingham as lord admiral. Bagg was the son of a merchant who had come to Plymouth – people hardly knew from where – and married a Cornish girl of no particular family. The son was able, hard-working, and got on famously – and so was unpopular. MP for Plymouth, he was described in Parliament by a Seymour, of that haughty family, as 'the bottomless Bagg'. The phrase stuck; everyone called him by it. All of this did nothing to prevent him from prospering: he seated himself at beautiful Saltram above the Plym and took to wife a Fortescue of North Devon, of that Norman clan. When Charles I and his queen came down to review the ships and troops for Cadiz, which Bagg had worked hard to set forth, he was knighted. We find Richard Trevanion, with three others, having to procure a ship of 200 tons for the expedition, and organizing its manning and victualling by the Cornish towns.

After the failure of the expedition Eliot turned sour, and his temper was not improved by the refusal of the favours he was asking for – Sir Richard Edgcumbe's colonelcy of militia and deputy-lieutenancy. Dismissed from his job as vice-admiral, he turned to attacking the favourite in Parliament. In 1627 he and Coryton, vice-warden of the stannaries, refused to contribute to the Forced Loan; they were briefly imprisoned. Affairs were coming to a head with the election of 1628, which was passionately contested with bitter feelings on each side. Eliot and Coryton managed their campaign with almost modern expertise and disingenuousness. The Court relied heavily on the deputy-lieutenants, Sir Reginald Mohun, Sir Bernard Grenville, and Richard Trevanion – all elderly – to carry the election; they put forward as candidates old Sir Richard Edgcumbe (whom Eliot had thought dead, hoping to step into his shoes) and Mohun's son and heir, John.

Sir James Bagg, rowing hard against the tide, reported the event: 'Here we had Bevil Grenville, John Arundell and Charles Trevanion coming to the election with 500 men each at their heels and lodged in towns together.' It was probably an exaggeration – but these were the freeholders, and they returned Eliot and Coryton. When the irate House of Commons met – in which Eliot took the lead with impetuous, ill-considered speeches – they sent for the ring-leaders among their opponents. Four gentlemen – two loyal Trelawnys, Walter Langdon and Sir William Wrey – were questioned at the bar of the sacred House and made to answer for their delinquency on their knees. They were then taken into custody. When the House sent its serjeant-at-arms down to Cornwall to call the offenders to book, Trevanion had his excuse: he had been taken some sixty miles away on domestic affairs, and could not appear.

Upon Parliament's dismissal, the loyal offenders were at once released; John Mohun was rewarded with a barony, John Trelawny with a baronetcy. After one more hopeless attempt by the king to come to terms with the Commons, where Eliot's intemperate oratory knew no bounds, Eliot was sent to the Tower. Here he remained obstinately determined not to yield and, after only three years, died – a martyr in the parliamentary and Whig calendar. He was probably a consumptive: hence his feverishness. It was no wonder that Charles did not want to assemble Parliament again, so long as he could do without it. For the next decade the traditional administration soldiered on – king and council, in which Laud had a considerable say (he was made to pay for it in the end with his head, by the vindictive gentry of the Commons). But events were to show that the monarchy could not in the long run manage to rule against the will of the upper classes, or even a significant section of them.

For some years a halcyon peace – such as is described by Clarendon in a famous passage – settled upon the land. Things resumed their old traditional course, or so it seemed: actually they were never the same again. The recalcitrants were bent on power, the outs determined to get in, and have their way in State and Church. Some leaders of the opposition were reconciled, notably Thomas Wentworth, henceforth hated as an apostate: his class brought him to the block.

When Pembroke fell ill in 1628 and was unable to fulfil his duties as lord lieutenant and lord warden of the stannaries, these were committed to the loyal: Lord Mohun and his father, Sir Bernard Grenville and Charles Trevanion, who had evidently rallied. At Lenten assizes in 1630 a dispute regarding the alehouses in the neighbouring little town of Tregony was referred to Trevanion and John Trefusis. They were to inform the mayor and corporation that thirty-six alehouses in that tiny place were too many, and to consider the number that should be licensed. When our hearts are wrung and sympathies organized for the impoverished state of the people, their poor health and inadequate diet, etc., we must not overlook their addiction to drink as a factor in creating misery for themselves.

The antiquated and lumbering royal administration broke against the passive resistance to king and archbishop's unpopular policy in State and Church, and the active resistance of Scots Presbyterianism, which stoked up the spirit of nationalism and religious fanaticism – irresistible when combined – over the Border. All the active and furious elements lined up behind the National Covenant to wreck royal government in Scotland and take over power. The scale of the resistance, the ardour, fury and madness, was totally unexpected, after so long a period of beneficent peace; a complacent, civilized government was ill-equipped to meet it. (The king was over-optimistic, but Laud was not complacent; he always apprehended disaster from the ugly spirit of rampant Puritanism.)

The king appealed to traditional loyalties, levies and forces, to his peers and natural supporters, to their patriotic spirit; but the country in general, or the effective part of it – the bulk of the gentry and urban middle class – dragged their feet. When war was undertaken along the border, against the inflamed Scots, soldiers serving abroad were summoned home by both sides. On the king's, were the Byrons. Sir Nicholas, uncle of the Sir John now at Newstead, was a professional soldier in the Netherlands. He was called home, made governor of Carlisle and a member of the council for war, his advice valued. With Lord Conway and Sir Jacob Astley, he was to report on defects in the ordnance office, which were glaring after the long peace, when people had had it too good for too long and many were spoiling for a fight.

During the brief and ignominious confrontation in the North in 1639, the 'Bishops' War', which heralded the greater struggle, Sir Nicholas served as colonel of a regiment. It was all to no purpose, however: the king had to give way to the embattled Scots, his civilized Church policy for Scotland in ruins. The populace won, led on by fanatical ministers like Alexander Henderson, propounder and propagandist of the Covenant – and with the connivance of ambitious aristocrats like Argyle, hungry for power. Much the same was true in England, where it was noted at this time that the earls of Essex and Holland, who were 'out', were 'much discontented', and the con-spiratorial Lord Saye and Sele, 'Old Subtlety', was in touch with the ablest leaders among the opposition, Commons men – Pym, Hampden, Holles, the odious Heselrig (who was to do so well out of the war) – determined to destroy royal govern-ment, drive out the king's ministers, and move in themselves. In the event, they did: Old Subtlety, previously hard up, made thousands out of it.

In January 1640 Sir Nicholas Byron was to go into the Low Countries to bring back a hundred serjeants and corporals and provide five hundred saddles. He was hard at work trying to equip the king's forces and improve the fortifications of Carlisle, in disuse with the long internal peace since the union of the two kingdoms. He was to make provision of sixty-four horse for the garrison, and to store corn and cattle in safe places along the border. In June he was commanded by the king to London.

The renewal of the war, and the straits the king was in, appealed to the latent loyalty of Sir Bevil Grenville and brought him over to his side. He wrote eloquently to Trelawny,

I cannot contain myself within my doors when the King of England's standard waves in the field upon so just occasion.... For mine own part, I desire to acquire an honest name or an honourable grave. I never loved my life or ease so much as to shun such an occasion, which, if I should, I were unworthy of the profession I have held or to succeed those Ancestors of mine who have so many of them sacrificed their life for their country.

Here was the spirit that led 'so many of them', indeed, to lay down their lives for king and Church in these next years.

For the present, all was to no avail. In July Sir Nicholas had to report mutiny in Astley's regiment from Berkshire and Oxfordshire: they 'would not fight against the Gospel, or be commanded by Papists'. These lies were, of course, the fruit of generations of Puritan propaganda, but, lies as they were, they were as usual enormously effective. Sir Nicholas was forced to get the trained bands from Hertfordshire to keep the regiment in order. In August he reports distraction in London: 'The King says, "Send Byron to them: he will take order with them" – but Byron has no mind to be made a moon-calf and advantage the King's service nothing by it.'

The king's service broke in his hands; on the Border his disorganized forces fell back before the Scots, who advanced into England – the first of their armed interventions, which ultimately decided the issue in the Civil War and won it for Parliament. The king tried to muster support from his peers; but Sir John Byron, stationed at Berwick, reported ill news of the situation. He hoped that the king's meeting with the peers 'will drive out those vipers we have been too ready to entertain in our bosoms. They might easily have been prevented ... had they been kept but twenty-four hours longer out of Newcastle, the whole army had disbanded; but now they have settled themselves so well.' The hungry Scots were irremovable: they settled themselves until they were paid off. Byron added that the Scots General Leslie's exaction of £350 a day from Durham 'will prove a fruitful precedent for the King's service, that hereafter Ship Money may be thought a toy'. It was indeed chicken-feed, compared with what the Civil War was to cost, or even the parliamentary taxation thought up by the ingenious business head of Pym. There was nothing for it but to call Parliament to pay them – and henceforth there was collusion between the embattled English Puritans and the Scots Presbyterians.

The elections to the Long Parliament of 1640 can hardly be described as hotly contested: they were a push-over for the gentry as a class, bent on power. In Cornwall the royal influence, exercised through the duchy officials, had no effect whatever.

Out of the forty-four members returned in November 1640, thirty-three were of the local squirearchy: the elections are the victory of a class more than of a principle.... The forty-four Cornish members were a homogeneous body. Led by Sir Bevil Grenville and Sir Alexander Carew, both members of the landed gentry to which two-thirds of the members belonged, the Cornish representatives were not yet organized into parties; the fundamental cleavage had not appeared. It would come with the trial of Strafford and the attack upon Episcopacy [i.e. the Church].*

Against the monstrous condemnation to death of the king's minister, Strafford, by Act of Attainder, i.e. a parliamentary murder, for no treason could be proved against him, eight Cornish members, in spite of insistent pressure and mob incitement, had the courage to vote. These honourable men were Richard Arundell, Joseph Jane, William Scawen, Robert Holborne, an Edgcumbe, and three who were also, like Bevil Grenville, to lay down their lives in the war – Sidney Godolphin, Sir Nicholas Slanning and John Trevanion.

The parliamentary leaders were determined to get all the levers of power into their hands, the control of army and navy, and of the Church. From the City, mobs were brought down to Westminster to exert pressure upon the king and the Lords, to bring down the bishops as they had done Strafford. From the Tower, that strong-point overlooking the City, the lieutenant, Sir Thomas Lunsford, was dismissed. Thereupon the king

* M. Coate, *Cornwall in the Great Civil War*, 24–5.

appointed Sir John Byron. The Commons again and again tried to get him out and, when the king would not dismiss him, attempted to get the Lords to join with them in getting the appointment into their hands. This the Lords refused as 'the King's peculiar right and prerogative'. So the Commons organized further mob pressure. Byron reported in January 1642 that the City was constantly picking quarrels, and that he could not promise 'to keep the Tower in the condition I am in'. The City had no cause for grievance; he had issued out arms for service against the rebels in Ireland, and powder for the navy (now under Parliament's control). The City should be appeased. Instead, there was a conspiracy to surprise the Tower, and Captain Skippon was posted with five hundred men on Tower Hill to overawe the garrison.

In February Byron was sent for, to appear as a delinquent on his knees at the bar of both Houses of Parliament. Royalist members were already absenting themselves from these deplorable scenes. Clarendon tells us that Byron begged the king 'to free him from the agony and vexation of that place, which had exposed his person and reputation to the rage and fury of the people, and compelled him to submit to such reproaches as a generous spirit could not brook'. After some reluctance the king acceded to Byron's request; Parliament was able to put in their own man in his place.

Byron was free to go and raise a troop of horse to fight in the king's service, one of the first to join him at York, and was with him when he raised his standard at Nottingham that summer.

IV

The Byrons in the Civil War

THE BYRONS were much to the fore and in the public eye during the Civil War, not only on account of their energy and exploits, but because there were so many of them serving the king. Sir John, the fifth head of the family at Newstead, was one of the foremost Royalist commanders in the field; as such, he was one of the small company excepted by Parliament by name from any possibility of pardon. In 1643 the king raised him to the peerage as Baron Byron of Rochdale; the first lord, it will be convenient to distinguish him as such among so many members of the family who were knights or colonels.

At the beginning of the war, in the Edgehill campaign, three of his brothers served in his regiment – Richard, Gilbert and William. Sir Richard, next in seniority, who was to succeed as the second lord, having an independent establishment at Strelley through his wife, raised horse for himself and achieved an independent command as governor of Newark. Sir Robert was for a time governor of Liverpool. Sir Thomas commanded the prince of Wales's regiment. Young Gilbert, who had been a lieutenant in the second Scottish campaign, served as a colonel in North Wales and governor of Rhuddlan Castle. Two of the brothers lost their lives in the war: Sir Thomas and Philip. Then there was their uncle, Sir Nicholas, twin-brother of their father, who, as a professional soldier in the Netherlands returned to be prominent early in the war. Born in 1600, he was a captain in the Low Countries, then a colonel of foot in the Scots war. In October 1642 he was governor of Chester for a time, with a large commission as colonel-general of Cheshire and Shrop-shire, which became a Byron stamping ground – though they stamped all over the Midlands.

They were a fighting family to a man, passionately devoted to the king's cause, as Mrs Hutchinson noted, where some families were divided. This was not often the case in Nottinghamshire, however, where all the nobility (with one exception) and most of the larger gentry were for king and Church; the lesser gentry, the urban middle-class, and often enough the common people, were with Parliament: Puritanism gave them their fighting ideology, and strengthened their backbone. A large element of class-interest and class-envy was observable in all this, usual enough in all societies.

John, Lord Byron, had had some military training in the Netherlands, as we have seen. He was a man of immense energy, unquestioning courage, and dogged pertinacity. He had professional competence and no nerves – nothing ever daunted him; by the same token, he had not much flexibility, and no subtlety or imagination. Thus he was several times caught out – but never gave up. One sees his personality and something of his qualities in the eloquent portrait painted by William Dobson at Oxford, on one of his visits during the war – a fighting tough: dark and saturnine, black eyes and sharp beard, a scar on his cheek, a curious uncomprehending expression in the fine eyes. Indeed, bluff and blunt, perhaps he did not see very far; neither a strategist nor much of a tactician, he just went straight forward, fighting all the way. But, though honest and not an intriguer, he was no fool and capable of writing down his own account of actions, with criticisms much to the point. The king had in him a servant whom he could absolutely trust, which was not always the case; and this was true of all the family.

We find Byron to the fore in so many actions from first to last, we can hardly track him in all his tireless campaigning across the countryside: with the king at the raising of his standard at Nottingham, thence to Oxford, Worcester, Shrewsbury, and back across country to Edgehill; next year, he played a prominent part in the South, at the battles of Roundway Down and the first Newbury. In 1644 he suffered a sharp defeat at Nantwich and was heavily engaged at Marston Moor, followed by another defeat back on the Welsh border, at Montgomery Castle. Lastly, there was his long defence of Chester

for many months, after most others would have given up:
it was one of the last Royalist strongholds to surrender,
in February 1646. Here one sees his qualities at their best:
honesty and loyalty without shadow, courage, endurance and
extreme tenacity. Perhaps 'dogged' is the word that sums him
up.

Byron had large estates, but, having recently put out a lot
of money for the purchase of Rochdale, he can have had little
cash to spare. The enormously wealthy marquis of Worcester
– who spent something like a million pounds for the king – lent
Byron £5,000 for 'mounting money', to equip a whole regiment
of horse. The Royalist cause had not the immense resources that
Parliament could command – the City of London, commerce,
command of the sea, the prosperous South and East – so the
king had to impose a great deal on faithful supporters. Among
these were the Oxford colleges; even Cambridge, so sadly infected by Puritanism, contributed its quota. At Nottingham the
town lent a barrel of gunpowder out of its store at Sir Nicholas
Byron's request.

Byron was on the march from Nottingham to Oxford, with
two of his brothers, when the country around Brackley rose
against the Cavaliers. The Byrons were at dinner on Sunday,
28 August 1642, when they were surprised. The country folk
took a number of prisoners and made a good killing in Byron's
richly caparisoned horse, a clothes-bag of sumptuous apparel,
a couple of hats full of gold, and some £2,000 in silver. The
brothers with their immediate followers took to horse and
managed to get away to Oxford.

We have a vivid account by the bailiff of their reception in
this uncertain time, when Sir John and his company arrived
outside the gates of the walled city at midnight on Sunday, 28
August. They might easily have been held up, he reported, by
the straitness of the passages by which they came, the weariness of
the horses and their attendants lack of arms. The mayor bade
the bailiff let them in (he was William Chillingworth, father
of the philosophic theologian, Laud's brilliant godson, fated to
die in the war). Then said the mayor, 'Have them to the Vice-
Chancellor, and let him do it.' So the vice-chancellor, Dr Pink,
and various fellows and scholars brought them in, the good
doctor going from inn to inn to take up lodgings and look to

the stabling of the horses. The mayor gave them wine and welcome, and free drink to the company.

So the vice-chancellor and Byron took control of the city, set a watch upon the gates and imprisoned opponents. Byron was careful to obtain the mayor's consent to his actions, and had the trumpets sounded in St Giles's Fields to that effect. Bullets were shot into Bailiff Heron's 'backside', i.e. of his premises; so the citizens were disarmed, the town's store of arms and ammunition collected for the king's use and put into the upper chamber of the tower in the Schools quadrangle. Byron's company dug up the stone bridge between the city and Botley, and began the work of entrenching and fortifying during their occupation.

The students were recruited to arms and, most important, plate and money were collected to be conveyed to the king's use. The problem was to get it where most needed. On 19 September Byron arrived with his convoy at Worcester, but found that the city was untenable, the walls and defences derelict. The Parliamentarian army under Essex was approaching, and the king ordered Prince Rupert to the rescue. In a brilliant action at Powick Bridge, Rupert inflicted a smart defeat with heavy loss upon the Roundheads, before their large forces could unite. The Cavaliers were able to withdraw with their treasure to Shrewsbury. Few were their losses, though one of the Byrons was wounded; the moral effect of the victory was great – it was the first set action of the war, and Rupert's name became an inspiration to the Cavaliers, a name of dread to Roundheads.

That autumn followed the Edgehill campaign, Essex's and the king's armies lumbering across country for the prize of London, neither of them knowing the whereabouts of the other in this early, amateurish stage of the war. Sir Nicholas Byron had managed to secure the arms and ammunition from Banbury Castle, 'valiantly surrendered by Colonel Fiennes, Lord Saye's son', said secretary Nicholas contemptuously. The Royalists held Fiennes to be a coward; he was to be unlucky yet again.

Byron was then ordered to assault the town, that stronghold of Puritanism, but the order was countermanded before Edgehill. Here Sir Nicholas was put in command of a brigade of foot, stationed half in the rear, with its back to Radway. John Byron commanded a brigade of horse in reserve, in the rear between Radway and Edgehill. The king's Life Guard was supposed to be under his command; but gallant young Lord Bernard Stuart pleaded with the king to join in the first assault, and the king gave way to him. This was a mistake, and it was followed by another. Byron's cavalry were so eager to attack (and take their chance of booty), that they did not fulfil their role of a reserve, when they might have turned the scales decisively – as Rupert observed reproachfully. The Roundhead horse broke; Byron 'thought there was nothing more to be done but to pursue those that fled, and could not be contained by their commander, but with spurs and loose reins followed the chase'.

Until the formation of the New Model Army and the ascendancy of Cromwell's Ironsides, the Cavaliers had a marked advantage in cavalry – naturally from their class composition. By the same token the Parliamentarian infantry were steadier and better. Essex's main brigades of foot advanced against Sir Nicholas Byron's and drove it back, Sir Nicholas himself wounded. Thus the battle was indecisive, though a strategic victory for the king: the road to London lay open.

As the king drew near to his rebellious capital, Byron's horse were quartered in and around Fawley Court, belonging to the Parliamentarian lawyer, Bulstrode Whitelocke. He provides an early example of the depredations committed on both sides. The Byron brothers had given orders that their regiment

should commit no insolence at my house nor plunder any goods. But soldiers are not easily governed against their plunder or persuaded to restrain it. For there being about 1000 of the King's Horse quartered in and about the house and none but servants there, there was no insolence or outrage usually committed by common soldiers on a reputed enemy which was omitted by these brutish fellows. There they had their whores with them, they spent and consumed 100 load of corn and hay, littered their horses with sheaves of good wheat. Divers writings of consequence and books which were left in my study, some of them they tore in pieces, others they burnt to light their tobacco. Some they carried away with them, to my extreme great loss and prejudice in wanting the writings of my estate, and losing very many excellent manuscripts of my father's and others', and some of my own labours.

They broke down my park pales, killed most of my deer and let out all the rest, only a tame young stag they carried away and presented to Prince Rupert, and my hounds, which were extraordinarily good. They ate and drank up all that the house could afford; broke up all trunks, chests and places; where they found linen or any household stuff they took it away with them, cutting the beds, let out the feathers and took away the ticks. They carried away my coach and four good horses, and all my saddle horses, and did all the mischief and spoil that malice and envy could provoke barbarous mercenaries to commit. And so they parted.

At Turnham Green the king, faced by the embattled strength of London's trained bands, turned back – it was the moment of Milton's sonnet 'When the Assault was intended to the City'. Byron's regiment fell back upon Reading, whence he reported in downright fashion that he wished to be relieved of his command: 'not for any impatience in myself, or unwillingness to undergo anything that may be for his Majesty's service, but to avoid the certain ruin of my regiment. Which, for want of accommodation here and all things necessary for the subsistence of men, hath been very hardly kept from breaking forth into a mutiny, and doth daily diminish, notwithstanding the best care I can take for the preservation of it.' His men simply could not be fed or lodged in the town, let alone taking in two or three troops more.

Here we see something of the other side of the picture. This kind of thing was to spread over most of the country, except for the monolithic Parliamentarian East: with the disruption of society came want and destruction; whole areas were devastated, ruin wrought upon castles, palaces, houses, cathedrals, churches, towns; there was pestilence and disease, and by the end, in some areas, especially in the North, actual famine. Such were the consequences of the idiotic Civil War.

On New Year's Day, 1643, Byron was escorting ammunition to the marquis of Hertford in Somerset (which suffered particularly from devastation later). At Burford he ran into a detachment of Roundheads seeking quarter, the night so dark that these were descried only by the glimmer of their matches. The Roundheads occupied the market place; Byron's foot fired on them from the houses round about; the horse then charged, beating them out of the town and pursuing them across country.

The king and Court were now firmly based at Oxford, the Royalist capital, strongly fortified and largely surrounded by water – the rivers east and west, Christ Church Meadows flooded on the south. We cannot follow the day-to-day activities of the Byron brothers; in the early stages of the war they fought in close association with, or under the command of, Prince Rupert. Fragments of their correspondence with him remain – we have already seen that John Byron commanded an eloquent style of straight talk. From Oxford in May a troop of his horse encountered a Parliamentarian contingent near Bicester, killing a score, including the captain, and taking a dozen prisoners.

In 1643 the Royalist cause was going briskly and looked like winning. In the West the Cornish Foot, by way of exception to the Royalist infantry in general, had accomplished fine feats all the way from Braddock Down and Stratton to the Battle of Lansdown, outside Bath, where they lost the best beloved of their leaders, Sir Bevil Grenville. Captain Atkyns paid tribute to them: 'These were the best Foot I ever saw, for marching and fighting; but so mutinous withal that nothing but an alarm could keep them from falling foul upon their officers.' The Cornish were devoted to their own leaders, but even Clarendon, who knew them fairly well, admitted that 'Cornish people are used to say what they think.'

In July, after their severe losses, they were cooped up in Devizes, with a far stronger army under Waller coming down upon them, and their own very able general, Hopton, nearly blinded and *hors de combat* from a gunpowder explosion. As a matter of extreme urgency, Byron's brigade of horse, with Wilmot's and Prince Maurice's, were dispatched to the relief of the Cornish. In the battle of Roundway Down, which was fought on 13 July, Waller had the advantage of occupying the hill, with a steep declivity in the rear, on the western side. Byron's brigade was on the right of Wilmot's, astride the road from Marlborough, north of Devizes.

Byron himself wrote an account of the action. Approaching Waller's Brigade up the hill,

the command I gave my men was that not a man should discharge a pistol till the enemy had spent all his shot, which was punctually observed. So that first they gave us a volley of their carbines, then of their pistols, and then we fell in with them and gave them ours in the teeth. Yet they would not quit their ground, but stood pushing it for a pretty space – till it pleased God (I think) to put new spirit into our tired Horse as well as into our men. So that, though it were up the hill and that a steep one, we overbore them and with that violence that we forced them to fall foul upon other reserves of Horse that stood behind to second them, and so swept their whole body of Horse out of the field.

The pursuit was furious to the edge of the precipice 'where never horse went down nor up before', and 'many of them broke their own and their horses' necks'. The scene where these characteristic human amenities took place – one pities the poor horses that had no responsibility for men's idiocies – is still called Bloody Ditch, and relics still fetch up.

The Cornish Foot now moved in to attack Waller's, divested of their cavalry. Byron rallied as many of his horse as he could, to join in the assault: 'Their officers thought it not fit to stand any longer, but such as had horses rode away as fast as they could, and too fast for us to overtake them. The rest blew up their powder and threw down their arms and betook themselves to their heels.' Many were cut down; the sensible surrendered. The Cavaliers claimed six hundred killed, eight hundred prisoners, and all Waller's guns and ammunition. It was a fine killing. Military experts consider it, as a work of art, 'one of the most interesting of the entire war'.

Impossible as it is to recover all the activities of those energetic brothers dashing about the country, we know that Sir Thomas was employed that summer in the relief of Basing House, the marquis of Winchester's great palace, which was to endure many months of siege, to end in destruction, pillage and massacre. Today, only a jumble of humps and hollows under the turf remain.

In September John and uncle Nicholas played important parts in the first Battle of Newbury, which should have held up Essex's advance to London, if it had not been mismanaged. John's account is highly critical of the gross error the Royalists made 'in not viewing the ground – though we had day enough to do it – and not possessing ourselves of those hills above the town by which the enemy was necessarily to march the next day to Reading'. This neglect enabled Essex to take possession of the dominating ridge south-west of Newbury. John Byron, in command of his brigade of horse on the right, was feeling his way round the flank of the hill, when he found the way blocked by a hedge, with a gap through which only one horseman could pass. As Byron was having the gap widened, his horse was wounded. The famous Falkland, the king's secretary of state, serving as a volunteer that day,

more gallantly than advisedly spurred his horse through the gap, where both he and his horse were immediately killed. . . . The passage then being made somewhat wide, and I not having another horse, drew in my own troop first and charged the enemy, who entertained us with a great salvo of musket shot and discharged their two drakes upon us with case shot: which killed some and hurt many of my men, so that we were forced to wheel off and could not meet them at the charge.

While Byron rallied his troopers, he sent in Aston's regiment, which 'beat them to the end of the close, where they faced us again, having the advantage of a hedge at their backs, and poured another volley of shot upon us, when Sir Thomas Aston's horse was killed under him, and withal kept us off with their pikes'. Military experts tell us that the Parliamentarian foot were 'stiffened by the London Trained Bands, who checked another charge by the gallant Byron, who had lost 100 men from his regiment alone. Had his efforts been followed up by the Royalist foot, Round Hill might yet have been gained.' Sir Nicholas Byron's brigade of infantry came forward and consolidated the ground held by the horse, but seems to have been unwilling to press home its attack.

Lord Byron was very caustic on the subject of the Royalist foot and no less critical of the king's decision to withdraw from the field.

This is generally confessed that had not our Foot played the poltroons extremely that day, we in all probability had set a period to the war – our Horse having behaved themselves with as much gallantry as could be. However, the advantage was extremely on our side . . . when we had beaten the enemy from the ground and drawn off a piece of their cannon, and might have done so by all the rest, had not our Foot played the jades and that intelligence was brought us of the great fright they were in, many of them stealing from their arms in the darkness of the night. We then, upon a foolish and knavish suggestion of want of powder, quitted all our advantages, and about 12 o'clock at night drew off all our men as if we had been the beaten party.

It seems that Byron was right and that the best opportunity of concluding the war quickly had been lost. For the drawn battle was a strategic victory for Parliament: the road to London lay open, and Essex's army was home. Byron's comments enable us to read further into his character – hot-tempered and uncompromising, not afraid to express his criticism of even the king's decision. Amid all these dangers and many more to come Byron seems to have had a charmed life, where so many others fell. For ourselves we may reserve the comment that once more the class structure beneath the conflict is revealed: the impetuous courage of the *élite* Cavalier horse, irresistible in the early stages of the war, was a wasting asset against the stolidity and numbers of the Roundhead infantry. The 'honours' of that day were with the London trained bands.

At the end of July Prince Rupert won his greatest triumph with the capture of Bristol, second city in the kingdom. A couple of brigades under Byron's command had been in at the kill, as we learn from his letter sent post-haste to Rupert on 27 July: 'I have sent my lieutenant-colonel back to Bristol to fetch back those men of these brigades who are stayed behind, and went this morning in so great numbers that there are very few left with the colours – the reason whereof is their discontent in that they think they are sent away at this time to lose their shares in the pillage of Bristol.' Rupert had sent them away; Byron now urged him to command that 'they shall have their parts as well as others ... and all who belong to those two brigades immediately to repair to their colours upon pain of death. And truly, sir, unless this be done, I shall carry as few back to Oxford as if I had received a defeat.... I see a mutiny like to arise amongst the soldiers unless they receive some benefit of your Highness's great victory at Bristol.'

Pillage – this takes us a little further into the reality of the Civil War. Byron's solicitude was purely military, the overriding necessity to keep his men to the colours. No doubt he got them, or most of them, back to Oxford. In November he was again at Brackley; a letter from thence to Rupert inducts us into further inhumanities of war: the sequel to spying, passing military intelligence, attempts to get opponents to betray their cause. He had been making offers to the governor of Aylesbury and others: 'The business of Aylesbury is discovered to the governor himself, who hath sent the poor woman that was employed betwixt us prisoner to my lord of Essex at Great Albans, where, I believe, she is hanged by this time. I suppose our failing of Newport [Pagnell] made him doubt of the possibility of effecting the other ... howsoever, I am sure he hath declared himself both a fool and a knave.'

He goes on to urge upon the prince his commissariat problems, which must have taken up far more of his time than fighting and prancing about the country.

All our quarters hereabouts are so eaten up that there will be no possibility of subsisting here above three or four days at the most, which I humbly beseech your Highness to take into your consideration. As likewise I may have the pay that was promised me for my regiment at my return – without which I must ride as a volunteer in your Highness's troop, for I am sure I shall have no regiment to command. And truly, sir, it would be much for the King's service, if your old tried regiments might have rest this winter that they may be strong and well recruited against the spring, and let the new levied troops learn their duty. For my own particular, if I may have but rest and pay for three months [i.e. for his men], I will undertake to make up my regiment in that time four hundred horse effective. I have given orders for the speedy bringing of all the shovels and spades in those parts.

We see that the country, which had had it much too good for too long under the king's personal government – without the distractions and discords of Parliament – was now being denuded not only of its surplus wealth but of necessities.

The effective turning-point came this year with Pym's masterstroke in calling in the Scots in the North to redress the balance in the South. The king hoped to offset this by calling in help from Ireland. Ormonde's cessation of hostilities enabled English troops to be released from service there to reinforce the Royalists in the North-West. Lying Puritan propaganda – the Puritans had no regard for truth – described these troops as native Irish and papists. They were, for most part, neither. A typical officer among them was Monk, a professional soldier of good West Country stock, a staunch Protestant. A prodigious future was in store for him.

The plan now was to send Lord Byron to the North-West,

pivoting upon Chester, as field marshal of the neighbouring counties. His job was to recover Cheshire from the control of the able Parliamentarian leader, Sir William Brereton; open the way for the reception of reinforcements from Ireland; build up an army with which to clear Lancashire and join up with the marquis of Newcastle against the Fairfaxes and the Eastern Association before the Scottish covenanting invasion, designed to convert England – think of it! – to Presbyterianism.

Already the Byrons were back in their native North-West. In October 1642 Sir Nicholas had been appointed governor of Chester and colonel-general of the forces in Cheshire and Shrop-shire. In February 1643 he had had his first encounter with the redoubtable Brereton, who had summoned the militia to meet him at Tarporley, midway between Chester and Nant-wich. Sir Nicholas's troops got there first, chose their ground to advantage, and in a brief engagement disposed of their opponents. The sympathies of the common people were with Parliament, however, and by March all the salt district around Nantwich was in their hands.

On 21 November Lord Byron left Oxford for his new and most responsible command with a thousand horse and three hundred foot. Marching by Evesham and Shrewsbury he reached Chester on about 6 December, to receive some five regi-ments from Ireland, including that of his brother, Robert, whose military career was to be mainly bound up with Ireland, where it had begun. His eldest brother lost no time in making his presence felt. On 26 December he reported, 'The rebels had possessed themselves of a church at Barthomley. I put them all to the sword, which I find to be the best way to proceed with these kind of people, for mercy to them is cruelty.' It is true that this was in accordance with the rules of war: the rebels had been summoned to surrender and refused – it was no more than Cromwell was to do at Drogheda. But, after this, Byron was anathema to Parliament: 'Bloody Braggadocio Byron', and 'inhuman upstart', referring to the recentness of his peerage, were the names for him in Puritan news-sheets.

He followed this up with a successful attack on Brereton at Middlewich, in which the Roundheads lost some three hundred men and as many prisoners; the Royalists had few losses, but Robert was among the wounded. Brereton fell back upon

Nantwich. There followed some unpleasant surprises for the Byrons, largely owing to overconfidence. Sir Nicholas was returning from Shrewsbury with a convoy of ammunition, when he allowed himself to be surprised at Ellesmere, the convoy overthrown, the ammunition captured, and a hundred prisoners taken, among them the governor of Chester, Sir Nicholas himself.

Nantwich was worse: an unexpected disaster. Lord Byron had been able to drive Brereton in upon Nantwich, clearing Cheshire, and he proceeded now to embark upon a siege. The effects of the intervention of the Scots were immediately felt: Newcastle was fully engaged, preparing to meet them, and this freed Fairfax to march an army to relieve Nantwich. Byron had no idea of its strength or the speed of its approach; he stuck doggedly to the siege when he should have retreated – there was time. He was caught with his forces strung out, divided in two by the River Weaver, swollen by a sudden thaw, the bridge wrecked – one of the chances of war. The Royalist wings fought well, Sir Robert Byron commanding the left. Fairfax's superior generalship blocked the attempt of Lord Byron's cavalry to get round the river to the aid of the stricken Royalist centre. The Parliamentarian infantry fought with stubborn determination and broke the Cavalier foot, putting the brigades of horse in imminent peril. The 'Bloody Braggadocio Byron' made off to Chester with his horse; his guns and baggage fell into Fairfax's hands, as did numerous prisoners – among them Monk – and over a hundred women camp-followers.

The consequences were decisive in this sector: no more hope of the grand strategy of forming a north-western army to oppose the Scots, or even of making the North-West itself a safe preserve for the king. Byron's limitations as a general were too obvious. Rupert had to be sent to save what he could. He had few troops with him, but two more detachments arrived from Ireland and with these the situation at Chester was stabilized for the time being. It was said that some hundreds of Byron's 'Irish' foot went over to the Roundheads – probable enough, since English troops serving in Ireland were likely to be more Protestant than not. It is another consideration against the ubiquitous propaganda, effective as it was, that the king's was the 'papist' cause.

From Chester Byron reported to Ormonde their ill-success, explaining that he had relied on Newcastle to prevent Fairfax's march, and that 'in this ill-affected country' he could never procure news of their approach but by sending out parties of horse. He excused his failure by saying that the ground where they fought was so enclosed that the horse could do little service. As for the foot, 'I could wish they were rather Irish than English, for the English we have already are very mutinous and, being for the most part these countrymen, are so poisoned by the ill-affected people here that they grow very cold in this service. And since the rebels here called in the Scots I know no reason why the King should make any scruple of calling in the Irish, or the Turks, if they would serve him.' There we have Byron delineated by himself.

An exception in this tale of woe was the behaviour of Colonel Monk, who had a commission from Prince Rupert to raise a regiment but marched as a volunteer and 'added great alacrity to the soldiers'. Sir Robert Byron, also writing to Ormonde, added a gloss that, though 'the regiment had their beloved Colonel Monk in the head of them, was no sooner charged but they broke and, being rallied again, the next charge ran quite away'. Some of them indeed went over to the Parliamentarians. Sir Robert gave no good account, either, of the surprise of his uncle's convoy coming from Shrewsbury – though superior in numbers, they were pounced upon and made prisoners before ever the alarm was given. Now both Sir Nicholas and Monk were prisoners. It was all a story of ill omen for the Royalist cause in the North-West.

From Chester Rupert had to dash across the Midlands to the relief of Newark, quite as vital a fortress on the east: strategically placed on the main route north and south, at the crossing of the Trent, in Royalist hands it impeded the southward drive of Fairfax and the Scots, and posed a threat to the hold of the Eastern Association upon Lincolnshire. Following Royalist defeats at Gainsborough and Winceby, Sir Richard Byron was made governor of Newark, to hold it fast – as he did.

We have an inimitable picture of the situation in the eastern Midlands from the pen of Mrs Hutchinson, in her style of lady-like condescension and well-bred malice. Her husband, virtuous man, had ensconced himself in Nottingham Castle and never let go, though the Cavaliers were all round him and even in the town. When 'Sir Richard Byron was come to be governor of Newark [in the summer of 1643], a house of my Lord Chaworth's in the Vale was fortified and some horse was put into it; and another house of the Earl of Chesterfield's, both of them within a few miles of Nottingham.' The malignants crept closer and closer, and Sir Richard made attempts upon the virtue of the citizens of Nottingham. 'Colonel Hutchinson, because the governor of Newark was his cousin-german, was forced against his nature to be more uncivil than to any other that were governors in that place. Whether it were that the dissension of brethren is always most spitefully pursued, or that Sir Richard Byron suffered under the same suspicions on his side, it is true they were to each other the most uncivil enemies that can be imagined.' Obstinacy was a Byron characteristic: each of them – Colonel Hutchinson was half a Byron – had his share of it.

Sir Richard began with an approach to his cousin: after all, among the Nottinghamshire gentry the Roundheads were a small minority (for all that, they included three regicides in Ireton, Colonel Hacker and Hutchinson). Sir Richard pleaded with young Hutchinson, 'out of that tender natural affection which he ever had for him', that he would save his estate for him if he would return to his natural duty to the king. Byron could 'plead you were an inconsiderate young man rashly engaged and dares assure himself to beg your pardon – but to keep a castle against your King is a rebellion of so high a nature that there will be no colour left to ask favour for you.' To this Hutchinson replied that Sir Richard 'might consider there was, if nothing else, so much of a Byron's blood in him that he should very much scorn to betray or quit a trust he had undertaken'.

Sir Richard's reply to this was a raid upon the town, let in by Alderman Toplady, a 'great Malignant . . . and no alarm given to the Castle. . . . The Cavaliers, being about six hundred, fell to ransack and plunder all the honest men's houses in the town, and the Cavaliers of the town, who had called them in, helped them in this work.' Attacked in turn by a troop of horse 'falling in with them pell mell, they had gotten Sir Richard Byron down and they had his hat; but he escaped, though his horse was so wounded that it fell dead in the next street. . . .

Their prisoners and plunder they sent away in boats to Newark; many of the townsmen went with them, carrying away not only their own but their neighbours' goods.' The Cavaliers were able to release the leading doctor in the town, Dr Plumtre, whom Hutchinson had imprisoned, 'not ignorant of his atheism' – this meant that he was not a Puritan; while, when the marquis of Newcastle summoned the colonel to give up the castle, Hutchinson replied that he 'scorned ever to yield on any terms to a papistical army led by an atheistical general'.

Sir Richard recognized that no further approach was possible to the stiff-necked Puritan, on his way to becoming a regicide. (At the Restoration it was largely owing to the influence of the Byrons that Colonel Hutchinson escaped the supreme penalty for his part in the murder of the king.) However, an exchange of prisoners was put through. 'Being almost all of them gentlemen,' says Lucy Hutchinson, 'Sir Richard Byron, for his brother's memory [they were from Sir Thomas's regiment, after his death at Oxford], exchanged them for prisoners taken when the town was first surprised.'

However, Sir Richard continued to tamper with the virtue of Nottingham's citizens; Mrs Hutchinson records her suspicions of a 'debosht malignant apothecary' and others. He varied these entertainments by blocking up the approach to the town across the river, and in November making a sortie to Melton Mowbray, capturing a number of prisoners. Among these was Captain Hacker, 'who had made a vow to pistol his own brother because he would not turn rebel, and was afterwards hanged for commanding the guard at the King's trial'. We do not learn this from Lucy, though she does tell us that the mother of Sir Richard's first wife had married Hacker's father: this man thus became the stepfather of the heir to Strelley, by Lady Byron's first husband. This Hacker 'had about £1,800 of the estate of young Strelley in his hands, which, he dying, his eldest son and heir, Colonel Francis Hacker was liable and justly ought to pay this money. Young Strelley died in France and left his estate to his half-brother, the son of Sir Richard Byron, who all the time of the first war was at school in Colonel Hutchinson's garrison at Nottingham.' Byron's son also was sent into France, and, as he was only a boy when the estate fell to him, Colonel Hacker tried to do him out of it. In this he was backed by Sir Arthur

Heselrig, the odious creature who scrounged Auckland Castle from the bishopric of Durham. Colonel Hutchinson managed to save the Strelley estate for Sir Richard's son and heir. Such were the amenities and courtesies, the civil family exchanges, during the war.

In March 1644 Newark was threatened by a strong force under Sir John Meldrum, with two thousand horse and some foot to Sir Richard's less than two thousand, all told. Meldrum stormed Muskham Bridge, destroying the regiment of Gervase Holles, who was away at Oxford. In consequence Byron is written down in Holles's *Memorials* as 'a person of a narrow soul and every way unequal to the charge he undertook. He, with no more soldiery than he understood, commands this shattered remainder of my regiment, not then above 250 men, as a forlorn to lie a mile from the town at Muskham bridge without relieving for four or five days together: which my Lieutenant-Colonel disputed not.' No doubt Byron was without the means of relieving the post, surrounded as he was by much superior forces. Everyone agrees that his tenacious resistance at Newark belied Holles's character of him: it was just the kind of thing people like to say about each other without any justice of mind.

In fact Sir Richard held on grimly until Rupert arrived, when Meldrum was caught between the two. This complete victory enabled Newark to hold out for yet another two years. Byron had advanced money of his own for its defence – along with other loyalists. In March 1645 the king himself wrote to Sir Richard that he would ever remember his care and courage, and offering to make additions to the town's charter as a mark of appreciation. Nothing could make up for £40,000 worth of damage when it was made a garrison town and one-sixth of it had been burnt. Today one sees the shell of the castle with its gaping holes looking down sadly upon the Trent.

The Byron brothers were spending themselves and their resources for the Cavalier cause, increasingly in vain and with diminishing returns as the king's fortunes turned downwards with the intervention of the Scots. We learn that at some time in the winter of 1643–4 Newstead was looted by a Parliamentarian party from Nottingham – some return for what Byron's troopers had done to Whitelocke's property after Edgehill. In those promising days, in December 1642, when the brothers were together at Oxford with Rupert, the loyal university held a grand degree day to boost morale: the eldest brother was made a DCL, the next an MA. The king, having little else to give, rewarded their services with knighthoods: Thomas at Shrewsbury on 27 September 1642; Richard, within the week, on 1 October 'in the field at the head of his company'; Robert on 12 May 1644, at Oxford; William on 25 February 1646, also at Oxford, before the end. In the Nottingham records we find Sir Richard agreeably promising a lease of St Anne's Well and a coppice to one Heywood, 'if that the King got the better'.

Sir Thomas was the first to fall, by a dastardly hand. He had commanded the prince of Wales's regiment at Edgehill, 'a very valuable and experienced officer', says Clarendon. He had been wounded at Powick Bridge, but more dangerously so at Hopton Heath, near Stafford, where he had made three gallant charges on 19 March 1643. 'Sir Thomas Byron, at the head of the Prince's regiment, charging their Foot, broke in among them; but they, having some troops of Horse near their Foot, fell upon him, and then he received his hurt, bleeding so that he was not able to stay on the field.' He had been shot in the thigh.

In December of that year Sir Thomas was attacked in the street at Oxford by Captain Hurst of his own regiment, over a dispute about pay. He was seriously wounded, but thought likely to recover. A week later the Captain was 'shot to death with five carbines. That afternoon the Lady Butler in Magdalen College shot herself to death with a pistol.' Byron lingered three months and died of his wound on 5 February 1644. He was buried in Christ Church Cathedral amid the growing number of victims of the war, 'on the left side of the grave of Lord Grandison, in a little aisle joining on the south side of the choir'. There they are, brought together by the fortunes of war – Byron and the young father of Charles II's notorious Lady Castlemaine. Sir Thomas's two sons had died as children; his widow was buried in Westminster Abbey in the heyday of the Restoration.

In June a younger brother, Philip, was killed. The combined army of the Scots and Fairfax was besieging York; Newcastle was putting up a strong resistance to overwhelming forces – in successfully repelling a fierce assault on the king's manor, young Colonel Philip Byron fell. The king ordered Rupert to march to the relief of his northern capital, with positive orders to fight. Rupert, with better judgement, was for once reluctant to take the offensive against much superior forces, particularly in cavalry.

Yet, seriously outnumbered as he was, Rupert almost brought off a victory; for long the issue was touch and go – both the Scots general and Lord Fairfax (not Sir Thomas) left the field, thinking it was lost, while Cromwell took advantage of a slight wound to withhold his presence. Nevertheless the well-disciplined charge of his horse and the intervention of the Scottish foot decided the day. Newcastle was late in bringing up his men from York, and Lord Byron's military talents did not shine. He was in command of the horse on the right wing, astride Kendal Lane, with cousin Molyneux in the rear. Once more Byron's simple impetuosity, driving right ahead with no tactical subtlety, was at fault. He advanced to attack Cromwell's Ironsides too soon, frustrating the fire of his own musketeers and losing the advantage of the ground. His first line broke and Rupert had to divert reserves to his imperilled right wing; he himself registered a crisp reproach, 'by the improper charge of Lord Byron much harm was done'. Had Newcastle arrived in time, had Byron's line held, Marston Moor might have been a Royalist victory. For long the issue hung in the balance; the longer it lasted, the greater the loss inflicted on the inferior side.

In the end, it all turned to disaster. 'Well over 3000 Royalists had been killed' – among these a high proportion of irreplaceable officers – and about 1,500 men captured. The grand marquis of Newcastle, who, like the marquis of Worcester, had spent nearly a million for the king, left the country in disgrace. A number of Byron's troops deserted, streaming off into Cumberland; he ordered his captain to pursue them and apply martial law if they refused to return. Rupert, with perhaps six thousand men, collecting stragglers as he went and picking up stranded detachments, crossed the Pennines to Chester, where he left Byron in command. He then continued on his way to Bristol, where in the South-West the king had had much better luck and won a notable victory in Cornwall. The war would continue.

From Chester Byron – as we have seen, no genius but indomitable – went doggedly on his way. Many small engagements took place out in the countryside, with varying success. In August, forcing the passage into Lancashire, at Haleford, he was un-horsed, but for his own person his luck held. Writing to Rupert, 'his most dear Prince', Byron reported: 'The night your High-ness lay at Ruthin, Marrow's horse were beaten' – the action took place 'on the spot where your Highness killed the buck as the Horse were drawing out'. We see that the war had its lighter entertainments, the killing of animals as well as men.

In September Byron suffered a shattering defeat. The Royal-ists' strength in North Wales and the Welsh border had con-centrated to retake Montgomery Castle (now but a shell from these events, the Herbert tombs in the church defaced beyond recognition). Byron had some four or five thousand men under his command, when the combined forces of his old opponent, Brereton, and Myddleton compelled him to break off the siege and fight for it. The Royalists were heavily defeated, Byron thrown back on Chester, the king's cause in North Wales crippled. Defeat was followed by recriminations, Governor Legh of Lyme accusing Byron of being responsible for the over-throw. He himself received some compensation, if not consola-tion, from being appointed gentleman of the robes to the young James, duke of York. We find a warrant to him, from the Court at Oxford, for £5,000 – though how much of this came through to him from the king's distressed finances we may doubt.

The Roundheads followed this up by pressing home the siege of Liverpool, of which Sir Robert Byron was governor. There was no possibility of defence, and Sir Robert surrendered upon terms: he and his officers might march out with horse and arms to any garrison except Chester. His uncle, Sir Nicholas, upon his capture, had been sent prisoner to the Tower. Sophie, Lady Byron, his second wife, appeared at Oxford to beg Ludlow, then prisoner there, to procure an exchange between them. Eventu-ally Sir Nicholas was exchanged for a Cheshire Parliament man, William Glegg. Money passed, for Lady Byron delivered household furniture, apparel, rarities, Dutch pictures and agate cups to a London merchant. One sees once more the erosion and loss of art-objects, which had delighted the eye of cultivated Carolines before the disastrous war. Shortly we find Sir Nicholas badgering Prince Rupert, the especial patron of the Byrons, for a commission.

Lord Byron was high in Rupert's confidence, for we find the prince dispatching him to Oxford to plead his cause for support. At the end of 1644 an angry Byron paid a visit to Oxford to plead his case for better support for the North-West. The fact was that the king's resources were drying up, while the New Model Army, under Fairfax and Cromwell, was being organized and trained to give the *coup de grâce* at Naseby.

In April 1645, beleaguered at Chester, Byron reported that he had only his own and Mostyn's regiments, whereof the officers, ignorant Welsh gentlemen, refused any strict duty. For the rest the garrison consisted only of citizens; there was little gunpowder in the city, and little money. Nevertheless, as the Parliament's forces grew in strength around him, he assured the king's secretary of state he would do his best as 'befitting an honest man and one whom I hope you shall not blush to own'. Brereton was well informed of the distress to which Chester was being reduced, as early as April 1645: 'they become every day more and more necessitated, fresh provisions being much wanting and very dear, and the poorer sort are already much distressed, their provisions being spent. It is most probable they will be in a mutiny.' That month, Brereton – quite as dogged as Byron, but now, with superior forces, in a position to press home his attack – captured two of the brothers, Sir Richard and Sir Robert. We can be sure that these distinguished prisoners were well cared for, for Richard had married Lady Brereton's sister: the fight was all in the family.

In May Lord Byron had an interview at Market Drayton with the king, on his way to the final disaster of Naseby. The king could do nothing for him – Chester had been utterly denuded of troops. Byron was thrown back on his own resources: here, with his back to the wall, he was at his best.

He found it necessary to dismiss Mostyn's regiment; then the garrison was insufficient for such a large circuit of wall (it mostly remains: one can still pace it, with those days much in mind). After Naseby the king was engaged in drawing together the remnants of his forces and marching to the North-West in the vain hope of effecting a junction with Montrose, who was already meeting defeat in Scotland. The king's approach forced Brereton's withdrawal, and for a week or so there was a respite during which some reinforcements from Wales and Ireland came in. Gone were the early days of idealism – always a mistake – on both sides: the conflict was degenerating into a brute struggle for survival. Even on the Puritan side the county committee was forced to complain to Brereton of 'the intolerable miscarriage of your troopers by robbing, spoiling, and plundering of the people; swearing, drinking and all kind of debaucheries'. Well, soldiers must live, and even Puritans are human, if not of an agreeable sort.

That September, from the tower of Chester Cathedral, the king was able to watch the unexpected and bloody reverse of his forces outside upon Rowton Heath. A part of the Roundhead forces under Colonel James fell back upon their main army under Poyntz. Garrison and townsfolk alike, perhaps spurred on by the sickness of hope deferred, rushed forth upon what they took to be a pursuit, into the jaws of an advancing army. There ensued a bloody slaughter, in which fell, among others, the king's handsome young cousin, Lord Bernard Stuart, whom we know from Van Dyck's splendid portrait, and – a more precious life – William Lawes, the most original composer of the time. The cultivated monarch was stricken to heart: 'nor was the King's soul so engrossed with grief for the death of so near a kinsman and noble a lord but that, hearing of the death of his dear servant, William Lawes, he had a particular mourning for him dead whom he loved when living and commonly called the "Father of Music".' The king, usually so dispassionate, was shocked by Rowton Heath, it was observed: perhaps by these intimate blows. He passed into Wales, no further hopes or strategy possible.

Of the two brothers, William and Henry Lawes, William – less well known to us through Milton's co-operation with Henry – was the more original genius, particularly in his instrumental music, becoming better known again today. In his own circle the poets mourned his loss: here is Aurelian Townshend, of the Court masques, celebrating the glory of the monarchy and the happiness of the realm in the glad days before the Civil War. *O fortunatos nimium*! Now:

> Brothers in blood, in science and affection,
> Beloved by those that envy their renown:
> In a false time true servants of the Crown.

In September there was news that Sir Nicholas was coming over from Ireland with reinforcements: we do not know what they were, but expectations were fated to be disappointed. At the end of the month the secretary of state wrote that the king was commanding provisions and horse to be sent into Chester from the Welsh side, still open. Charles himself had got back to Oxford, whence he moved on to Newark in the hope of diverting Roundhead forces from Chester. He hoped that Byron would secure Anglesey, and particularly Caernarvon Castle. In October Byron received the first summons to surrender the city, now blockaded on all sides. He replied with spirit: 'We neither apprehend your condition to be so high, nor ours (God be thanked) to be so low, as to be threatened out of this city.' The Parliamentarian commanders rejected his requests. Thereupon he replied, 'Your refusal of our reasonable offer we have received, which argues you intended not that you pretended, which was the sparing of the effusion of Christian blood.'

The effusion went on, not only among the military; citizens were dying of want or disease. Among them were Byron's sister-in-law, Philip's widow, and her infant daughter. In December he sent his wife to the king at Oxford to beg relief – he could not hold out else to the end of the month. In the event he held on for three months longer.

In November Beeston Castle surrendered; it had engaged a considerable number of Parliamentarian troops, now freed to increase the stranglehold on Chester. A second summons to surrender followed; the reply was a sally of Cavalier horse, which Brereton described as 'the most adventurous and gallant that they ever made'. Further taunts followed between Byron, joined by the mayor of Chester, and Brereton. 'When we call to mind those ancient and honourable privileges and immunities granted heretofore to the citizens and freemen of Chester, we cannot but wonder at your impertinency in urging that as an argument to withdraw us from our allegiance.' Sir William was quite equal to that and flung back: 'Your rebellion and obstinacy is not the way to preserve the ancient privileges granted to that city.' In December unfit horses were turned loose outside the walls, and extra mouths – people who did not belong there – were allowed to leave: two of Lord Kilmorey's servants 'desiring to live at peace', for example. (Kilmorey was the father of Byron's second wife, Eleanor.)

Seven thousand troops were now besieging Chester. Within was starvation. Byron proposed an exchange of prisoners to Brereton. He had gone into the treatment of Roundhead prisoners and found that 'notwithstanding the siege, they have been provided far better than those of ours in your possession. We shall so far remember charity begins at home and, as your design is to reduce us by starving, not to suffer the plentiful provision of prisoners to straighten those who faithfully serve in the garrison. If you send any provision for them, it shall be faithfully given.' An exchange of prisoners took place.

In January a third summons was sent; we are told that 'the citizens were exceeding troubled that the Lord Byron had rejected it. A mutiny in city this morning about provision – cannot hold out a fortnight, so many will be starved.... Divers Welsh are dead from hunger. Five Welsh died last Sabbath day, were starved, formerly there died twenty-five in one week.' Byron wrote in his own hand : 'Keep your foolish senseless paper to yourselves and know there are none in this city such knaves or fools to be deluded thereby' – a characteristic fling.

It is possible that such obstinacy paid – at least for himself and his officers: since there was nothing for it but negotiation, he got better terms. The Parliamentarian army was itself suffering privation and disease. In mid-January negotiations began. Byron to Brereton: 'You may be confident that nothing can necessitate me to treat upon other than favourable conditions.' One of the thirty-six conditions Byron made was very understandable, after the Puritan record of iconoclasm: 'That no church or churches within the city be defaced, that all that belong to the cathedral enjoy their places, and all rooms and furniture [i.e. church fittings] be preserved from violence or profane abuse'.

Brereton to Byron: 'I should not have expected proposition of so high demands as those you have sent. We know your wants are great, your hopes of relief desperate. I will not trouble myself with answering the particulars of your unparalleled demands.' Byron to Brereton: 'Those demands of mine, which you term unparalleled, have been heretofore granted by far greater commanders than yourself – no disparagement to you –

to places in a far worse condition than, God be thanked, this is yet. Witness the Bosse, Breda, and Maestricht.' Byron was, as a professional soldier, attempting to come it over Brereton who was not, though an abler leader. He had no difficulty in riposting: 'I cannot believe that you conceive the war betwixt the Hollanders and the Spaniards is to be made a precedent for us. Neither can I believe that such conditions as you demand were granted to the Bosse, Breda, or Maestricht.'

On 25 January the last hope of relief from the Welsh forces, in which Gilbert Byron was colonel of a regiment, met with a repulse. Lord Byron had to moderate his demands. It is significant that he had to drop the one about the cathedral clergy keeping their places – impossible for a Parliamentarian to accept, now that Parliament, to buy the Scots, had accepted the nonsense of establishing Presbyterianism in England. (Already Cromwell's victorious army was as opposed to stiff-necked Presbyterianism as to uppish Anglicanism.) The condition, as accepted, now read simply: 'That no church within the city, or evidence, or writings belonging to the same, shall be defaced' – and one wonders whether this was kept. Those native Irish who had taken part in the rebellion of 1641, who – with the intolerable Scots covenanters – had brought on the war, fanatics both, were to be made prisoners.

On 3 February 1646 the residual Cavaliers marched out with the 'honours' of war, if that is the word for it. Anglesey was still in Royalist hands, along with several of the great Welsh castles, which would require reduction or starving out. In accordance with the king's wishes Byron assumed command of Caernarvon, and held out there as long as possible – until 4 June. Once more obstinacy paid: the Cavalier officers got the benefit of the articles, including himself and his brother William, engaged in the defence; and the town was saved from plunder.

The first Civil War virtually over, Byron left the country for Paris, where he was provided for by his appointment as governor to the duke of York. It was as well, for in England he was excepted by name from all pardon and his estates confiscated. We catch a glimpse of Sir William Byron in April 1646 when the Committee of Both Kingdoms at Whitehall reproved his doughty opponent, Colonel Mytton, for giving William a

pass to go to the king with two servants. Henceforth there were
to be no passes for the Byrons. The following February Parliamentary troops seized all Lord Byron's goods and chattels, his
estates already sequestered for his malignant 'delinquency'.

Meanwhile the king had come to terms with the Scots, as
discontented with Parliament now as before with him, and this
brought on a renewal of the war: the second Civil War. Lord
Byron was using his influence in Nottinghamshire to stimulate
the loyalists in preparation for the expected Scots invasion
under Hamilton. Thus inspired, Gilbert Byron made large
offers to Colonel Hutchinson's deputy, Captain Poulton, to
render up Nottingham Castle. Lucy Hutchinson confirms:
'which proposition he thought not fit utterly to reject lest the
Castle – being then in a weak condition and the soldiers discontented – some of his under-officers might more readily embrace
it and betray both the place and him'. Poulton reported to the
colonel, who, *sans peur et sans reproche* as ever, 'advised him to
hold his cousin on in the treaty till he himself could go to London and provide for the better securing of the place'. Having
done so, 'when the place was well provided, Captain Poulton,
who was too gentle-hearted to cut off Mr Byron under a pre-
tence of assenting to him, sent to him to shift for himself, which
Mr Byron accordingly did. And now the insurrection began
everywhere to break out.'

The Royalists seized the strong fortress of Pontefract Castle,
to which numbers of them rallied from all quarters. By mid-
June 1648 so many were concentrated there that the place was
eaten up. Some three hundred horse, under Gilbert Byron,
Michael Stanhope and Sir Philip Monkton, made for Don-
caster and into the Isle of Axholme, Puritan countryside which
they could live off and plunder with all the better conscience.
The hue and cry after them was up in all Lincolnshire. Making
south for familiar Newark, surrounded on all sides they turned
at bay in a large beanfield by Willoughby church. There was
a fierce, hacking soldiers' battle, in which no quarter was given
and many were killed, including young Stanhope. Colonel Gilbert Byron was captured 'and carried prisoner to Belvoir Castle,
where, being in distress, although he was an enemy and had
not dealt handsomely with Colonel Hutchinson in endeavour-
ing to corrupt one for whom he was engaged, yet the Colonel

sent him a sum of money for his present relief; and after procured him a release and composition with the Parliament'. Thus Lucy – but were they not cousins? And the Byrons in turn would be able to get Hutchinson off a much worse sentence when the day of judgement arrived with the Restoration in 1660.

Meanwhile Lord Byron had got back to this country and seized Anglesey, hoping to raise North Wales and Lancashire, on the arrival of the Scots. The plan was an important element in deciding the duke of Hamilton to invade by the western route through Lancashire. There his large army was caught strung out along the roads and, at Preston, routed and smashed by Cromwell. Byron's plans for a junction came to nothing; in any case, North Wales was too exhausted and war-weary to rise.

There remained Ireland, where Robert served most of his military career. At New Year 1649 the marquis of Ormonde wrote from Kilkenny to Lord Byron, urging the prince of Wales to come to Ireland: he assured Byron that three parts were devoted to him, and that the fourth might be won over or reduced, i.e. Owen Roe's Catholics or Jones's discontented Puritans. He submitted detailed proposals for the prince to follow, and for Lord Byron's course sailing on Captain D'Arcy's frigate. Byron evidently reached Ireland, for we have a mention of him serving with Ormonde this year. No further details transpire, and shortly he went back to Paris in attendance upon his young charge, the duke of York.

V

Civil War and Sequel: the Trevanions

WE MUST RETRACE OUR STEPS to the war in the West, and the part of the Trevanions in it. All commentators on the Civil War today realize how intensely regional and local it was. Apart from the main campaigns and great battles, like Marston Moor and Naseby, it was waged as a series of localized conflicts, chiefly in the North, North-West, South and South-West. The campaigns in the West have an interest of their own, and are particularly well lighted since Clarendon was mainly concerned with and better informed about this area. It even has a sad charm upon it: the heroism and unexpected achievements of the Cornish Foot – the best to fight on the king's side; the deaths of practically all their leaders in the field:

> Gone the four wheels of Charles's wain:
> Grenville, Godolphin, Trevanion, Slanning, slain.

Cornwall was by no means a homogeneous unit, a monolith on the king's side, as is usually supposed. At the beginning it looked rather evenly divided. The Parliamentarian leader, the virtuous second Lord Robartes, was the richest man in the West. His father had made a fortune of £300,000 from the tin business, usury and mortgages: he bought his peerage with a payment of £10,000 to Buckingham. When Parliament made this a ground of complaint against the man whom the king was delighted to honour, the duke was able to reply that Robartes had before this offered £20,000. He was supported by Bullers, Boscawens, St Aubyns, Eriseys, the Rouses of Halton (close relations of Pym), Nicolls, a Prideaux and a Trefusis; of the

Carews, Sir Alexander lost his head as a traitor to Parliament, caught going over to the other side, while John Carew lost his as an unrepentant regicide at the Restoration.

The king's supporters, it is true, were more numerous and, in Cornwall, far more popular – no one loved Lord Robartes: he was too virtuous and too rich. The irreducible nucleus of the Royalist leadership was to be seen among those Cornish MPs who had had the courage to vote against Strafford's indefensible attainder, against mob pressure applied at Westminster: their names were placarded among those fifty-nine for popular obloquy outside Parliament. Among these were Sidney Godolphin the poet, Richard Arundell of Trerice, an Edgcumbe, Sir Nicholas Slanning and young John Trevanion. Sir Bevil Grenville, 'the most generally loved man in Cornwall', according to Clarendon, took no part in these debates.

Cornwall hesitated, as indeed did most of the country, on the brink. In 1642 the county sent up its petition, supported by some 7,000 inhabitants and most of the gentry, against any alteration of government in Church and State, i.e. against the revolution pushed forward by the majority of the Commons at Westminster. A sensible proposal was made in the West that Devon and Cornwall might opt out, but the revolutionary party in Parliament would have none of that. Their representatives in the county, declared the Royalist Joseph Jane, were 'a passionate company'.

Then the rumour ran that Cornish folk would not make up their minds until 'harvest was gathered in'. The Parliamentarians thought that the county was fairly secure for them – or so they were assured by Lord Robartes, who always exaggerated the influence his wealth and prominence could command there. For when the king's commissions of array came down – perfectly legal as they were – the county's trained bands responded to them, and still more to its natural leaders, Grenvilles, Godolphins, Mohuns, Arundells, Trelawnys, Bassets, Killigrews, Trevanions – from one end of Cornwall to the other.

In organizing the county for war Francis Basset, its sheriff, and Sir Nicholas Slanning, governor of Pendennis Castle took the lead. The county, populous for its size, was poor – unlike the agricultural counties of eastern England. Its main resources were tin-mining and the tin trade, under the control of the duchy (appanage of the prince of Wales – always to be distinguished from the county); its numerous ports and creeks, with their shipping and fisheries (and scope for privateering); and its girdle of castles and strong places, from Launceston to St Michael's Mount. Basset organized the financial side of all this; Slanning, as an expert, the munitions and shipping, the privateering from Pendennis.

A professional soldier, trained in the Low Countries, Slanning had been made governor in 1635. Born at Bickleigh near Plymouth in 1606, he was at Oxford, where he displayed a partiality for experimental and mechanical science – unlike Bevil Grenville, who there 'fell upon the sweet delights of reading poetry and history in such sort that I troubled no other books'. Slanning went thence to the Inner Temple, then abroad. Like the Byrons, he returned to serve in the Scots war. In the Short Parliament he was member for Plymouth; to the Long Parliament he was returned for Penryn, but did not sit long. Clarendon, who visited him when mortally wounded, says that Slanning told him 'he had always despised bullets, having been so used to them, and almost thought they could not hit him. . . . He professed great joy and satisfaction in the losing his life in the King's service.'

The great historian gives us a pen-portrait of him, 'of a small stature, but very handsome and of a lovely countenance, of excellent parts and of invincible courage. He was of a very acceptable presence, great wit [i.e. intelligence], and was well beloved by the people.' We have no such portrait of Jack Trevanion, as everybody called him – a nickname which signified his popularity. Born in 1613, he had married at twenty, in 1634, Anne, daughter of John Arundell of lovely Trerice, then a comparatively recent Elizabethan house, with its decorative gables and plasterwork within. One can imagine the wedding procession that December day along the lanes to the parish church at Newlyn East, the jollifications in that great hall –

> when our nuptial day was done
> And tapers burned to bedward . . .

Jack was Nicholas's junior by some seven years and seems to have followed his lead. They were the closest comrades, brothers in arms throughout the famous western campaign of 1643, and in death were not divided.

Jack raised his own volunteer regiment, as did Slanning, Sir Bevil Grenville, Sir Richard Vyvyan, Richard Arundell of Trerice; there were at first five regiments of foot, subsequently raised to seven. Jack's father, Charles Trevanion, made vice-admiral of the Cornish coast in 1643, subsequently brought together one of these. The father, like Grenville and Slanning, was an Oxford man too, having matriculated from Oriel in 1611, at seventeen – so now, forty-eight in 1642, he was getting on, for those days. He had plenty of work on his hands as vice-admiral – until his son and heir's death in the field, when he in some sort took his place. Because of the disappearance of the Trevanion papers, with the end of the family, we have only the minutest traces of the work that was done, and how they did it. At the end of 1642 Trevanion writes to the vicar of St Austell urging the support of the clergy for 'the Western Army or dragoons' and appointing a meeting. At the end of January 1643 money was paid to St Ewe church 'for our soldiers who fought at Braddock Down'. One sees what key-points the churches were in the parishes.

Jack Trevanion led his men, a regiment of some seven hundred, in each action all the way from Braddock to the storming of Bristol, in which they were decimated and he was killed. In the winter of 1642–3 a storm drove three Parliamentarian ships into Falmouth, well supplied with arms and money. This came in handy to meet the Roundhead incursion over the Tamar under their general, Ruthen. Opposed to him was the admirable Sir Ralph Hopton as commander, one of the ablest of Cavalier generals. The two forces – not large, as yet amateurish and feeling their way – clashed at Braddock Down, at the east end of splendid Boconnoc Park, across the Liskeard road. Hopton decided on attack, waiting only for prayers to be said at the head of each squadron: they were at Mass, Puritan propaganda put it.

Grenville, though no trained soldier, led the van, charging down one slope and up another, so that they 'strook a terror' into his opponents. 'But it was the Cornish infantry that won the day', pushing home the victory to a rout. 'Both our Horse and Foot were suddenly routed', wrote a Roundhead officer, 'and every man divided and dispersed, ran and rode as fast as fear could carry them towards Saltash.' Few were killed, but a good number of prisoners were taken, with five guns, which were 'to be the mainstay of Hopton's artillery for several years'. Ruthen and his officers escaped across Saltash passage; some small boats were swamped in winter weather, the men drowned. The chief effect of the victory was psychological – people used to say 'moral' – as at Powick Bridge by Worcester: victory encouraged the Cornish, though the trained bands refused at first, as often elsewhere, to go beyond the bounds of their county.

The Earl of Stamford, leading a second incursion into Cornwall by the northern route, now drew back from Launceston. Sir John Berkeley, with the regiments of Grenville, Slanning and Trevanion, pursued him; Hopton, with Mohun's and William Godolphin's regiment, advanced from the south. In a skirmish in the misty dawn at Chagford, Colonel Godolphin's brother, Sidney, was killed: a tragic loss to his side. An exquisite poet – though he had not had time to write much – he was a rare philosophic spirit, comparable to Chillingworth, another victim of the war. An Oxford man, he was an intimate of the brilliant but fated circle around Falkland at Great Tew, upon whom the war fell so hardly. Like all of them, except the first genius of them all, Thomas Hobbes – an outsider in everything – Godolphin was a religious spirit:

> There is no merit in the wise
> But love, the shepherds' sacrifice;
> Wise men, all ways of knowledge past,
> To the shepherds' wonder come at last:
> To know can only wonder breed,
> And not to know is wonder's seed.

A very delicate and tiny man, it was this scrupulousness of conscience that made him engage himself in action, for which he was ill fitted.

He loved very much to be alone, being in his constitution inclined somewhat to melancholy and to retirement amongst his books. He was of so nice and tender a composition that a little rain or wind would disorder him, and divert himself from any short journey he had most willingly proposed to himself. [Nevertheless] out of the pure indignation of his soul and conscience to his country he had with the first engaged himself with that party in the West. And though he thought not fit to take command in a profession he had not willingly chosen, yet as his advice was of great authority with all the commanders, being always one in the Council of War, and whose notable abilities they had still use of in their civil transactions, so he exposed his person to all action, travail, and hazard. And, by too forward engaging himself in this last, he received a mortal shot by a musket a little above the knee, of which he died in the instant.

His friend Falkland was to fall similarly, later in the year, at Newbury.

There followed a check, once more from Cavalier over-confidence – as with the surprises the Byrons experienced in Cheshire. Stamford and Chudleigh concentrated and combined their forces in time for an engagement at Sourton Down in April. Hopton occupied Beacon Hill, but had not enough troops to man it. Slanning and Trevanion joined him. Lord Mohun and Sir John Berkeley were 'carelessly entertaining themselves in the head of dragoons' when they ran into the Roundheads. The Cavaliers had much the worst of it and were forced to retreat across the Cornish border. Stamford pursued them into Cornwall, and took up a strong position above Stratton, now known as Stamford Hill. Though without his cavalry, he had over 5,000 foot, the Royalists only half that strength. Hopton determined that 'they must either force the enemy's camp, while the most part of their Horse and dragoons were from them, or unavoidably perish'.

The Royalist attack was then uphill: Hopton and Mohun from the south, William Godolphin and Sir Thomas Basset from the north, two columns from the west, one under Berkeley and Grenville, the other under Slanning and Trevanion. The battle began at five o'clock in the morning and continued till the afternoon; by which time Hopton's converging columns gained the top of the hill, and the Parliamentarian army broke and fled, the earl of Stamford with them. The victory was complete: 300 good fellows killed, 1,700 prisoners, thirteen cannon, ammunition, baggage and a Parliamentary £5,000. The victory was greeted with great enthusiasm in Cornwall, of which one catches a whiff in Francis Basset's lyrical letter to his wife at

the Mount: 'Dearest Soul, O dear soul, praise God everlast-
ingly. Read the enclosed. Ring out your bells. Raise bonfires,
publish these joyful tidings, believe these truths.' One remem-
bers the pacific Walpole's 'They now *ring* the bells but they will
soon *wring* their hands.' Sooner or later humans do – but at
that time, not yet.

With such heady wine of success the Cornish were ready to
follow their leaders all the way into Somerset, where there followed, on 5 July, the comparable battle of Lansdown outside
Bath. Once more Hopton mounted converging attacks upon
the Roundheads, now commanded by his former friend Waller,
entrenched on Lansdown Hill. The battle swayed to and fro
and was a bloody one. This time the Royalist horse behaved
badly. Hopton said that of 2,000 only 600 stayed in the field,
the rest bolted for Oxford, convinced that the day was lost. The
Cornish infantry saved the day; Atkyns reported, 'Now did
our Foot believe no men their equals, and were so apt to undertake anything that the Hill upon which the rebels stood well
fortified could not deter them.'

At the crisis of the battle, when the Royalists faced defeat,
Sir Bevil Grenville led a last advance up the hill, massed pikes
in the centre, musketeers on his left, a body of Cornish horse
to cover open ground on the right. Captain Atkyns described
the scene for us vividly:

As I went up the Hill, which was very steep and hollow, I met
several dead and wounded officers brought off, besides several running away, that I had much ado to get up by them. When I came
to the top of the Hill I saw Sir Bevil Grenville's stand of pikes, which
certainly preserved our Army from a fatal rout with the loss of his
most precious life. They stood as upon the eaves of an house for steep-
ness, but as unmovable as a rock. On which side of the stand of pikes
our Horse were I could not discover, for the air was so darkened by
the smoke of the powder that for a quarter of an hour together there
was no light seen but what the fire of the volleys of shot gave: 'twas
the greatest storm that ever I saw.

Grenville was pole-axed on the spot where his monument
now stands; his serjeant-major and captain-lieutenant dead
beside him, the latter with the enemy's colours he had won
round his arm. For many generations Bevil Grenville's was a
name to conjure with in Cornwall – no doubt now forgotten.

At the time his was an irreparable loss to the Western Army. Sir John Trelawny wrote, as if there were any consolation, to the widow:

Seeing it hath pleased God to take him from your ladyship, yet this may something appease your great flux of tears that he died an honourable death, which all enemies will envy, fighting with invincible valour and loyalty the battle of his God [the other side were fighting for 'God' too], his King and his country [so too Parliament claimed]. A greater honour than this [we know what Falstaff thought of 'honour'], no man living can enjoy. But God hath called him unto himself, to crown him with immortal glory for his noble constancy in this blessed cause.

Be this as it may, claims just enough were made by the Oxford poet, William Cartwright, himself to die there of fever that year and be buried with those other war victims in the south aisle of the cathedral, in his poem on Grenville's death:

> Whence, in a just esteem, to Church and Crown
> He offered all and nothing thought his own.
> This thrust him into action, whole and free,
> Knowing no interest but loyalty;
> Not loving arms as arms, or strife for strife,
> Not wasteful, nor yet sparing of his life,
> A great exactor of himself, and then
> By fair commands no less of other men.

Though Lansdown was technically a victory – Waller drew off and the Royalists remained in possession of the field – they had suffered grievous losses, several able officers among them, and were short of ammunition. Then occurred one of the malign accidents of war: in an explosion of gun-powder their commander-in-chief, Hopton, was temporarily blinded. The Cornish Foot withdrew to Devizes, where, with very few cavalry, they were in imminent danger of being surrounded by the concentration of superior numbers. The emergency was appreciated at Oxford and, as we have seen, Byron's and Wilmot's brigades of cavalry were sent to the relief of the Cornish Foot.

We have noted Byron's account of the cavalry action and the disastrous driving of Waller's horse precipitously down Roundway Hill into the 'Bloody Ditch'. To complete the disaster the Cornish Foot marched up the road from Devizes, catching the disordered Roundheads in flank. Waller's army dissolved that unlucky 13 July. The road was open to Bristol, the greatest prize in the West.

The storming of the city followed within a fortnight, on 26 July. The forces inside were much inferior in strength, but the natural defences of the place were strong, within two branches of the river dominated by its walls and ditches. Bristol was fiercely defended, though its governor was Saye and Sele's unlucky son, Nathaniel Fiennes, whom the Cavaliers despised and whose fate it was to have to surrender the second city in the kingdom. The Cornish Foot were allotted the south-eastern defences, Redcliffe Gate and Temple Gate. Flushed with their victories they attacked much too soon, at three in the morning, alerting the enemy all round the perimeter, before Rupert could co-ordinate the attacks in the arc from north to south-west.

The Cornish attacked in three brigades: Slanning in the centre, with Trevanion; Colonel Buck on the right, their major-general Sir Thomas Basset on the left. They paid heavily for their impetuosity, the ditch before them proved too deep, their scaling ladders for the wall too short. They were driven back with heavy losses, particularly among the officers leading them. Buck managed to reach the wall, but was struck off by a halberd into the ditch, where he died. Basset was hit, Slanning and Trevanion mortally wounded within a few yards of each other.

Clarendon describes these events vividly, for he came down to the city with the king some days after; he was with Slanning before he died, and reported his words.

On the Cornish side fell, besides Major Kendall and many other inferior officers [Lieutenant-colonel Moyle, serving with Rupert, was killed on the north side, with young Lord Grandison], Colonel Buck, a modest and stout commander and of good experience in war ... Sir Nicholas Slanning and Colonel John Trevanion, the life and soul of the Cornish regiments: who, being led by no impulsion but of conscience and their own observation of the ill practices and designs of the great conductors – for they were both of the House of Commons – engaged themselves with the first in the opposition, and as soon as Sir Ralph Hopton and those other gentlemen came into Cornwall, joined with them. Being both of singular reputation and good fortunes

there, the one in possession, the other in reversion after his father,
they engaged their persons and estates in the service ...

They were both very young, of entire friendship to Sir Bevil Grenville, whose body was not yet buried. They were both hurt almost
in the same minute and in the same place; both shot in the thigh
with a musket bullet, their bones broken the one dying presently [i.e.
immediately], the other some few days after.

A closer report says of Jack Trevanion's wound, 'It swelled,
grew black and stank: whereof he died about midnight.' In his
autobiography Clarendon gives a brief character of him: 'He
was a steady young man, of a good understanding, great
courage, but of few words – yet what he said was always to
the purpose.' In the *History* he improves the occasion:

> Both had the royal sacrifice of their sovereign's very particular sor-
> row, and the concurrence of all good men's. And, that which is a
> greater solemnity to their memories – as it fares with most great and
> virtuous men whose loss is better understood long afterwards – they
> were as often lamented as the accidents in the public affair made the
> courage and fidelity of the Cornish of greatest signification to the
> cause.

Bristol was won, though not by the Cornish. Their losses in
men were irremediable, and those of their leaders, wrote Joseph
James, cast 'a general damp upon the people, so that, though
they retained their loyalty, they lost much of that life which
appeared in their first actions'.

The Western Army was never again the same.

Jack Trevanion left quite a numerous family, for a young man,
by his wife, Anne Arundell. Of his four sons the eldest, Charles,
carried on the family at Caerhays. John and Richard we shall
hear more of: they both had active naval careers. Little is
known of the third boy, Hugh, who lived on the farm at
Newham. Of the two daughters, Amy married Joseph Sawle
of Penrice – the neighbouring estate to that where I write; and
Mary, who went to live in London, died unmarried: we have
her will.

The first thing we learn is of a suit for the wardship of the
young heir, by William Killigrew, serving as governor of St
Michael's Mount, in a letter of 5 January 1644 to Lord Percy,
general of the ordnance. He writes that the king had already

granted the vice-admiralty of Cornwall to the child's grand-father, so, 'if I might have it, the wardship should not prejudice me very much. But the King will give no forfeited estates now; if the Prince had done it in time [i.e. as Duke of Cornwall], his favour had made me happy.' Killigrew goes on to complain that 'the King expects great things from hence and yet will not give me credit to oblige one man in the county'. Killigrew wanted an honour for 'the industrious Sheriff (Francis Basset); but

it happened that the King's first denial found the Sheriff and me at my Lord Mohun's house [Boconnoc], where, upon my cold account of his own hopes, his lordship thought fit to laugh at the Sheriff, and to show such contempt to me and his Majesty's promised favours to such as should merit from him in the county as begat a breach with me, such as shall never more bring me under his roof.... The King hath lost above £100,000 this Christmas for want of nine or ten whole culverin at the Mount's Bay, and the like may happen again at the next storm.

Such were the people the king had to contend with and, if possible, content; as Queen Elizabeth I said, there was no satisfying the 'insatiable cupidity' of men. I do not know if Killigrew got the wardship of the young heir – it is unlikely. Francis Basset got his well merited knighthood, so did Charles Trevanion; Killigrew had to wait till the Restoration, when he received a baronetcy from Charles II, who was much more easy-going and cynical about such things. At the Restoration Court all the gay Killigrews were in clover.

When, in the summer of this year 1644, Charles I himself pursued a Parliamentarian army under Essex and Robartes into Cornwall, it was the king's army that carried off the honours. Charles, though not trained as a soldier, learned the trade in the course of the war and proved a competent com-mander. He showed at his best in this campaign, cooping up a large army in the narrowing peninsula and forcing their sur-render. Lord Robartes had persuaded Essex into this unpromis-ing venture, optimistically exaggerating his influence and naturally anxious to look to his property.

In the campaign Jack Trevanion's father took his place, rais-ing an additional regiment from the much depleted Cornish: they had had some two hundred men killed at Bristol. In the tighten-ing cordon around Essex's army – both armies scouring the

countryside for provisions and eating it up – the king's head-
quarters were fixed at beautiful Boconnoc. It was, however, a
recognizable Cornish summer, wet and windy, the landscape
obscured by moorland- and sea-mists. We can follow events from
the notes of delightful Richard Symonds, a captain in Lord Bernard Stuart's troop of horse, whose engaging passion was for
antiquities and history, particularly genealogy and heraldry.
Any time he had to himself he employed in visiting churches
and houses, noting down monuments and inscriptions, antiquities, stained glass windows in hall or church, with their coats
of arms and the information they gave. Since most of these have
disappeared, many of them being destroyed in the war, his notes
are invaluable, and show him to be one of the endearing characters out of that destructive time.

He tells us that Charles Trevanion and Francis Basset were
knighted at Lord Mohun's house – this must have given Killigrew food for thought – as also young John Arundell of Lanherne, 'under age, being a ward, which frees his wardship'. He
was to marry Jack Trevanion's widow. We can re-create the
scene that summer from Symonds's jottings: the gay party of
Roundheads surprised at Lord Mohun's house – several of them
killed, a Dutch quartermaster escaping by putting off sword
and hat, and pretending to be a servant of Lord Mohun's. The
twenty-five quarterings of the Mohuns in the great parlour
where the king lay one night; the little church next door
crammed with their monuments – now all vanished; the king
another night lying, with his servants about him, under a hedge
in a field (there was a rumour of an attempt upon him); his
narrow escape from a stray shot at Bodinnick (the place afterwards known as the King's Walk); when the weather cleared,
starlight over the down at night.

At Fowey Symonds noted the coats of arms commemorating
the marriage of John Trevanion of Edward iv's time to Jennet
Treffry of Place, the great house overlooking the town. There
they were in the hall: the Trevanion coat, argent, on a fesse
azure, between two chevrons gules, three escallops or. The Trevanion arms appeared again in the south aisle, the Treffry aisle,
of the church below: those of the son and daughter-in-law, Sir
William Trevanion and Anne Edgcumbe.

Cornwall and the Cornish people were utterly exhausted by

these campaigns and losses, hundreds of the menfolk killed, including a number of foremost leaders of that war-time generation. The little county was impoverished by the marching and
marauding of several armies in those years, let alone supplying
and provisioning, the drain of her chief resources from tin to
support the king's cause. Before Fairfax's invasion of 1646 the
Royalist army melted away. Sir Charles Trevanion's regiment
was opposed to Fairfax at Launceston, but 120 of his musketeers
surrendered. Hopton surrendered in March. There was no
point in holding out any longer, though an indomitable
remnant, under old John Arundell of Trerice, held out at
Pendennis to the last, marching out at the end, tattered and
starving, but with 'honour'. Even in those last forlorn days,
one of the Killigrews, Sir Henry, received his death wound
there.

After all the ardours and endurances, the sufferings and ultimate defeat, there was the devil and all to pay. The whole
country was in misery and want, the victorious Parliament at
its wit's end for money to pay its army and navy, determined
to inflict reparations upon its opponents, those who had been
loyal to the king. An immense documentation of this penal victi-
mizing of the Royalists remains – 'compounding' for their
'delinquency', as it was called. There is no doubt that a large
number of families of gentry were permanently crippled, and
some, having to sell their all, ended. In Cornwall the Langdons
came to an end; one hears no more of Joseph Jane's family,
though he resorted to his pen unrepentantly to defend the king
against the aspersions of Milton's *Eikonoklastes*. Families of small
gentry, like the Polwheles, were permanently damaged and
contracted in their estate, though they managed to hold on,
and continue. The effects must have been felt, with richer
families like the Trevanions, for a generation, if not longer; with
some, permanently.

Richard Symonds reports to us the common estimation of
leading families' wealth in Cornwall, on an average much less
than elsewhere; the county was so small and by far the largest
holding, with coignage and tin rights to boot, was that of the
duchy, which went to the upkeep of the prince of Wales, as
it still does today. The Arundells of Lanherne, though Catholic
recusants, owned more land than anybody; probably the

Edgcumbes came next, with a reputed income of £3,000 a year. Lord Robartes was richer than anybody in cash, not in land. Lord Mohun was thought to be worth £2,000 a year, Sir Charles Trevanion £1,500 a year.

Immediately upon Trevanion's surrender Sir Thomas Fairfax, who was a gentleman and had the sympathies of his class, wrote to Speaker Lenthall on Trevanion's behalf suggesting a moderate composition for his 'delinquency' (Puritan semantics for loyalty). It seems to have had no effect, for in 1648 his fine was set at the usual one-tenth of his estate: he was to raise £665 10s 8d. This must have been crippling, in addition to the expense of raising two regiments for the king's service. In 1650 the fine was confirmed, with a penalty added. Next year the Commonwealth Committee for the Advance of Money assessed him to pay £300 – was this the residue, or the total, of his fine? In January 1652 he petitioned that, since he was not well and living more than two hundred miles from London, might the county commissioners consider his case? He submitted that in 1642 he was £3,480 in debt. The commissioners certified that he had paid £240 in the country – he was to pay £25 more in three weeks. In March 1652 his discharge was granted. But in September 1653 it was found necessary to add some rents in Devon, omitted by his solicitor. The fine on this was set at one-third, i.e. £49 15s. In February 1654 this was paid and he was discharged – twelve years after the beginning of the war! It is just one example of the kind of thing going on all over the country: a high price to pay for one's 'convictions'.

The family was still not quit of these depredations. In March 1652 Jack Trevanion's widow petitioned for the discharge of Efford House and mills (near Bude) and lands in Newlyn East, which had been leased by John Arundell of Trerice to his daughter Mary. The county commissioners were to certify particulars. All through the Commonwealth, investigation of such complications continued. Next month Jack's young son and heir Charles begged the discharge of Pellamounter in Newlyn East, leased to him by John Arundell of Trerice, for whose delinquency it had been seized.

The country could never settle down under the rule of Commonwealth or Protectorate, a Puritan minority at Westminster under whatever guise. The only issue determined by the Civil War was that, in the ultimate settlement, Parliament would have its place. This was foreshadowed by the king's agreement with Parliament, against the army, which brought him to the block after the explosion of the second Civil War in 1648. The report went that the malignants were stirring in Cornwall, inspired by Sir Charles Trevanion. But Cornwall was too exhausted to move – as Lord Byron found was the case with North Wales.

In May 1650 a Royalist colonel was in the West sounding support for a rising. Sir John Berkeley and Colonel Slingsby were flushed out of hiding at Caerhays – suitably remote and sequestered, with every opportunity of landings from France upon the beach below. Sir Charles, Sir Nicholas Prideaux and 'old Mr Arundell', i.e. of Trerice and the heroic defence of Pendennis, were seized, but set at liberty upon their engagement not to serve. In 1651 a Royalist informer reported that Sir Charles Trevanion was 'a man of great power among the people'. Once more in 1654, in the crisis that led to Cromwell taking upon himself more than monarchical power as Lord Protector, feelers from Charles II at Breda were put out – but the group was discouraged by the previous arrests.

In July 1659 young Charles Trevanion had a pass to go 'beyond seas' – we do not know upon what mission. But the West Country gentry took a decisive part in the restoration of the king, through the relationship of the Grenvilles with General Monk, in the key position to bring it about; Bevil Grenville's son, John, and Peter Killigrew, 'Peter the Post', were principal emissaries. Before the happy Restoration old Sir Charles had died. His grandson Charles, now head of the family, was a member of the 'Cavalier' Parliament of Charles II's reign, sitting for Grampound from 1661 to 1679. He was one of the group in Parliament to press for the victualling of Tangier, in which Mr Pepys was so masterfully concerned.

Disturbing consequences of the upheaval to society caused by the war went on for years. In December 1660, Hugh, Jack's third son, settled at Newham, was petitioning the treasury regarding a fine in the manor of Treluggan contracted with the king's commissioners in 1645. In the following year Hugh was petitioning regarding copyhold lands held of the duchy – the

rates were approved and the steward of the particular manor
was to grant a lease accordingly. We hear no more of Hugh,
who never married, died in 1696 and was buried in St Mary's
at Truro. Administration of his property was granted to his
mother in 1699, then Lady Arundell of Lanherne.

In 1662 the eldest son, Colonel Charles, receiver of taxes for
Cornwall, wished to compound for felling twenty acres of
wood in the duchy manor of Helston in Trigg, near Camelford;
and he sought the reversion of the lease of the duchy park at
delightful Restormel and Trinity, where the medieval chapel
had been (now a Regency Gothic mansion looking down the
valley of the Fowey). Charles II's government was bombarded
by petitions and requests from impoverished Royalists for compensation for their losses. In 1665 Colonel Charles Trevanion,
reciting that his father had been slain at the head of his regiment
at the storming of Bristol, and that his grandfather had injured
his estate by constant adherence to the late king – together
advancing £4,280 (he appended an account) – prays that he
might be spared fines of £1,094 14s 4d for duchy lands for which
he had contracted.

During 1669–70 there was a lawsuit between Charles, as late
receiver of taxes, and his deputy, Mr Trevanion of Gerrans and
Gray's Inn, a lawyer. It concerned the cost of the transport of
£12,460 to Exeter in his majesty's wagons. Affidavits flew to
and fro, processes were stopped, there were the law's customary
outlays. What allowance was to be made for transporting the
tax-money from Cornwall? Both Colonel Charles and Charles
Trevanion of Gray's Inn were called to the treasury; Mr Willis,
head collector for Cornwall, was summoned up. Lawyer Trevanion petitioned for a further allowance: in June 1670 he proposed £199 10s for his charges. As a sop he suggested means
for getting in arrears of £269 5s 7d – which would well cover
his expenses.

Among a number of sureties for the revenue of the duchy
in 1673 he appears as Charles Trevanion of Crego (one of the
family properties). The nephew was again receiver of the royal
aid, a euphemism for tax, in 1673 and also a commissioner for
recusancy, i.e. fines on Catholics for refusing to attend church,
re-awakened at this time of the Test Act: Parliament's reaction
to James, heir to the throne, declaring himself a Catholic.

Actually some members of the family did become Catholics, as we shall see.

In the reign of Charles II two of Jack Trevanion's sons, John and Richard, looked to the Royal Navy for a career. John was the second son, baptised on 2 April 1638 in the tiny church of St Michael Caerhays, on its windswept hill above that familiar valley running down to the sea. He was entered at Queen's College, Oxford, where he subscribed in March 1657, and went on as a student to Lincoln's Inn; but the navy was more in his line, the sea in his blood. In 1667, at twenty-nine, he took possession of his ship, the *Dartmouth* frigate, as captain at Bristol. This was the last year of the second Dutch war. Trevanion reported to Secretary Coventry that he had provisions for 145 men for one month, but repairs were needed and stores required before going to sea. The usual delays supervened: a month later the ship was still unrigged and unfit for careening. He had spared thirty men whose wages were due: he hoped that they would have done better service than newly pressed men, who might run away every day. In August he reports to Sir William Penn from Bristol that he has arrived from Youghal and is bound for Milford, with four vessels laden for Sir Jeremiah Smith's squadron.

In November of next year we learn from Pendennis that he had left in the *Dartmouth* to form part of a convoy for Sir Denis Gauden's pleasure-boat. In the early months of 1669 there was a fuss at Plymouth over the captain's caning of the purser of the *Dartmouth*. The purser wrote to Pepys with his complaint, adding that the captain had clapped him into the bilboes atop the foc'sle for ten hours in cold weather. Others said that the purser had wronged the captain: while Trevanion was ashore others of the officers had put the purser under arrest. It seems that the captain had received much provocation from the purser, who had not provided beer for the ship but taken up wine; his accounts were five years in arrears, his creditors threatening to clap him in gaol. The clamorous purser continued to pursue Pepys, but a court martial dismissed him and justified the captain, with a hint that he should be more careful with his cane in future.

In 1672 Captain John was killed at the murderous battle of

Sole Bay, in the third Dutch war, fighting under James, duke of York, to whom he was gentleman usher. Admiral Kempthorne reported, 'Of my division I wanted only Captain Trevanion, the rest were in order. As soon as we came near the *Royal James* we discovered a ship on board him' – the smoke from the firing was such that they could not descry before. Trevanion is listed among the many 'persons of quality and gentlemen slain' in that tough action. A couple of years later his mother's lease of Restormel Park was renewed in 'compensation for the life of John Trevanion', for a £50 fine to the receiver of the duchy and 53s 4d for a heriot upon his death, since he had been a duchy tenant.

We have much more information about the youngest brother, Richard, Jack's fourth son. In the second Dutch war we find him captain of the *Marmaduke*, in 1666. In September 1671 he was captain of the *Richmond* at the Nore, one of the convoys for the herring fishery, on the eve of the third Dutch war. Next year he was captain of the *Bonaventure*, of 46 guns, 220 men; in September, captain of the *Dreadnought* at the Nore with the fire-ships, and in command there. In November he arrived at Woolwich, hoping to dock, if the navy commissioners would order a survey of 'the stinking beer we have on board' – a familiar complaint for centuries. In December he wanted his medicine chest recruited; the ship, having been in the Straits, was very sickly and now ordered out again. In 1676 he sent his compliments to Lord Ossory from Genoa Mole.

He was commander of the *Suadados* in 1682, and carried a number of his company with him when promoted to command the *Hampshire*. In 1685 he was commander of the squadron that captured part of Monmouth's forces at Lyme Regis. Thenceforward we find Trevanion in close association with James II, whom Monmouth's hare-brained rebellion encouraged to proceed further with his Catholic policy – crazy in a madly Protestant country – that led to the Revolution of 1688.

At the end James lost his nerve, daunted by his nephew's threatening approach, deserted by the Protestant members of his family, the country turned against him by his own folly. On his first attempt to fly he was sent back. For his second attempt, towards the end of December, he ordered Captain Trevanion and Captain Macdonnel to prepare a shallop to leave at midnight. The two captains showed the king the way to the boat, with the young duke of Berwick, his illegitimate son by Arabella Churchill. The tide was against them, and the wind blew so hard that it was 6 a.m. before they got to the Swale. Trevanion proposed going on board a Hamburg vessel to refresh themselves and await the tide. The king preferred Trevanion's own ship, the *Harwich*; the captain replied that, though he could answer for the fidelity of the officers, he could not for the common seamen – a significant pointer.

James and his company made for the smack in waiting and took Captain Trevanion's boat in tow, the gale not lessening. They were some twenty in all. In the tiny cabin there was room only for James and Berwick. Hungry as they were, Trevanion went to fry his majesty some bacon. The frying pan had a hole in it, but the Captain stopped it with a pitched rag, and tied an old furred can about with a cord to hold some drink. This aroused the king's mirth: 'he never ate nor drank more heartily in his life.'

They had a difficult passage, landing at Ambleteuse at 3 a.m. on Christmas Day, in time for James to hear early Mass. His great ancestor, Henry of Navarre, had thought it worth attending Mass to win Paris; his miserable grandson thought it worth losing three kingdoms. (The ribald Judge Jeffreys had summed up crisply: 'The Virgin Mary was to do all.') When Madame de Sévigné met the absconding monarch she was astonished to observe him chattering unconcernedly about the loss of his kingdoms as if it were someone else's mishap.

Captain Richard, having thrown in his lot with the self-dethroned monarch, was made groom of his bedchamber at St Germain and remained in close attendance on James until his death in 1701. He went to Ireland with him in 1690, in the absurd effort to reconquer his lost kingdoms which ended with William III's victory at the Battle of the Boyne. James did not acquit himself well on the field, and quitted early. 'It was ten at night after the battle that he entered Dublin, in a very silent and dejected condition, and with very few attendants', of whom Trevanion was one. James told the duchess of Tyrconnell – Sarah Churchill's sister – that all was lost, and left again at 4 a.m. with a company of a dozen 'whereof Trevanion and Stafford were chief'.

Trevanion was provided for at St Germain; he was an executor of King James's will and was present at the melancholy scene around his death-bed. Some three years before, at New Year 1698, Richard had been granted a warrant to return to England, no doubt for a brief visit. It was peace-time, after the Peace of Ryswick.

Evidences of other members of the family touched by Catholicism remain. While James was king in England, he made a point of selecting Catholic officers for his army. In a list of gentlemen suitable for his guards in 1686, we find the name of John Trevanion, eldest son and heir of Colonel Charles at Caerhays: 'His father has a good estate but has disinherited him for being a Catholic. He is a handsome young man.' The Revolution of 1688, if nothing else, persuaded him of the error he was making, for in the event he succeeded his father properly in the estate. But his brother Charles became a Jesuit.

This Trevanion often went, in those penal days, by his mother's name of Drummond (*her* mother had been a Cornish Lower). Born at Caerhays in 1667, he entered the novitiate of the Jesuit order in 1685, under the name of Drummond, and was professed a full Jesuit eighteen years later. From 1695 to 1699 he served in the Suffolk district, from 1704 in the London area; he lived his surreptitious life at Richmond, where he died, aged seventy, in 1737. Another Catholic fleck remains in a visit by 'Mrs Trevanion' – probably his sister, Mary Winifred – to the English Benedictine nuns at Pontoise in 1686.

From their wills we descry that Richard and his sister were in fairly prosperous circumstances. As late as 1716 Richard was assured of 200 *livres* a month by James II's son, the old Pretender. He made his will in 1720,* his chief property in England being a mortgage of £1,500 upon the estate of his brother-in-law, John Sawle of Penrice. He bequeathed this mortgage, with interest at five per cent, to his only child, Anne Fitzwilliam, a widow with three children. His granddaughter Anne was to receive £1,000 of the mortgage, his grandson Charles £300 of it. For thirty years, i.e. from 1688, Richard Trevanion had been deprived of his rights and benefits as an Elder Brother of Trinity House; all such profits and arrears as might be recovered he left to his daughter and grandson Charles.

* Prob/11/575, f. 184.

He left her his goods and chattels, specifying his silver watch; to Councillor Morragh a silver cup and cover; to his servant all wearing clothes, except his best suit, which was to go to his grandson Charles, who was also to have two cases of pistols, two beds with all tapestry curtains, furniture and linen from his chambers, closet and kitchen – presumably his apartment at St Germain; 'what provisions of wine and wood' were to be Mr Devereux's. He had left in keeping with Garret Devereux 100 new *louis d'or*; of this considerable sum he left 900 *livres* to Councillor Morragh, 100 *livres* each to Clara Devereux, Catherine Butler and Ned Howard, his servant. He was owed a debt of some 2,300 *livres* by Mr Arthur Bauginer at Paris – this was bequeathed to his grandson.

His sister Mary Winifred, of St Giles in the Fields, unmarried, made her will in 1689, 'sick in body but of sound and perfect memory'.* To her aunt Penelope Plowden, of that Catholic family, she left £214, and to her cousin Mary 20s for a gold ring. To brother John Trevanion £200 'with all the interest that is due to me for the same'; to his wife 'my mother's picture set in gold'; to brother Charles a £5 piece of gold; to grandmother, the Lady Arundell, 40s; to aunt Mary Trevanion, 20s and a silver cane marked with her name. This, Colonel Jack's younger daughter, was 'of Somerset House'; was this a grace-and-favour lodging, or was she a maid-of-honour? 'Lady Elizabeth Dryden, wife to Mr Dryden' was left 40s. Dr Lower, the eminent physician, was also a cousin: he was left £5, and smaller sums went to his wife and children. Further small amounts were bequeathed to servants and dependants of her mother and aunt Plowden: to 'my maid Elizabeth Julian £7, and all my linen and wearing clothes, except my damask napkins. To my dear mother £50.'

Of remaining members of the family we have few evidences. Upon the forced surrender of borough charters in March 1685, a move designed to make them, and consequently their return of MPs, safe for Tory supporters of the monarchy, Charles Trevanion of Caerhays was appointed alderman and JP for Truro – removable only by the king. He was similarly nominated for Tregony, along with cousin Richard as senior mayor. Charles, whose mother had been a co-heiress of the Lowers of

* Prob/11/449, f. 15.

St Winnow, died at Caerhays 'on the night of the great storm, 26 November 1703' – which left a swathe of destruction across the West Country. Various members of the family were parked out in various farms on the estates, almost wholly within the delicious countryside we call the Roseland, the triangle between St Austell, St Mawes and Truro: Trevanion country. Richard Trevanion was a captain of foot in the militia, under Richard, Lord Arundell of Trerice (promoted to the peerage for his services in the Civil War: Charles II had little else to give, except to his mistresses – and their bastards he made dukes). This captain was bred up in William III's wars, and served in his campaign in Ireland and Flanders. In 1690 he was in the earl of Bath's regiment (Bevil Grenville's son). He resided in the parish of Veryan; his son Richard married a Verman, who owned the manor of Lamorran, with its woods along the creeks of the Fal.

Whatever the reason, a quarrel blew up in a Holborn tavern between John Verman and the captain. A characteristic episode, when human fools carried swords – they fought a duel in Red Lyon fields at night, their seconds being Captain Carew and Mr Trevanion on one side, Mr Raleigh and Mr Buller on the other. Mr Verman and Mr Buller were dangerously wounded. Captain Richard survived to end his life as governor of Pendennis Castle.

Of Charles Trevanion of Crego, Hals the antiquarian gossip – a kind of Cornish Aubrey – tells us an amusing tale. This was the lawyer who brought suit against his nephew; apparently he was a projector too. He procured an Act of Parliament to enable him

to undertake to make the river Fal navigable as far as Crow hill in St Stephen's; and though his first summer's work seemed to favour his design, bringing the salt water by two or three sluices above Tregony bridge, the place of its old flux and reflux, yet by reason of the great and rapid confluence and washes of the Fal river in the winter season after the foundation of those sluices being made upon mud or osier ground, where the sea was driven aback as aforesaid, were undermined, fell down. However the good undertaker was not discouraged at this misfortune but re-edified the same the summer following; and so on for many summers after with great skill, cost and charges. But alas! still the lofty current of the river Fal, in winter season, was such a malicious and invincible enemy to this noble project

that, as before, it continually undermined the walls of those sluices
. . . so that the very worthy gentleman aforesaid hath spent the greatest
part of this fine estate and given over his undertaking as too difficult
and unprofitable an enterprise.

However, it procured him his return to the Parliaments of
1679, 1681 and 1685 by the voters of Tregony, for what that
was worth; and the project was his only progeny.

VI

Civil War and Sequel: the Byrons

JOHN LORD BYRON'S SANGUINE HOPES of raising North Wales, Cheshire and Lancashire on the approach of the Scots under Hamilton, and his plans to surprise Nottingham Castle and Oxford, collapsed with the unexpectedly rapid crushing of the Royalists in the second Civil War in 1648. After the execution of Charles I Byron was proscribed by name, and banished, along with the king's sons and a number of unpardonable opponents such as Sir Richard Grenville, as an enemy of the Commonwealth. From Ireland Byron passed to Jersey – where Clarendon was beginning to write his *History* – and shortly on to Paris. Byron had been appointed governor to young James, duke of York, by Charles I; at one point one hears of him writing in invisible ink to ask loyalists for aid for him. The exiled Court was full of quarrels, the queen herself a mischief-maker, and Byron had his enemies. He had a rival wanting his job, who took advantage of Byron's visit to Brussels to make trouble. Young Charles II, early inured to a necessary cynicism where humans are concerned, solved the problem by declaring James *sui juris* and free to choose his own attendants. Byron ceased to be the duke's governor, but remained his officer.

In England the Council of State ordered Lady Byron's apprehension, for holding correspondence with the enemies of the Commonwealth. She was committed to Peterhouse for examination, and bound in £200 for good behaviour. Byron had already made interest with Ormonde on behalf of the young duke of Buckingham's estate in Ireland – all he had left to live upon, everything else confiscated. In 1651 Byron was reporting to Ormonde from the Louvre, where Queen Henrietta Maria was residing, the mischief made by her concerning the duke of York. (In spite of all that had happened in England – and against Charles I's express orders – the silly woman was constantly trying to make her sons turn Catholic.) In September, 'the foolish intrigues of our little Court are so unworthy of your Excellency's consideration'. The following year, 1652, Byron was delivered from it all by death; he had no children by either wife. He had married his second wife, Eleanor, to console himself during the siege of Chester. She was a young woman, daughter of Lord Kilmorey, one of his colonels there: Pepys heard that she became Charles II's seventeenth mistress while in Paris.

The next brother, Richard, succeeded as second lord and, though a less ardent and impetuous personality, had to fill something of his brother's place. In the movement against Cromwell's Protectorate in 1655 Richard was named to lead a rising in Nottinghamshire. An informer reported to Thurloe, the extremely able head of Cromwell's intelligence system, that Byron told Lord Wilmot that he was 'much pleased they had so much confidence in his little carcase as to choose him for their leader'. Nothing eventuated. Newstead was searched – no arms there – and the place denuded. Byron remained in London; one report says that he was briefly in the Tower. It is agreeable to learn, from Puritan humbugs in 1658, that Richard Byron, 'another carnal rich man', had drawn the parish of Aston-on-Trent to refuse tithes for not administering the sacrament.

In 1659 the end of the Puritan *épopée* was in sight, after Cromwell's death; though, even now, the dominant army had no difficulty in squashing Booth's premature rising in Lancashire. The crux of the matter was, as Mrs Hutchinson puts it with disgust, that 'the Presbyterians had long since espoused the Royal interest, and forsaken God and the People's cause, when they could not obtain the reins of government in their own hands and exercise dominion over all their brethren'. This is just what John Milton said. The fact was that the two wings of the governing class, Parliamentarian and Royalist, had realized their folly in allowing themselves to be divided, for jumped-up army officers – cobblers, butchers, artisans – to lord it over them. One has a case in point in Lord Robartes, who had withdrawn in dudgeon after the army's triumph, to become a key figure, lugubrious sourpuss as he was, in the government of the Merry Monarch at the Restoration.

Byron was back at Newstead when his father-in-law, Sir George Booth, led his premature rising in Lancashire. Byron hoped to secure his (former) stronghold, Newark. The opportunity slipped by, but in August he got together a hundred or so troopers in the forest, six miles north of Nottingham. The county militia turned out and chased them in disorder through the town. Nothing disagreeable happened to Byron – the end was too visible on the horizon. Mrs Hutchinson reports, however, that he 'thought that no gentleman ought to be unprovided of arms in such an uncertain time', and so ordered down a trunk of pistols from London. Not daring to fetch them from the carrier himself, for the suspicions upon him, he got Colonel Hutchinson to secure them on his behalf.

Mrs Hutchinson's *Memoirs* were written after the Restoration, so she was anxious to bring forward any little acts of friendly compliance on the part of her husband, and tone down his responsibility as a regicide. Indeed his relationship with his Byron cousins stood him in good stead: in her petition to Parliament on behalf of her husband, she cites both Lord Byron and Sir Robert as witnesses to Hutchinson's opposition to the Protectorate.

The property upheaval caused by the Civil War was immense. There was the impoverishment to both sides caused by wartime expenditures and taxation; all this fell more heavily on the Royalists, redoubled by the swiping fines for 'malignancy' – compounding compelled the sales of many estates, and many more changed hands. All this besides the devastation and destruction: the country laid waste by 'human folly' in the view of Swift, whose clerical grandfather suffered heavily from depredations, the magnificent castle in his parish above the Wye today a ruined monument.

The financial losses to the Byron family were immense, and provide a typical example of the complexities that ensued: charges upon estates for trusts, marriage and family settlements, mortgages and debts to be offset, claims made, true and false.

All this provided a roaring trade for committee men and lawyers – no wonder they made fortunes out of these miseries.

John, the first lord, had mortgaged lands to the marquis (then earl) of Worcester in 1630. In 1642 he and his heir, brother Richard, had sold Over and Nether Colwick to Sir James Stonehouse of Essex for £23,000: £14,000 down, while £9,000 remained in Stonehouse's hands. Charges upon this were an annuity of £460 and arrears to Sir Nicholas Byron's lady, Anne. Their mother had a claim of £2,100 for her dower. John's creditors had lent him £20,000 before the war; to meet this he had sold part of his estate. He owed Sir Thomas Alcock £1,040. Now in 1647 Sir James Stonehouse owed eight years' rent to four Byron brothers, £40 a year each, 'in arms against the Parliament'. Sir James Stonehouse was ordered to pay £3,000 of his debt immediately, 'to be employed for the defences of Plymouth and Lyme'. Meanwhile the committee for sequestrations was felling the timber of both Newcastle and Byron – no time was to be lost; the timber had to be sold at best, the money paid in. The encumbrances on the estate were to be met. By 1651 'the tenants have a great sum in their hands'. No doubt: people lower down the social scale profited from the confusion and the opportunities it created. Here is another aspect of the social upheaval, disregarded by historians. After the Puritan Revolution, the Restoration was a real reaction, and no wonder!

Since there was such a large number of claimants on Byron's estate, the committee for compounding made a general order that his estate was to be disposed of to the best advantage, the rents received by the several county committees in which the lands lay, while the claims were to be tried at law. Byron's aunt Mary claimed £1,000, or interest on it, settled on her by her grandfather as her portion. Till the wars she had received £80 a year; after Lord Byron's sequestration, nothing. Sixty years old, she had no other livelihood.

In 1653 Lady Byron, 'widow of the pretended Lord Byron' (Parliament did not recognize his Royalist title) claimed dower out of the estate of George Warburton of Cheshire. She had brought a marriage portion of some £2,000–£3,000 to her first husband, Peter Warburton, who died a minor, and his brother George succeeded to his estate. She married Byron when

Chester was held for the king and was with him in England, France, Ireland and elsewhere. She is now at her father's, Lord Kilmorey's, at Dutton, Cheshire, and claims her jointure. 'Is this to be paid, and with arrears, if she do not demand them by reason of some dealing with the said George Warburton, being affectionately both of one side?'

In 1649 uncle Nicholas's affairs come up: his first wife, Anne, was ordered to appear, to show by what right her dower was claimed upon lands in Colwick and Snenton. She did not appear – was presumably dead: the claim could conveniently be disallowed. There were a number of claims upon Sir Nicholas's estate at Gaines Park in Essex, mostly debts. In 1650 Sir Thomas Alcock was under obligation to pay £50 in trust for him. Next year his second wife, who was Flemish, had a pass to go into Flanders with two servants. As late as 1657 Ernestus, son and heir, was assessed to pay one-tenth on the estate he inherited – £90.

By the articles of surrender of Rhuddlan Castle, Colonel Gilbert Byron was granted three months to make his peace with Parliament. He had taken the National Covenant and the Negative Oath; in spite of this his fine was fixed at a half – £350! In 1649 this was reduced to one-sixth: he paid £146 13s 4d and was discharged. Two years later he had to compound for the arrears on his annuity: one-sixth, i.e. £40. It reminds one of today's penal taxation imposed by Parliament in the social revolution of our time.

In June 1646: 'Sir Richard Byron of Strelley, since September last, has lived in Parliament's quarters.' His fine, at one-tenth, amounted to £120. In 1651: 'Robert Byron of Newstead is not yet sequestered, but his small estate is liable.' And so it went on.

Of course, we must remember that on the other side many made their fortunes. The Leveller, John Wildman, built up a fine estate out of sequestered Royalists' properties, and even secured a knighthood after the Revolution of 1688. The odious Heselrig seated himself in princely state at Auckland Castle, belonging to the bishopric of Durham. Lugubrious Puritan preachers waxed fat – John Milton complained of it – like Cornelius Burgess in the deanery at Wells. (Was he a forebear of Guy Burgess, Communist spy and traitor? A direct line of descent leads from the Puritan Revolution to that of today.)

When so many loyal families were impoverished or ruined, it naturally led to a heavy burden of claims upon the Restoration government, which its finances could never meet. We can trace sympathetically something of the problem it had to face with our two families. The government did what it could; it could never restore completely the financial position they had enjoyed before the lunacy of the war, or all the lands and estates lost. However, it handed out pensions, appointments, pittances, 'honours' – these were cheapest. The Cavalier joke that the Restoration Act of Indemnity and Oblivion was one of indemnity for the king's enemies and of oblivion for his friends was not quite fair.

Royalist families were not slow in pressing their claims, and reminding the king of their services; from their petitions we gain a great deal of interesting information otherwise lost. Three months after the Restoration, Sir Ernestus Byron and three colleagues received warrant to seize certain goods of Charles I and his queen, having discovered in whose custody they were detained. (Colonel Hutchinson was only one of many who had purchased pictures from Charles I's fabulous collection.)

We learn from a petition on behalf of Gilbert Byron's widow and five children that he had been one of Charles I's attendants when he went to the House of Commons to arrest the five MPs in June 1642, followed him to York, was sent to the queen in France, was in several battles, fortified and defended Rhuddlan and was taken prisoner trying to get into Colchester. Some years after, he died of his wounds, a comparatively young man. His wife had spent all her own property providing for him and the five children, whom she had had to put out among friends on the failure of her former petition. In May 1661 she was granted a pension of £100 per annum, put up to £200 in September. Lord Byron's widow got a pension of £500: her services were of a more remunerative kind. Gilbert's widow petitioned for a place as keeper of the sweet coffers or dresser to the queen. As late as 1671 Gilbert's daughters were granted a pension of £100 per annum each, since they had no other means of support.

In November 1660 Sir Thomas Byron's widow petitioned for repayment of £700 her husband had lent the king for his own regiment when prince of Wales, and a pension for her carrying secret letters and intelligence, for which she had been plundered and imprisoned. The lord treasurer would try to pay the debt at £100 or £200 per annum 'as the Exchequer now stands'. Of course, payments and pensions all suffered from chronic delays and obstructions, were often for years in arrears. Two years later the widow had 'as yet received no relief'. By March 1665, when Eleanor Lady Byron was dead, her pension was two and a half years in arrears, a sum of £1,125: warrant was made out to her executors for 'her husband's many good services'.

How was the peerage itself to be kept going at Newstead, denuded and impoverished? Richard, now lord, petitioned in 1661 for the revival of the silk farm, and for £600 from fines on goods forfeited for non-payment of customs: warrant was given for the latter. This was in return for the surrender of the grant Charles 1 in his need had made him of three hundred of the best trees in Sherwood. In 1666 he asked for the sole right to purchase refuse lops and tops felled in the hays of Bricklave and Billhay in Sherwood. Next came up the question of the sums he had expended for the defence of Newark, for which he held tallies. The treasury minuted that these were to be settled when the customs were considered; but, after some consideration, 'unless the Parliament do help, the King cannot pay these debts'. Several months later Lord Byron and his sister Dorothy were called in. 'They shall be considered when there is money.' Meanwhile, brother William 'late of Newstead is outlawed for debt'.

At the outbreak of the second Dutch war the navy commissioners approved Lord Byron's offer of 2,000 loads of timber from Newstead, good and fit for service; hoys were wanted for transport to London. He wished to have the monopoly of the refuse wood which was useless to the navy from the forest near where a great fall of his own wood was being made for ship-building. Two Harwich vessels were lent him for transport of timber to Chatham. Wartime hazards at sea and unreasonable rates for carriage absorbed the price he obtained: he refused to fell any more trees; he had so much lying at Gunthorp, and knew not how to get it to Stockwith on the river. His timber fetched £2 10s to £3 10s per load. In 1667 the commissioners of prizes lent him the captured *St John Evangelist* of Amsterdam and *St Peter* of Rotterdam to carry timber. Next year the king directed that Byron should keep these prizes, in consideration of his services and sufferings. In 1669 the navy commissioners lent him the *Chick* to carry planks to Hull, where he had a ship loading.

He had not ceased to serve. In the alarms of 1666 with the Dutch off the coast and in the Medway, Byron's troop of horse lay at Lynn and kept watch on the coast towns thereabouts. Next year he was given a commission in Prince Rupert's regiment – quite like old times, twenty years before. He had got his warrant for selling the refuse wood from Sherwood, but three years later it was questioned: it was only the lord treasurer's and they must have the king's. Moreover the warrant related only to the offal wood *then* on the ground. A new warrant was granted. In 1674 he was to have £500 royal bounty as compensation for the wood to which he had pretensions in Sherwood. Over this there were complications about payment of taxes. Byron pleaded that £100 and more had been paid, but that the steward who had his orders to pay his assessment had left his service and died, while the acquittances were lost or mislaid. This dispute continued after Richard's own death in 1679, in his seventy-fourth year – luckiest of the family, it may be said.

What, meanwhile, of Robert's Irish career? He had, as a young man, served the king there before the outbreak of the Rebellion, which raised such a panic in England. Thence he had come over to fight in the North-West, where he had had to surrender Liverpool. At the Restoration he returned to serve in Ireland; on leave upon important service to the king in 1661, his 'entertainment' was to suffer no check. He at first was granted the lands in Enniscorthy which had been given earlier to the regicide, Wallop; but these had been transferred to the earl of Southampton and others. Sir Robert wished to exchange for lands of Fleetwood's regiment in the barony of Fews.

In 1663 he acquired a lease of Ardgowl, county Limerick, and was proposed for master of the ordnance. Ormonde, restored to power, had no objection but pointed out that it would be an economy to have Lord Dungannon, who would then surrender his claim to the marshal's place. Ormonde proceeded to urge consideration for Lord Byron's sister, the widow of Sir Thomas Lucas, whose grants had proved ineffectual. Her sufferings and those of her family merited the king's special consideration. This was no more than the truth: the Lucases, like the Byrons, had been torn to pieces in the king's cause. They were now engaged in picking up the pieces and fitting them together.

In 1664 Sir Robert applied for command of the troop late of the earl of Kildare, only to find that the lord lieutenant wanted it for himself: 'Sir Robert Byron shall have the next that shall fall.' He had lately been made master of the ordnance, and was now a member of the Irish privy council. He should have received £400 for his exploit, during the Rebellion, of capturing two of the leaders, Art Roe McPatrick and Art Moyle McMahone, but there had been no money in the treasury. He might now be paid from any funds by his own procurement, though not from ordinary revenue. Over in England early in 1665, when there were disturbances in Southwark, he was ordered as lieutenant of the king's foot guards to march with two companies of them to quiet the place. A young Thomas Byron received a commission in Sir Robert's company.

In Ireland Sir Robert had a regiment of foot, of which he was both colonel and captain. We hear of a young John, ensign in the king's regiment of guards there: this was his nephew. In 1665 Sir Robert put in his memorandum of supplies necessary: £5,000 for repair of the king's castles and forts; £3,000 for cannon – no great guns in all Ireland, except at Dublin and Dungannon; £1,000 for wagons and building materials; 1,200 tents – £2,400. In the next year he reported on the state of arms and ammunition in the country. He was necessarily involved in the complicated business of the land settlement after rebellion and Cromwellian conquest: Charles II's government tried to steer a middle path, more favourable to Irish landholders. Lord Byron had asked for compensation to the tune of £2,000 per annum out of the estates of those who had opposed the Restoration. The reply was: 'This cannot be – they are appointed for reprisals [claims for forfeits] only, vested in the King.' Lord

Byron received an annuity of £500 for life, out of the English exchequer. Sir Robert got one-third of the 'lapsed money' and one-third of the lands and tenements in lieu of the same – in accordance with the Act of Settlement.

In 1671 there followed a brief contretemps: Sir Robert and others were dismissed for signing a petition about pay. Charles II, under constant pressure for cash from every quarter, blew up uncharacteristically. The storm was soon over, and they were all reinstated. But, in 1672, the new lord lieutenant, the earl of Essex, wanted 'a more diligent and younger man' at the head of the ordnance. In the following year Sir Robert was anxious to sell his command, which Essex refused: 'If I should suffer men, as in his case, when they grow old or infirm, to dispose of their commands, I should scarce ever have any opportunity of obliging any gentleman in a thing of this nature' – and the person he recommended was altogether improper. Sir Robert ceased to badger him: shortly after, he died. Young Lieutenant John was given command of his uncle's company. Sir Thomas Byron's widow was to share, with a number of others, in the benefit of the lottery to which they were reduced to raise funds. Lord Conway was willing to give Lady Byron, presumably Sir Robert's widow, £1,000 for her reversion: she had been 'left in great want'.

A few scraps remain that may properly be called part of the sequel to the Civil War, particularly in Ireland. James II's unfortunate incursion upset the more moderate and friendly landsettlement of the Restoration, which was the intention of his brother Charles II and represented the wishes of their father, Charles I.* William III, having to reconquer the country, in effect went back to and confirmed Cromwell's unsympathetic settlement.

In 1685 Sir Edward Byron, baronet, received of the royal bounty, a gift of £500. He was the son of Sir Ernestus, therefore a grandson of Sir Nicholas. He was captain of a foot regiment, and had served for some years in Ireland. In 1697 he petitioned for lands, in the new share-out, to the value of £100 a year. The lords of the treasury found that the lands in the list he had

* For this *v.* my *Milton the Puritan*, 142-3, and *The Early Churchills*, cc. iii, iv.

put in were worth more like £400 per annum, and his petition was referred to Ireland for probation. In the event he received lands of £100 per annum for ninety-nine years, out of forfeited lands in Kerry and Galway: 1,216 acres, 'for many good and acceptable services performed'.

At Newstead the second lord was succeeded by his son William, third lord: not much to him – the epic days were over. He married first, at twenty-four, Penelope, daughter of Viscount Chaworth, of the family of Nottinghamshire neighbours we have already met. They lived at Wiverton, south-east of Nottingham, towards the Leicestershire border. Only a fragment of their old gate-house remains, for Lord Chaworth fortified the house in the Civil War, and it was destroyed. The church has disappeared; but some of their Tudor tombs remain in the neighbouring church of Langar. Penelope produced a son and heir, another William, in 1670, but died in Dublin in 1682. In 1685 Lord Byron married, at Westminster Abbey, a daughter of Sir George Stonehouse, evidently of the family with which his uncle, the first lord, had had such intricate financial relations before the war. William, and his son William, took their place in the commission of the peace as deputy-lieutenants for Nottinghamshire, though we hear little of them. In 1695 the third lord died, and was buried in the church at Hucknall Torkard; he cannot have been old.

His son took his seat in Parliament as the fourth lord, on 20 January 1696, and was shortly named among those to be attached for not attending. In 1699 he was at the Loo, William III's country palace in Holland: he and a friend were there for a couple of days, and hunted once, 'which proved a damned chase, and won't give a very good character to our sport'. Back at Newstead complaints were made of his felling in the forest: he pleaded that this was by ancient grants, but the felling was stopped until he could prove his rights. He was able to secure the naturalization of one Lewis Barber who had gone out of England with the first lord and settled in France, but remained a Protestant. Byron was a teller in the Lords on the Irish Forfeited Estates Bill, and next year voted in the majority for the acquittal of Lord Somers from impeachment. He was evidently friendly to William III's government.

A sea-faring Richard Byron was in intimate attendance on William III, for he was commander of the king's personal yacht, the *Fubbs*. From its inventory we can see the indomitable little monarch on those journeyings to and from Holland, in his actual surroundings: the bedchamber with bed curtains of silk-fringed red serge, window curtains and table carpet; the state room with four beds and a dozen cane chairs; the gun room and captain's cabin with one close stool; the twelve basins and twelve chamber pots. In 1705 Byron is petitioning for the *Fubbs*'s share in the immense Spanish treasure captured in Vigo Bay. Lord Treasurer Godolphin agrees, but wants to know what proportion this would come to. The commissioners of prizes were to examine what was done for others in like cases. The captain sets forth his services in Admiral Rooke's expedition to Cadiz, and prays for the same proportion as the *Isabella*. In this year 1706 Byron transferred to the *Cleveland*, evidently another royal yacht – perhaps the *Fubbs* was superannuated – for it is the lord chamberlain who gives warrant to the master of the great wardrobe for the delivery of its furnishings.

The fourth lord himself became close to the royal family with his appointment as gentleman of the bedchamber to Queen Anne's consort, Prince George of Denmark. To the day of his death he received a pension of £600 a year, 'for good causes and considerations us hereunto moving' – evidently not so much for present services as for the immense losses the family had endured in the Royalist cause. In 1714 he put in a memorandum asking consideration as to five hundred trees from Sherwood for the repair of Newstead, probably much in need of it, and the enlargement of his park. This was the age of 'improving' landlords; but the good work was entirely undone by his successor.

He was three times married, before producing an heir. First he married Mary Egerton, daughter of the third earl of Bridgwater, a Cheshire family; she died of smallpox six weeks after her marriage and was buried at Hucknall. His second wife was Frances Williamina, daughter of William III's intimate friend from youth, Willem Bentinck, first earl of Portland, by his Villiers wife. This marriage produces an echo in the mind, for William III's mistress was Elizabeth Villiers, countess of Orkney, Swift's wise old friend who saw through everybody and

everything, especially in politics. Thirdly, Byron married
Frances, a young daughter of the fourth Lord Berkeley of Stratton, who confessed, 'I am going to dispose of one of my
daughters to Lord Byron, a disproportionate match as to ages,
but marriages not offering every day, I would not miss an
opportunity, though attended with never so many inconveniences.'

This takes us back again to Civil War days, for the first Lord
Berkeley of Stratton had fought with the Western Army all the
way from Stratton to Bristol, a comrade of Jack Trevanion and
the others; and Berkeley had succeeded the first Lord Byron
as James, duke of York's mentor and companion in France.
It was this late marriage on 3 December 1720, at Kensington
where Lord Byron would have his apartment in the palace, that
produced an heir, another William. A later memorandum
refers to a royal gift of 110 ounces of gilt plate on the christening.
In spite of his handsome welcome into the world, this William
has come down in history and tradition as the 'Wicked Lord':
he succeeded when his father died at Newstead on an August
day in 1736.

Portrait of John, first Lord Byron, by Dobson.

Newstead Abbey, Nottinghamshire home of the Byrons.

The church of St Michael, Caerhays, where the Trevanions were buried.

Caerhays Castle in Cornwall, the Trevanions' home for many generations.

Admiral John Byron, the poet's grandfather, as a captain at the time of his marriage.

Sophia Trevanion at the time of her marriage to Captain John Byron, by Rosalba.

Pen and wash caricature
of William Trevanion
being carried off from
Exeter College to
Queen's, from the
Oxford Almanac of 1755.

Monument to William
Trevanion, last of the
male line, in St Michael's,
Caerhays.

Newstead-Abby Nottinghamshire.

Newstead Abbey Lake, with the toy fort of the 'Wicked Lord',
William, fourth Lord Byron, in the foreground.

'Mad Jack' Byron, the poet's father, and the marchioness of
Carmarthen, with whom he eloped.

Augusta Leigh, the poet Byron's half-sister, by Sir George Hayter.

Lord Byron the poet by Thomas Phillips, 1814.

Medora Leigh, an 1829 engraving (*opposite*).

'Bifrons' in Kent, the house
Lady Byron lent to Georgiana
and Henry Trevanion.

Byron's cousin and hero,
Captain Bettesworth in St
Michael's church, Caerhays.

VII

Augustans:
The 'Wicked Lord'

SEVERAL CIRCUMSTANCES conspired to bring the Byrons and Trevanions close together for the next century. In the first place, William, fourth Lord Byron and John Trevanion, head of the family at Caerhays from 1703 to 1740, married two daughters of Lord Berkeley of Stratton: the first Frances, as we have seen, the second marrying Barbara, so that the Byrons and Trevanions became cousins. They both had Court associations, with their comparable Royalist background in the Civil War. Henceforward too we find a strong naval element in both families, the younger sons making their careers, some of them their mark, in the navy.

We cannot follow the spreading tree of the Trevanions in the West, nor the cadet branches of the family in any detail; but one or two members are worth mentioning, where their careers illustrate the naval theme. That of Sir Nicholas Trevanion, who died in 1737, achieved a note in history. As a young captain of the *Dunwich* he served in the expedition to Newfoundland in 1697. The French had overrun the island, and the naval expedition under Desborough achieved nothing. Young Trevanion had been present at the commander's consultations; the latter's course of action was abortive and he was himself found guilty of neglect on his return. Trevanion was called in to give his evidence at the admiralty inquiry, though a fellow captain, meeting him on the 'Change, cautioned him against appearing 'where they would be badly handled'.

The next notice of him is a considerable exploit. At the beginning of Marlborough's war, in January 1703, Trevanion in the

Dover, of fifty guns, captured the *Comte de Toulouse* with three hundred soldiers on board. We find traces of him on active service at sea all through the war, sailing from the Nore in 1704; in 1708 in Barcelona Roads to transport troops from Catalonia for the reduction of Minorca. In 1712, as captain of the *York* man-of-war, he captured a prize, about which there was some dispute whether the queen was not entitled to its forfeiture. Knighted by George i, he ended as commissioner in control of the navy at Plymouth from 1726 to 1737.

He seated himself conveniently at Molenick, not far off, in St Germains parish, and did well for himself by marrying a well-off widow, already twice married. She was the widow of a Lombard Street goldsmith and banker when Sir William Coryton married her, by whom, gossip Hals tells us, 'though a very aged woman, to recompense that defect he had much riches or wealth'. After his death she married Sir Nicholas Trevanion of St Germans, who followed in marriage the Delphic Oracle's direction, and Dion's –

> Refuse no woman ne'er so old,
> Whose marriage bringeth store of gold.

Her monument in St Germans church sounds another note: 'A Lady of most Exemplary Virtue and Piety.'

Sir Nicholas's cousin John succeeded to Caerhays in 1703, and married, first, a daughter and co-heiress of Sir Francis Blake of Ford Castle in Northumberland, who gave him no children and died in 1725. In the following year he married Barbara Berkeley, who gave him three: William, Frances and Sophia. He sat in Parliament for Tregony, 1705–8, and for Bodmin, 1708–10. In 1709, during the last year of the Whig ministry – Godolphin, a non-party man, was forced to rely on the Whigs for support of Marlborough's war – Trevanion put in a petition for the reversion of the lease of Restormel Park, originally granted to Colonel Jack's widow. She had devised it to her grandson, who obtained a lease in reversion, 'then and now living at St Germains outlawed for treason'. The reply from the treasury came down: nothing can be done till it is known whether this Richard Trevanion is alive or no. We know that he was.

In 1710 the Tories got their revenge in a nation-wide electoral upheaval. The reality behind it was that the nation, and the queen, were sick of the war, which had been going on ever since 1702, and longing for peace, which the Whigs were unwilling to make. On top of this Lord Treasurer Godolphin, who despised the party spirit of the religious sects, made the mistake of prosecuting a silly clergyman, Dr Sacheverell, for an inflammatory sermon. This provided a good election cry: the Church in danger. In Cornwall the election was a victory for the Tories, as almost everywhere: it resulted in a mob of unmanageable right-wingers, who gave Harley, another sensible moderate, as much trouble as they had given Godolphin. The elections for the county, with their considerable electorate of freeholders, were more significant than those for the boroughs; also more honorific and, in case of a contest, much more expensive. A county election, moreover, could last over a couple of months.

The Cornish election was indeed symptomatic, with its reverberations from the Civil War, loyalty to the Stuarts – Parliament had decided on the Protestant Hanoverian line succeeding Queen Anne – and its Jacobite affiliations. (If James Edward, the Old Pretender, had had the sense to become an Anglican, he might have pulled it off; for the Hanoverians were Germans, and very unpopular. But the Old Pretender had no sense – like his father, James II, who lost everything for lack of it. The Hanoverians always knew which side their bread was buttered.)

At the Restoration the Grenvilles had decided – it was a grand time for snobbery – to call themselves Granville. Now in 1710 Sir Bevil Grenville's grandson, George Granville, a pompous and extravagant man, who lived in stately splendour at Longleat by right of his wife, decided to challenge the Whig county members. These were Hugh Boscawen and James Buller, whose families, be it noted, had been on the side of Parliament during the Civil War: hence now Whigs. Granville was a Jacobite; John Trevanion was selected as his fellow candidate, and that family, as we know, had its Jacobite affiliation, with uncle Richard still with the Old Pretender at St Germain.

Harley, unlike Godolphin, kept his ear to the ground. In October 1710 a report went up to him from Liskeard, where

the meeting of our gentlemen yesterday was the greatest ever known on such an occasion. Mr. Boscawen and Edgcumbe [Sir Richard] made a rude opposition to reading Lord President Rochester's letter [lord president of the council, the queen's uncle], which the gentlemen of the county much resented. The letter was read and applauded, and it was agreed to set up Mr. Granville and Mr. Trevanion in opposition to them. The towns are in a good disposition and expect a good return.

Harley's agent was then going to visit the corporations, who mostly returned the MPs for the towns, and to meet Mr Granville.

The election went on for two months, and cost Granville some £4,000! We do not know what it cost Trevanion – a pretty penny, it may be surmised. Yet it was said that bribery was heavier on the Whig side: needs must, for the Tory was the popular side. They had a good cry in the rhyme:

> Trevanion and Granville, sound as a bell,
> For the Queen and the Church and Sacheverell.

The Court, the clergy, most of the country gentry and the mob were for the Tories. The Whig *Flying Post* summed up the fun: 'For bespeaking and collecting a mob, £20. For Roarers of the word Church, £40. For several gallons of Tory punch on church tombstones, £30. For a majority of clubs and brandy bottles, £20. For Dissenters-damners ... committing two riots, demolishing two houses, for a gang of Aldermanabusers, for a set of notorious liars, law and charges in King's Bench, £1460.'

The size of the majority gave Harley great trouble, and the right-wing, organized in the October Club, fell to the leadership of his rival, the unprincipled St John, later Lord Bolingbroke. Granville was left with £1,500 of his expenses still to pay, and applied for help to Harley, who gave him a peerage as Lord Lansdowne. Trevanion considered himself not sufficiently rewarded: Granville asked Harley to 'find some way to put him in good humour', before he came up to town to join the malcontents.

However, being a member of Parliament gave opportunities for advancing the interests of friends, however grand, and of clients, however small. In 1711 James Trengrouse reported to Harley, now lord treasurer and earl of Oxford, that all four surveyors of the tin blowing-houses in Cornwall had been put in their places by Lord Godolphin during pleasure; during the last election they had acted in opposition to the two Tory candidates. Trengrouse had the recommendation of these knights of the shire and prayed for one of the surveyorships. Here we have the stuffing of politics at all times and in all places. Next year we find Trevanion forwarding complaints against the postmaster at Bodmin and recommending one John Williams for appointment; and, next, supporting Robert Freeman for tidewaiter in the port of London. This was, after all, what MPs were for; it does not appear from the record that John Trevanion was for much else.

When George Granville moved up to the House of Lords, his place as knight of the shire was taken by Sir Richard Vyvyan, another Jacobite. Upon the Rebellion of 1715 they were both popped into the Tower.

Trevanion seems to have concentrated his energies, such as they were, on improving Caerhays – though he gets little credit for it from his contemporary, the antiquary Thomas Tonkin.

Mr. John Trevanion has . . . bestowed a great deal of money in buildings, gardens, etc., on this place. But, as there is nothing of regularity observed, it may more properly be called a pleasant romantic seat than a complete habitation; and, although it faces the south, yet it lies too much under an hill, and is therefore cold and damp in winter. The house [i.e. Trevanion] anciently stood to the north of the present towards the brow of the hill, according to my opinion in a far better situation. The place where it was built is still called the haller, that is, the hall; but the odd desire of our ancestors to settle in our valleys and to get, as they called it, in the *lewth* [Cornish for lee], inclined one of the Arundells to remove the house to where it now stands.

In short, John Trevanion had not seen fit to rebuild Caerhays in newly fashionable classical style, as a number of Cornish gentry were doing at the time – perhaps his medieval house was more in keeping with romantic Jacobite sympathies. That he was proud of the place and its gardens, his work there, is evident from his will.* This he made in 1737, when he was seventy; he died three years later, in 1740.

He began with a large charitable bequest, '£100 to poor persons in Cornwall'. His widow, Barbara, was a youngish woman:

* Prob/11/708, f. 53.

like her sister, Frances, who married Lord Byron, she had married an elderly widower, so that the children were all under age. The only son, and heir, William was thirteen at his father's death. In addition to her marriage settlements the widow was to have the gratification of £400, all her jewels, and as much of the plate as she wished. The residue might be sold for the education of young William. Generous remembrances follow to members of the family and to servants: £50 to his godson, son of Hugh Trevanion, late of Windsor. (Hugh had had grace-and-favour lodgings in the castle, for in 1712 he had received payment 'for lodging her Majesty's chaplains'.) To Sir Nicholas Trevanion went £10 for mourning, and to his daughter Mary, 'my god-daughter, £20'. To his godson, Thomas Plowden, son of a cousin, he bequeathed £10 for mourning. He left a house-keeper, Mary Polsue, a fair annuity, on condition that she lived 'in the mansion house at Caerhays and [looked] after the house and furniture'. One of the executors was his brother-in-law, the eldest son of Lord Berkeley of Stratton.

Decisive for the future of both Trevanion and Byron families was the provision that he made in case of the failure of male heirs. His elder daughter Frances – called after her aunt, Lady Byron – was next in succession to her brother William, named for his uncle, Lord Byron, and she would succeed to the Caer-hays estate. The younger daughter, Sophia, would receive an inheritance of £12,000, which would leave the family for the Byrons, on her marrying her cousin, the fifth lord's younger brother. Elaborate instructions were laid down for no less than nine members of the family in succession, in case of failure of heirs to his young children. 'And it is my desire ... that every person who by this my will shall be from time to time entitled to possession of my capital mansion ... shall sufficiently main-tain, support, and uphold the houses, gardens, walks and park at Caerhays, and leave the same so well and sufficiently repaired, maintained and upheld to the next person in re-mainder. ...'

John Trevanion must have loved that lovely place.

The career of his cousin, William, fifth Lord Byron, was in every way a contrast. Where John was quiet and respectable, devoted to his family and to Caerhays, William was very far from a family man, led a life which brought him notoriety and the sensation of a trial for murder before the House of Lords, and ended by well-nigh wrecking Newstead. Even before he died legends were circulating about him in the vicinity, as a devil incarnate, and he became generally known as the 'Wicked Lord'.

He was not particularly bad or wicked – except, according to my standard of values, in neglecting and nearly ruining New-stead, laying waste the park, selling its pictures, etc. He was certainly eccentric and irresponsible – spoiled, perhaps, by his early succession to the peerage at fourteen, unbridled, undisci-plined, extravagant in the way that eighteenth-century aristo-crats were liable to be; and, in the end, a resentful recluse, soured by the way life had worked out – serve him right for a fool. Fancy throwing away such a heritage!

Born in 1722 he started a career in the navy, becoming a lieutenant at an early stage; he gave that up on succeeding to Newstead in 1736, though he retained his naval fixation. One of his extravagances was to sail vessels on the lake there for mimic sea-fights. He built a couple of forts to add to the illusion of war – in a contemporary engraving one sees one of them, the flag of St George floating above it, the noble Gothic façade of the abbey across the lake. For the coming of age of his son, William, in 1770 he had quite a large boat brought overland for yet another battle. Fighting was in the Byron blood: I think we can say of this one that he was an ungrown-up boy, a spoiled adolescent.

His career began in orthodox fashion well enough for a young blood. He served as captain in the duke of Kingston's regiment, with his neighbours, Lord Robert Manners and a Sutton, against the Jacobite invasion under the Young Pretender in the '45. They marched as far as Preston. We hear of him hunting with popular Lord Granby and Lord Rockingham; there were festive race meetings at Nottingham, cock-fights at Newark. He was grand master of the Freemasons from 1747 to 1752. In 1747 he married a Norfolk heiress, Elizabeth Shaw, with £70,000. That should have steadied him up a bit; instead, it increased his extravagance and he treated her badly.

He was already fairly well known as a rake in London, prob-ably, as we are told, from an attempt – typical enough of young bloods of the time – to carry off Mrs Bellamy, the actress. He built a little castle on a rise among the trees, the scene of lively parties which, no doubt, rumour exaggerated into orgies. It all cost money, and by 1760, when Horace Walpole visited Newstead, trees had been sacrificed on a large scale.

Horace, of course, loved the romantic Gothic ruin,

the very abbey. The great east [actually west] window of the church remains and connects with the house; the hall entire, the refectory entire, the cloister untouched with the ancient cistern of the convent and their arms on it, a private chapel quite perfect. The park, which is still charming, has not been so much unprofaned; the present Lord has lost large sums [gaming, no doubt] and paid part in old oaks, £5000 worth of which have been cut near the house. In recompense he has built two baby forts, to pay his country in castles for the damage done to the Navy.

We have seen that the oaks of Sherwood Forest provided the best timber for the ships of the navy. In their place, he 'has planted a handful of Scotch firs, that look like ploughboys dressed in old family liveries for a public day! In the hall is a very good collection of pictures, all animals; the refectory, now the great drawing-room, is full of Byrons'. A dozen years later this fool was reduced to selling most of the pictures. Think what a Horace Walpole would have done to cherish such a place and add to its collections – a grander Strawberry Hill, the real thing!

In 1763 Lord Byron became, appropriately, master of the royal staghounds of Sherwood Forest. A couple of years later came the catastrophe that ruined his life. A club of Nottinghamshire gentlemen met regularly at the 'Star and Garter' in Pall Mall, and here Lord Byron had the misfortune to kill his neighbour, and cousin, Mr Chaworth. Horace Walpole reports for us the typically idiotic tiff that led to the killing. There had been 'a dispute between the combatants whether Lord Byron, who took no care of his game, or Mr. Chaworth, who was active in the association, had most game on their manor. The company had apprehended no consequences and parted at eight o'clock.' It was a dark January night in 1765.

Lord Byron, stepping into an empty chamber and sending the drawer for Mr. Chaworth, took the candle from the waiter and, bidding Mr. Chaworth defend himself, drew his sword. Mr. Chaworth,

who was an excellent fencer, ran Lord Byron through the sleeve of
his coat and then received a wound fourteen inches deep into his body.
He was carried to his house in Berkeley Street – made his will with
the greatest composure and dictated a paper which, they say, allows
it was a fair duel, and died at nine this morning.

This kind of thing was a not infrequent occurrence. But it
made a sensation in the eighteenth century, because Byron was
a peer. 'Lord Byron is not gone off, but says he will take his
trial – which, if the coroner brings in a verdict of manslaughter
may, according to precedent, be in the House of Lords and
without the ceremonial of Westminster Hall.' The coroner
brought in a verdict of murder, so there was to be a State trial
in Westminster Hall after all, with the greatest possible *éclat*.
Eighteenth-century society loved a spectacle, especially a grand
trial with a death sentence hanging in the air. Tickets were selling at six guineas apiece. Horace Walpole asked his old crony,
George Montagu, if he would like one: 'I can secure you a ticket
for Lord Lincoln's gallery.' But George 'would not be a specta-
tor of such a scene for anything'.

Horace, writing to Mann in Florence, affected a lack of interest in the 'solemn puppet show. I, who should like the trial of
a Laud or Strafford as a wholesome spectacle now and then,
am not interested about an obscure Lord, whose birth alone
procured his being treated like an overgrown criminal. This
quarrel was about game, and the very topic should send it to
the quarter-sessions.'

However, when the trial took place in April 1765 all London
was there, headed by two royal dukes, York and Gloucester,
and the archbishops of Canterbury and York. The lord chancellor was lord high steward for the solemn occasion: this was
Lord Northington, who said, 'If I had known that these legs
were one day to carry a Chancellor, I'd have taken better care
of them when I was a lad.' He and the royal dukes processed
into the hall in full state, long trains borne behind them, with
much bowing and curtseying and reverences, and resounding
'Oyez, Oyez, Oyez!'

The lord steward (whose daughter's husband was to be killed
in a duel) held forth with some complacency: 'Your lordship
will reflect that you have the happiness to be tried by the
supreme judicature of this nation, that you can receive nothing

from your peers but justice, distributed with candour; delivered, too, under the strongest obligations upon noble minds,
honour. These considerations will, I hope, compose your lordship's mind, fortify your spirits, and leave you free for your
defence.'

The facts did not differ much from what Walpole had heard,
but Byron's defence was better than expected. Chaworth
apparently had confessed that he had been rather short with
him, so Byron had had some provocation. Also Chaworth was
a big fellow, well known to be a good fencer; Byron was a small
man, who had said, smarting under injury (or an inferiority
complex), 'I have as much courage as any man in England.'
Witnesses were examined; when Byron had called Chaworth
from the stairs into a back room, a waiter went in 'with a
poor little tallow candle, which was all the light, except a dull
fire'.

Byron said, 'Draw!' When Chaworth saw his sword half-
drawn, he whipped out his own and quickly gave Byron the
point. He thought that he had mortally wounded him in the
breast, when actually the sword was entangled in his waistcoat.
Byron shortened his sword and ran Chaworth right through,
close to the navel. The master of the tavern burst in to find
them grasped in each other's arms. Chaworth yielded his
sword, Byron did so with reluctance. Byron said, 'Good God!
that I should be such a fool as to fight in the dark.' When Hawkins, the surgeon, arrived he found that Byron's sword had gone
in one side and out the other. Chaworth said that he forgave
Lord Byron and hoped the world would.

In the end 119 peers voted Byron guilty of manslaughter
only, four of them voted him not guilty at all. He thereupon
claimed the right of a peer under a statute of Edward VI, and
was discharged. The lord high steward ritually broke his white
staff in two, and the procession re-formed: the officers of the
chancery two by two, like animals out of the ark, the royal dukes
and archbishops, finally the lord chancellor, all with elaborate
bows to the throne.

How much one appreciates the idiocy of human affairs – just
the kind of thing to arouse Swift's *saeva indignatio*!

Horace Walpole, a kinder man, came round a little after the
event. 'The prisoner behaved with great decorum, and seemed

thoroughly shocked and mortified. Indeed, the bitterness of the world against him has been great, and the stories they have revived or invented to load him very grievous. The Chancellor behaved with his usual, or rather greater, vulgarness and blunders. Lord Pomfret kept away decently, from the similitude of his own story.' He, too, had killed a man in a duel. To Mann Horace reported later that it was Byron's former faults that 'had given handle to ill-nature to represent him as guilty of an event which truly it had been very difficult for him to avoid. He escaped with life, and recovered some portion of honour, if that can comfort him, after the publicity made of his character and the misfortune of killing an amiable man, but one not blameless in the late instance.'

Chaworth may have forgiven Byron, but the world did not: eighteenth-century society was apt to be very hard on people who broke – or, rather, who were exposed in breaking – its rules. The exposure was such a breach of decorum. Walpole confessed himself sorry for the honour of the family and for Byron's sister, Isabella, Lady Carlisle, whom he knew. Mrs Delany, Lord Lansdowne's niece, gushing as ever, wrote, 'How good! How like herself was our most dear friend's [the duchess of Portland] carrying Lady Carlisle down to Bulstrode, at a time when it must have been shocking to her to have to be in town! I am glad the sad affair has ended to her satisfaction.'

Isabella Byron, too, seems to have had her share of light-headedness. Something may be allowed her for the circumstances of her marriage. A year older than her brother, at twenty-two she was married off in 1743 to an elderly widower, twenty-eight years her senior, the fourth earl of Carlisle. Lady Mary Wortley Montagu, no mean judge, thought the young lady 'very agreeable, but if I am not mistaken in her inclinations, they are very gay'. She had fifteen years of gaiety with her old man, and when he died he left her a mere £1,000, some silver and her customary jewels. If she re-married, she would lose everything except her marriage-settlement. This was rather mean of him; but it did not prevent her from marrying a man much her junior the next year.

Horace Walpole tells us, in 1759, that she 'is going to marry a Sir William Musgrave, who is but three and twenty; but in consideration of the match and of her having years to spare, she has made him a present of ten, and calls him three and thirty'. Lord Carlisle had died the year before, leaving a vacancy in the Order of the Garter. Lord Temple, the great Pitt's insufferable brother-in-law, at once asked for it: 'If he would have been contented to ask first for my Lady Carlisle's garter, I don't doubt but he would have obtained it!' The rumour ran that Lady Carlisle was rather free with her garters.

As for Byron, the world closed against him, and he shut himself up at Newstead, becoming more and more morose. Next year he was removed from being master of the royal staghounds. He had hoped that his son and heir, another William (born in 1749), would recoup his own losses by marrying an heiress. Instead of that the young man went off with his first cousin, Juliana, daughter of his father's younger brother, John, Admiral Byron and Sophia Trevanion. William, son and heir, died young in 1776, at only twenty-five. He left a son, another William, who was killed at the siege of Calvi in Corsica, in 1794. It was the fifth lord's younger brother, the admiral, who had the naval career that the elder evidently desiderated, and garnered fame and reputation where the fifth lord had achieved only notoriety and ill-fame.

His wife, not unnaturally, left him. Perhaps he had already taken his servant Betty to him – 'Lady Betty', as she was known. An old valet testified to his lordship's eccentricities. Worse than eccentricity, he seems to have developed a scunner against Newstead, selling off all the deer in the park for much less than market value, felling more and more timber to denude the place, selling the pictures, even leasing the mines at Rochdale at a derisory rental.

One sees in all this no very obscure resentment at what he had made of his life, wreaking a revenge upon Newstead. Thus the 'Wicked Lord' became something of a legend, in the manner of the countryside and country folk. He was supposed to be evil and to worship devils – because he had brought back a Pan and a satyr from Italy and set them up in a wood: it was said that he paid homage to them. His ill-treatment of his wife – since she did not set foot in Newstead again – was transformed into drowning her in the lake. He would dine alone with his pistols laid before him. When the poet, his great-nephew, succeeded him as a boy at Newstead he took the 'Wicked Lord's' sword and pistols for his playthings. It is not difficult to see where the element of diabolism in the poet came from.

VIII

Admiral Byron and Sophia Trevanion

THE 'WICKED LORD'S' YOUNGER BROTHER, John, was born at Newstead on a November day in 1723. His characteristics were such as to suggest that the elder may well have been jealous of him: no evidence of any friendly feeling exists, and the peer evinced no interest in his brother's family that was going to succeed him. William was a small, cocky little man, with perhaps a sense of inferiority to account for some of his antics; John was six feet tall, powerful and strong, a fine figure of a man, rather handsome and full of self-confidence. He left school early to join the navy, probably enough when 'his bedmaker evinced his abilities in the field of Venus'. This was the kind of thing that was said now and again of the rising, and indeed risen, sailor: his sexual prowess was impressive. For all his time away at sea – and he was at sea most of his time, a fully employed professional sailor – he gave his wife nine children, and there were other activities in between.

At fourteen he was an able seaman, on convoy duty between Newfoundland and Lisbon. At sixteen he was recruited by Anson as a midshipman on board the *Wager*, the storeship for his famous expedition which was to recapitulate, in some respects, Drake's voyage round the world. Anson, too, captured a Spanish treasure-ship, which made his fortune. But the *Wager*, a heavy, slow-going vessel, was shipwrecked on an island on the desolate coast of Chile, north of the Straits of Magellan, where the mountains come down to the sea. Years later Byron brought out his *Narrative* of the appalling hardships and sufferings they had to endure – and made name and fame for himself. Oddly

enough, at all the critical points of his career, when he might
have had success like others no more deserving, he was beset
by storms and bad weather – as if the devil were in it – to such
an extent that sailors, with the superstition of their profession,
used to be certain there would be stormy weather whenever
they were under his command. They called him 'Foul-weather
Jack', and the name stuck.

We need not go in detail into the harrowing happenings to
the crew of the *Wager*. John Byron was young and tough, or
he would never have survived. As it was he fell ill – from a surfeit
of seaweed fried in tallow grease, he said. Many of the men
died, from scurvy or simply of starvation. The decisive facts
were these. Anson had appointed a rendezvous, in case of
separation in bad weather, at the pleasant island of Juan Fernandez off the coast out in the Pacific. The *Wager*, with her
stores, was wrecked on the rocks, but most of her men got
ashore. There blew up a difference of opinion, a mutinous disagreement with the captain – always dangerous, often fatal, in
such circumstances – who wanted to build boats from the
wreckage and make north for Juan Fernandez. After a good
deal of muttering, pillage, treachery and some murder, a party
formed under the lead of the gunner, and the majority opted
to go back south through the Straits of Magellan and so home.
Most of the men who went by majority opinion never got back.

They left the remnant in appalling circumstances, having
taken the yawl that had been built and most of the stores. Young
Byron stood by the captain. He happened to have with him
Shelvocke's account of the wreck of the *Speedwell*, and the
measures he took which brought him through. Byron's read-
ings – the captain was seriously ill – gave them hope and a
promise of escape. They built a couple of small boats, in which
they made up the coast, though constantly forced to turn back
by the *cordillera* coming down to the sea, with no evident passage through, and they could not get round the obstacle of a
mountainous headland, which Byron named the Dome of St
Paul's, of which it reminded him. At last, after many efforts,
they discovered a portage and carried their boats through the
passes. After months, and various adventures among Indians,
they reached a Spanish settlement at Chacao, where the inter-
preter was an old Cornish buccaneer, born at Falmouth,

captured forty years before in the West Indies. Young Byron, recovering health and strength, had another kind of escape – from a Creole lady who fancied him and wanted to marry him.

Ultimately they got passage on a French ship, which took them to Brittany, where, since war was still on, they were held captive for many more weary months. It was not until 1746 that Byron was repatriated, now a grown man of twenty-two matured by such an astonishing variety of adventures. He at once made for his sister, Lady Carlisle's house in Soho Square, where he became an interesting figure in her gay social life. Later on, after Carlisle's death and the breakdown of her marriage with the youthful Musgrave, she was thought to go beyond the bounds of decorum. She certainly gave her Byron temperament a free fling, going off to live in Provence on her own, moving restlessly from garrison town to town – Nimes, Aix, Montpellier – dancing all night, painting, versifying: '*garnison – fréquent repas – fort agréable à tous les officiers*'. For twelve years she remained abroad, almost as eccentric as Lady Mary Wortley Montagu who disapproved of her levity.

Young Byron now received rapid promotion, and was at once made captain of the *Syren* frigate and, two years later, of the *St Albans* cruising to the Guinea coast. On an August day of that year, 1748, he married his cousin Sophia Trevanion down at Caerhays. When their grandson the poet wanted to take his seat in the House of Lords, he needed to establish the legitimacy of their marriage, for there was no certificate of it. A clerk had to be sent down to Cornwall to collect affidavits of the event, when it was found that it had taken place in the private chapel of the old house, not in the parish church. With Sophia, £12,000 left the Trevanion estate: on her brother's death without children, her sister and she were the co-heirs. No wonder the poet's grandson, the earl of Lovelace, commenting on his grandfather's love for his half-sister Augusta, speculated that there was something to be said for marrying close relations and keeping the money in the family. After all, the Ptolemies were bound to marry their half-sisters.

The marriage in itself seems to have been happy enough, though it brought Sophia many worries, especially over her children and her husband's career at sea. Nor was he faithful to her, though there were no major scandals, as with her son, the poet's father. One can hardly expect an eighteenth-century sailor, and an aristocrat, not to kick over the traces occasionally. One such amorous adventure, described in an anonymous novel, may have some basis in fact, for it has the right West Country background. Mrs Thrale described her friend Sophia as 'wife to the Admiral *pour ses péchés*' – and no doubt there were several of these. The sea-officer and his wife were described as keeping a hospitable and liberal home (where a too-good-looking chambermaid was found in the master's bed: hence the sequel to the tale). Byron was in command of the guardship *Augusta* at Plymouth for a couple of years, and was then promoted to the *Vanguard*.

At the outbreak of the Seven Years' War he commanded the *America* in Pitt's attempt on the French coast, at Rochefort, which proved a fiasco; thereafter Byron was kept cruising off Brest under Anson, blockading reinforcements for Canada. In 1760, in the *Fame*, he was put in command of a squadron to demolish the fortifications of Louisbourg, key fortress to the colony, and subsequently mopped up satisfactorily all the enemy shipping in the Bay of Chaleur.

The Peace of Paris of 1763 saw British power at its apogee, all North America within the empire: it could not, and did not, last. In the next year Byron was put in command of a voyage, which should have had historic significance. Though it was given out that the objective was the East Indies, it was really intended to follow up Anson's expedition, in which Byron had served his apprenticeship, and to penetrate the Spanish preserve of the Pacific once more. The *Dolphin*, in which Byron sailed, along with the *Tamar*, was the first ship to be copper-sheathed. Byron was a thoroughly competent and professional seaman; he kept his crew in exceptionally good health, and made a most expeditious voyage round the world in only twenty-two months.

But that was not the point of the exercise: from the point of view of discovery the voyage was entirely nugatory. (Even the wreck of the *Wager* had left its memorial on the map in Wager Island.) The commodore showed himself to be unimaginative and to have no instinct for discovery. The straight course he took across the Pacific – as if to get back in the shortest possible time – led him to by-pass all the islands he might have discovered; certainly if he had zig-zagged in the manner of Wallis or Cook. Upon Byron's return with no results the *Dolphin* was immediately sent out again, under the command of Samuel Wallis, a Cornishman of no family; but he opened out a part of the ocean till then unknown, containing the Low Archipelago, and the Society Islands and many more, and returned home the discoverer of paradisal Tahiti.

Byron did light on one of the Gilbert Islands, which he named for himself. The Royal Society expressed its disappointment at such poor scientific results. He did not adhere precisely to his instructions; it is thought that he was driving at the re-discovery of the Solomon Islands, and that, in his account of the voyage, he exaggerated the difficulties of the seas, particularly the heavy swell, he encountered. However, he probably took part in the planning of Wallis's voyage; his own inaugurated the series which culminated in Cook's clearing up the main outstanding problems of the Pacific.

It is perhaps disappointing, though characteristic and revealing, that what little survives of the admiral and Sophia's correspondence is concerned with money. It is also characteristic of the time: people in society constantly lived beyond their means, put on a show that was beyond their resources to keep up with their aristocratic friends and what was expected of them, with the result that they were continually racked by money worries and in debt.

At New Year 1775 Sophia is writing to their agent, Sykes, that she is 'sorry to trouble him for more money', though, as at Christmas her whole quarter's allowance was due: 'I have no scruple as to my husband. . . . I have on coming home so many things – alas – to pay – it distresses me – nay near makes me mad – if I can't save it out of next quarter – what will become of me – I know not.' Her breathless punctuation in dashes reminds one of the similar habit of the poet. His father, Mad Jack, makes his appearance in a characteristic light. Sykes had advanced him 5 guineas, and Sophia wrote: 'I have settled his not taking ill your sending him no more – as I have pretended *to be angry* you let him have *even that* – be so good to call here about twelve with my money [she wanted £50 or £60], but if he should be in the room do not give it me while he stays –

but I will call you out of it to take it – if not able to get rid of him otherways.'

At this time Jack was a youth of eighteen, and this was the way he would be for the rest of his life, always dunning somebody for money. One sees something of what Sophia had to put up with from her family. At the end of the year it is the Admiral who is pressing for money. He had been down to Bath to see Sophia who had been ill, 'but the journey has half ruined me; add to this that I have no less than thirteen workmen to pay every Saturday'. Apparently they had a country house at Pirbright, for thence he writes to Sykes to advance £20 to his daughter, Juliana, widow of her cousin William, the fifth lord's son and heir. She was now marrying Sir Robert Wilmot, who was expected next week, and 'I should be ashamed that she should be obliged to ask him immediately upon their marriage for £10 or £20. ... For it would appear very much to go to him without a single shilling in her pocket.' The Admiral then raises the demand to £100, £50 to be supplied immediately. 'I have heard lately that Sir Robert is a man of very good fortune as well as character, so that I hope they will do very well together.'

Juliana was a favourite with her mother; her son, Robert, held with the poet's wife over the separation and was in consequence disliked by him.

Next year the poet's father, at Frankfurt, is drawing upon Sykes for £44, since his creditors would not accept a bill drawn upon his mother. 'I have wrote to Grosvenor Square [their London residence] about it and desired my mother to repay my father.'

In December 1785 Sophia writes angrily to Sykes that she is 'charged with the carpenters' bill at Grosvenor Square, which [she] had as much to do with as with the carpenters here [at Pirbright]. The wine sent to Bolton [i.e. Bolton Row] was half of it drunk while the Admiral was there.' It had been given to her, and so was the post-chaise and the ten guineas in her sickness. 'As for paying off the chariot any more than the job horses to Carter, they were not to be called my expenses as I never desired either and had long objected to both. To save blame elsewhere I was to be the nominal spender – I was the housesteward to follow directions and then because I did as I was

ordered was accused of dishonesty.' At this Sophia's Cornish
temper flares up: 'It's a bad representation of Lord Howe's to
the Navy', and she quoted a captain's reply to him, 'You seem
to have forgot you was not always the great man you are now
become and that you have heretofore wanted money still more
than I do.' She threw this back at Sykes, adding, 'I well remember and ever must what *I am* and you are.'

After Sophia's death there was in 1793 a chancery suit to
settle the question of her dowry, £12,000, which had gone out
of the Trevanion estate into the maw of the Byrons. It had,
with her consent, been made use of and appropriated to the
Admiral. It was directed, therefore, that £2,400 of this should
be regarded as a debt of the Admiral's estate, to be paid to and
applied among the children. Here were the expectations Mad
Jack was constantly anticipating; by the time of this decision
he was already dead. One does not know if his share came to
his son.

We must return to the naval career of Sophia's husband. For
some three years he served as governor of Newfoundland (1769
to 1772), and in successive years was promoted rear-admiral,
then vice-admiral. The revolt of the American colonies was
upon us: Choiseul, Pitt's opposite number in France, had pro-
phesied that by taking Canada and removing the threat to the
colonies, Britain would lose them. They were now – not fully
realized on either side of the Atlantic – of an age and maturity
for full independence.

Byron was fully employed at sea, and given an important
command in 1778 and 1779; he had no better luck than before,
particularly with the weather. A strong French fleet under
D'Estaing had got across the Atlantic to give support to the
Americans. In April 1778 there was an alarm that Byron's ship
might not be able to get out of Plymouth harbour – this was
not easy in all winds – to pursue D'Estaing. There were delays
in setting sail; in May Lord North was amazed to hear that
Byron 'is but just gone from London'. George III sent an overland express to Byron to get on board immediately his reinforcement appeared off Plymouth. Commodore Hood sent the advice
that Byron should urgently steer direct for New York; thence
he could sail north with greater facility than south from Halifax.

In New York the British were awaiting Byron's fleet with much anxiety. Everything there depended on Byron's reinforcing Howe in time, when their united forces would be strong enough to overthrow D'Estaing. In July Lord George Germain wrote, 'We are still pursued with misfortune in Byron's fleet being so little advanced and having one of his ships disabled. There is a great deal due to us from fortune and I hope our luck will turn before we are quite ruined.' It did not. Late as he was in getting away Byron met with foul weather on the way over; the *Cornwall*, a big ship of seventy-four guns, parted company in the gale. When he arrived off New York, he wisely did not stand in with his great ships in such weather, but got into Rhode Island. We learn from George III's correspondence, 'had Byron's squadron not met with a storm D'Estaing's fleet must have been destroyed. If any part of Admiral Byron's fleet arrives in time, Lord Howe may still act with success.' The *Cornwall*, had managed to make New York and joined Howe in pursuit of D'Estaing, who had sailed for the West Indies.

Off Cape Cod, Byron met with an appalling storm. In September Lord Carlisle wrote, 'No news yet of my uncle. We are very apprehensive for him.' In November the Admiral wrote to his nephew describing their experiences: 'Drove fast, carried no sail – lost sight of ships – in danger of drifting on Nantucket Shoals.' Next day he was joined by Commodore Graves (of the family that succeeded the Sawles, Trevanion cousins, at Penrice), but D'Estaing had escaped. 'I look upon myself as the most unlucky fellow that ever was, and shall have no thoughts of home till I have had one fair meeting with D'Estaing.' So far from that, his fleet now needed refitting.

Byron had no luck: it appears that to achieve greatness one needs to command luck, in addition to everything else.

Not until mid-December was he able to pursue D'Estaing to the West Indies. There, while the British were in superior strength, the French were able to take shelter under the guns of Fort Royal in Martinique. Nothing would draw D'Estaing out until Byron drew off to St Kitt's to see the trade fleet safely away to England. In the interval D'Estaing was heavily reinforced with ten ships of the line, and captured and pillaged Grenada. Byron had no news of the reinforcement and, when he returned, gave chase to D'Estaing with his twenty-five ships of the line. Byron was now decidedly inferior and, in the action that ensued, got the worst of it. He was not defeated, but neither had he gained a victory; it was even rumoured that he had not sufficiently supported Admiral Barrington's squadron, though the latter honourably denied this and affirmed that Byron had done everything practicable to give him assistance. The French, now a fourth stronger, withdrew and Byron went back to St Kitt's.

The operations had resulted in frustration, failure and checkmate; in England, expecting victories at sea, they made a sensation. People blamed Byron; parties were formed, some for, some against. All this, in that small society of the English governing class where everybody knew everybody, bore hardly on the Admiral's wife. We can tell something of the feelings aroused from the exchanges between her friend Mrs Thrale and Dr Johnson. 'Poor Mrs Byron', wrote the great doctor, 'I am glad that she runs to you at last for shelter: give her what comfort you can. Her husband, so much as I hear, is well enough spoken of, nor is it supposed that he had power to do more than has been done.' Mrs Thrale 'felt for dear Mrs Byron's misery', but was relieved to hear that 'the Admiral behaved quite unexceptionably, and that – as to honour in the West Indies – all goes well'.

When Barrington returned he spoke up well for his chief, and in October Byron, who was suffering from 'a nervous fever', was given provisional permission to return. The Admiral arrived in October; the admiralty wrote him a letter of appreciation of his services. The tender heart of the Great Bear, Dr Johnson, continued his condolences: 'You shall not hide Mrs Byron from me; for if she be a feeler, I can bear a feeler as well as you, and hope that in tenderness for what she feels from nature, I am able to forget or neglect what she feels by affectation.... Fondle her and comfort her.'

Sophia's anxieties were being added to by her scapegrace sons. Her second son, George Anson, had already been in trouble over a bastardy order at Nottingham; now he was bringing back a wife from Barbados after only three weeks' acquaintance. 'Poor Mrs Byron seems destined for mortification and humiliation; yet such is her native fire and so wonderful are her spirits that she bears up against all calamity.' Dr Johnson to Mrs Thrale: 'Poor Mrs Byron is a feeler. It is well that she has yet power to feel. Fiction durst not have driven upon a few months such a conflux of misery. Comfort her as you can.' Mrs Thrale embroidered on the theme of the humiliation Captain George Byron was bringing 'for this proud family' – though it was little compared with what the eldest son John, the poet's father, would accomplish. Dr Johnson: 'Poor Byron's tenderness is very affecting. Declining life is a very awful scene.' Then, 'Dear Mrs Byron, she has the courage becoming an Admiral's lady.' Later, after further family troubles: 'Mrs Byron has been with me today. I sent her away free from the anxiety she brought with her.'

Sophia was a bluestocking, an intimate of Mrs Montagu, Mrs Boscawen and young Miss Burney, among whom the cult of sensibility and the feelings ran high. Patriotic Fanny Boscawen, widow of her admiral, summed up the feelings of these ladies. 'Admiral Byron has not a speck, after all our infamous newspapers; he and Barrington have never had the least disagreement, and the latter professes to admire, respect, and love his Commander. What pity that all this combining should yet have been ineffectual for want of the means, and that our enemy should be so much superior in force that were inferior in valour.'

The Admiral, though exonerated from blame, was not employed again. The victory which had eluded him was won two years later by Rodney, at the Battle of the Saints, which enabled Britain – after confronting half the world with the revolting colonies – to make a not dishonourable peace. Ironically enough, it was George Byron, then senior cruiser captain in the *Andromache*, who brought Rodney the intelligence of the French fleet coming out from Martinique in April 1782, which enabled him to overthrow French naval power in the West Indies.

Mrs Byron was very much a personality in her own right, as one can appreciate, away from the Admiral – as she often was – among her own female friends. They all agreed that she had too much sensibility, was very much up and down, having an engaging vivacity in society but often plunged in despair by the worries and troubles of her family. Perhaps it was this recognizable affinity of Celtic temperament that drew her and Hester

Thrale, who was Welsh, together. Mrs Byron was the more
engaging of the two, for Mrs Thrale was that rather rare thing,
a female egoist, herself always in the foreground. Sophia was
not in the least an egoist, indeed she had a palpitating heart
for others and was too much affected by their troubles and
follies. Her portrait shows her beauty and refinement. We know
her best from the letters of her women friends: her own have
not been collected.

When Hester was staying at Exmouth for the benefit of the
health of her second husband, Piozzi, she wrote, 'Who would
ever think my dear Mrs Byron a native of these western
counties where, I am told, 'tis never very hot, nor very cold;
that it never thunders, and never snows: I could scarce have
imagined so quiet and steady a climate.' Sophia was all nerves
and heart, always doing good deeds for others. In her last years
she grew somewhat febrile; Hester suggested, in the affected language of the circle, that she would make their favourite doctor
'tie that too active soul tight in its thin wire cage, lest it should
beat the house down with fluttering so'. Sophia did not have
the intellectual pretensions which attached Mrs Thrale to Dr
Johnson, but she had more practical talents. Hester relied on
her to replace an unsatisfactory Irish butler who drank, or find
her servants, or help her to get a woman cook 'who can do interesting dishes – no great boiled leg of mutton for Piozzi. We want
such a woman as you kept, to make little dainty messes for the
Admiral.' That was evidently one way of contenting that demanding husband.

In the early stage of their friendship Mrs Thrale had not fully
appreciated Sophia, measured against the effulgence of Mrs
Montagu, who easily assumed leadership of the circle, with her
airs and graces, her intellectual condescension. One sees her
at a *conversazione* in Grosvenor Square, blazing with diamonds –
she was as rich as she was pretentious – 'solid in judgment [she
was from Yorkshire], critical in talk'. Dr Johnson was good-
humoured; Piozzi sang. Sophia sat back; but it was she who
had the intuition to say, as Piozzi fluted away to Hester, 'I suppose you know that that man is in love with you.' And she was
capable of a crisp judgement: she summed up a rather forward young lady as 'everybody's admiration and nobody's
choice'.

In the games these ladies played, awarding marks for their eminent qualities, Mrs Byron came only shortly behind the unbeatable Mrs Montagu. She was her equal in worth of heart, surpassed her in good humour and useful knowledge, was not far behind in conversational powers, though much below in ornamental knowledge (Mrs Montagu knew Greek). If Mrs Montagu, in food, was *'soupe à la reine'*, Mrs Byron was 'provincial toast'; in animals, if Dr Johnson was obviously an elephant and Miss Burney a doe, then Mrs Byron was a zebra. 'Mrs Byron ... a creature of animated elegance, who loves me tenderly, claims all my kindness from her warmth and brilliancy.'

Then Mrs Byron made a mistake. Married to a sailor, and with a family such as hers, she was not shockable. Mrs Thrale was. Sophia lent her 'an ingenious poem about the geranium, but so obscene I will not pollute my book with it.... Though strongly tempted to copy or get it by heart I have done neither, without any comment.' Later, Hester prided herself on having helped forward Mrs Byron's salvation, along with Mr Thrale's. 'Mrs Byron, too, another flighty friend whom I love better than she deserves is distressed just now – her husband is supposed to have forborne fighting in this last affair, the loss of the Grenada Island, and she is wild with grief.' When Hester eventually met Admiral Byron it was: 'Mrs Byron rejoices that her Admiral and I agree so well; the way to his heart is connoisseurship, it seems, and for a background and contours, who comes up to Mrs Thrale, you know.'

Oddly enough, before the trial for murder when life turned sour for him, the 'Wicked Lord' had been something of a connoisseur too. His old valet said that his 'dear late Lord, whenever there were any very rare and costly articles of virtu or art on sale in London, would order horses to his carriage and set out at a moment's notice to purchase them.' After his exposure he seems to have turned to despair and destruction.

Dr Johnson, old and ill as he was, was in love with Mrs Thrale, and jealous of anyone else possessing her. To begin with, he had no remembrance of meeting her friend, Mrs Byron: 'perhaps her voice is low.' Then to Hester at Brighthelmstone: 'Miss Byron and, I suppose, Mrs Byron is gone. You are by this time left alone to wander over the Steyne and listen to the waves.' Or it is, 'Mrs Byron, and anybody else, puts me out of your head.'

Mrs Thrale's marrying Piozzi, an Italian singer, put her family and almost all her friends against her; Dr Johnson behaved very badly and ended their relations. Sophia naturally did not take to the husband at first. Hester decided to go off to Italy with her treasure – a better bedmate than Dr Johnson would have made. 'My sweet Burney and Mrs Byron will perhaps think they are sorry; but my consciousness that no-one *can* have the cause of concern that Johnson has, and my conviction that he has no *concern at all*, shall cure me of lamenting for friends left behind.'

When she came back from Italy, she found herself cut by most of her former friends – but not by Mrs Byron. By New Year 1788, 'Mrs Byron is converted by Piozzi's assiduity: she really likes him now.' This, of course, riveted the friendship. When the returned couple went off on a tour to Hester's native heath in North Wales – she was born a Salusbury – Mrs Byron made and sent Hester a beautiful purse, which accompanied them everywhere. Still, Mrs Piozzi was looking forward to seeing her 'dearest Mrs Byron settled in Bolton Row [near Berkeley Square] and glad to make comfortable chatting parties before Christmas'. In June 1788, 'My sweetest Mrs Byron has ever experienced the vicissitudes and varieties of life in an uncommon degree.'

This was certainly true. Before the Admiral's death they had both been worried by the extravagance of their elder son, John,

for whom they have paid and paid again, till I think they have been obliged to go into a small house and put off their carriage. He crowned it all by marrying without her knowledge – he said, a fortune of £6 or £700 a year.* But I fear that don't quite answer, and all this mortification will be but of little use to him, who is going on just in the same way. This is the outline of the poor woman's misery, and the detail must have been terrible.

Thus an informant of Mrs Piozzi's, writing to her in Italy. She next reported the Admiral's death in 1786. 'Do you know that Mrs Byron is a widow; he has left her almost all his fortune, amounting to £1600 a year; £2000 to Lady Wilmot, and £500

* Evidently Miss Gordon, the poet's mother.

to that scapegrace Jack, who has behaved in a most shocking manner to his mother, and goes on as usual like a rascal.' This was the poet's father. Lady Wilmot was their daughter, Juliana, who had first married the Wicked Lord's son, heir to the title; on his early death she had married Robert Wilmot. Their son took the side of the poet's wife at their separation, and so was detested by the poet.

We have a portrait of the once-beautiful Sophia in old age from Hester, comparing her with another lady of their circle.

How differently age affects different women! Mrs Byron and Mrs Cholmondeley – of the same rank in life, much about the same degree of beauty too – a style of prettiness that inspired passion more than symmetrical proportion is ever found to do: in short, two women for whom their contemporary men would have willingly run through fire. How they look now! Mrs Byron has lost all face, but retains that elegance of form and manner that still strikes you with the idea of a decayed *belle*, a lady of quality more battered by sickness than subdued by age. Mrs Cholmondeley is not to be compared to her – original want of birth tells. Byron was born a woman of fashion, Cholmondeley became one at fifteen.

Hester always pays tribute to Sophia's elegance and style, her vivacity and mercurial temperament, but she also singles out her quality and high breeding. She was an aristocrat; so were the Byrons – but, though her cousins, what a family to be married into!

In the critical summer for the Admiral of 1779, Sophia was ill. The doctors ordered her to Bath, but she would not go, expecting the Admiral home: she drank the waters at Islington instead, 'much sunk in spirits and emaciated'. Next year she was able to go down to Bath, where all the Burneys visited her at the Belvedere. She was far from well, but her 'charming spirits never fail her, and she rattled and shone away with all the fire and brilliancy of vigorous health'. When the Admiral returned and was exonerated, her spirits perked up. She resumed her good deeds for others. Now she is looking after Hester's furs for her while away, she improves the occasion: 'Whatever is obtained with difficulty grows precious in proportion. How did I get your dear friendship? Dear, *dear* Madam, take care of your health and blunt down sensibility a little; for 'tis a too warm heart makes hot the palms of your white hands, I know.' Now Mrs Byron's kind heart was looking after Mrs Lambert. Hester has to finish her book about Dr Johnson, and 'then we will come home and settle snug for the winter in Hanover Square and tell old stories, and thank God who has given me a calm pleasant evening, after a noonday storm that had very near destroyed me.'

After a West Country tour to see the beauties of Mount Edgcumbe Mrs Piozzi stayed at Bath,

where I have passed the most happy and the most miserable of all possible hours ... and I do love the place passionately and the waters gratefully. This town fills apace; if Captain Byron does not come soon and secure a house, he may be disappointed of one to his mind, though the buildings increase every day. There is no place where one lives so *well* for so little money, no place where so many beauties meet, no place where there are such combinations of gaiety and such opportunities of snugness. Town and country, health and society are to be found at Bath, which is now improved beyond my power of praising it.

Now it was Hester's turn to congratulate Sophia on a son's preferment, 'and I might say preference showed by Lord Chatham'. Since the second Lord Chatham was at the admiralty, this would refer to the naval son, George, not scapegrace Jack. Hester was glad that Mrs Byron was going to have some happiness and pleasure – that of saving poor Edward's life. 'But if he is destined to spend it in India or the Madeira Islands, I greatly fear his forgetting his benefactress, as those are no good places to learn virtue, however they may benefit health. . . . Your son's deserved good fortune and admirable behaviour, public and private, is a cordial you much wanted.'

In 1789 Hester is touring in Scotland and Ireland. 'My dear Mrs Byron deserves the best letter that ever was written for her good taste and judgment in desiring to hear about Edinburgh and Dublin rather, as she says, than about Lisbon or Madrid – because they interest a rational English reader much more nearly.' Then, at the opening stage of the French Revolution: 'Are you thinking of the French government at all? It takes up attention reasonably enough: some will have it that they are going to be free now, and *then* how they will eat us up! – for freedom was all they wanted. Well, the English are always hated somehow by every other nation, go where one will.' Hester asks the old lady to follow their tour on her map. 'Were you ever much a reader of Johnson's *Tour to the Hebrides*? 'Tis one of his first-rate performances.... I look it over now every day with double delight. Oh, how the Scotch do detest him!' It does not appear that Sophia was much of a reader – in this respect *very* inferior to Mrs Montagu.

Mrs Piozzi's complacent English expectations of a liberal turn in France were shortly belied. 'But these Frenchmen! these frantic fools! When one reads of their cruelties and reflects on that theatre of gaiety and good humour – Paris – more a scene of sorrow and bloodshed in this dreadful manner...' The newspaper 'hourly brings new horrors, I hoped exaggerated – yet private letters confirming public accounts – what can be said?' Next, 'When will your poor heart cease fluttering so? I am sincerely sorry for your persecutions.'

Her family brought her little but worry and trouble. 'Mrs Byron is now old and infirm, and apparently in her last stage of existence – Lady Wilmot's death last year [her daughter Juliana died in 1788] broke her up and she could never recover to be what she was before. But not a daughter ever goes near her, and the only son that should be her comfort [i.e. George] is in India.'

Sophia's health was declining fast, though her vivacious spirit kept her going. 'Why will you be always doing exploits of valour in the Park? walking through it at midnight one time, and crossing it in a storm at another!' Mrs Byron's danger was in being so *thin*, but Bath should restore her health. 'It always did, and we shall meet at old Greenway's Cold Bath, I hope. Dear Mr Hay is tender and gentle, and Dr Harington will be *so* attentive, and I will come morning, noon and night to see how your sweet spirits mend. Mr Piozzi says he will have a share in your cure as soon as you can bear the sound of his forte piano.'

Alas for her hopes! At Bath Sophia was in her last illness. We have a touching note to Hester in shaky hand, but with a little flare of the old spirit. 'Don't be overcome with the *little cant* of grief of my daughter, Mrs George Byron, when I am no more – tell her black becomes her and she will forget it all – once more adieu – I think I have not many more hours to love, thank, and beg you never to forget your S.B.'

Nor did she: with her passion for writing everything down – fortunately for us – Hester sketched her old friend's personality and character. 'Nobleness, elegance, animated beauty – promptitude of wit, capacity for thought – could no longer avail her, it seems; no longer keep body and soul together, though against the general foe few ever made more vigorous resistance. Sweet soul! in her way she loved *me* dearly, and her last letter to me – how fine a thing it is!'

In their way Mrs Thrale-Piozzi's letters point quite as sharp a contrast between her and Sophia Byron as she once made between the latter and Mrs Cholmondeley: in everything she wrote one notes the egoism and the archness, the intellectual condescension. Nothing of that in Sophia Trevanion! Mrs Piozzi pleased herself with the thought of putting up a little monument to 'poor dear Mrs Byron in the Abbey church at Bath, where she is buried' – her burial was on 12 November 1790. None of her family took the trouble to put up a memorial to her, though Captain George did to his own wife. And Hester's project came to a literary end in the epitaph she composed, from which we do, however, discern traits of Sophia Trevanion in life:

> From some cold spot near this sad stone that lies
> Byron's re-animated dust shall rise.
> You then that idly range and thoughtless tread
> These melancholy mansions of the dead,
> You that in wit or birth or beauty trust
> Reflect that lovelier Byron is but dust;
> That now no more her high descent we trace
> In each fine feature of th'expressive face;
> While polished ease with sprightliness combined
> In every sentence spoke the vigorous mind....

There is no evidence that Sophia Byron in later life went down to her old home at Caerhays, though in 1786 her scapegrace son Jack absconded to that remote spot to escape creditors – or to extract money from his wealthier cousins. His uncle, William Trevanion, had died there in 1767, not yet forty, leaving no children. He had married Anne Barlow of Pembroke – this Welsh connexion probably came through the dowry of his Berkeley mother. He sat in Parliament for Tregony for the last twenty years of his short life, and this enabled him to command his reward. He attached himself to the opposition interest of Frederick, Prince of Wales, to whom he became groom of the bedchamber in 1749, and from whom he obtained the auditor-ship of the duchy in 1751 at £220 a year, which probably covered his election expenses. His official career ended with this. Evidently he suffered from ill health. His chaste white monument in the little Trevanion aisle in the church on the hill says as much. Though Swift warns us not to take the epi-taphs on monuments in churches for gospel truth, this seems to describe Trevanion as he was:

> A mind th'Almighty wisdom framed so pure
> To teach the world what virtue could endure:
> That faith, on His unerring will relied,
> Shines more approved, as more severely tried.
> Through years of pain, th'appointed task sustained,
> The sufferer died: the saint his heaven regained.

Evidently the last of the male line of Trevanions at Caerhays was an invalid.

We know from Borlase what the old mansion Trevanion in-habited was like: the interior plastered with arms and mottoes (like the historic house of Place at Fowey, where the Trevanion coat still exists): the chestnut parlour with Queen Elizabeth's arms. The chapel, in which Sophia married her sailor cousin in the summer of 1748, adjoined the gate-house – within was painted heraldic glass; it was demolished in 1808. Up at the church a little stone covers a child who died in infancy: 'Isabella Byron, daughter of the Hon. John and Sophia Byron; born the 5th September 1751, and died January 15th, 1752.'

On William's death the provisions of his father's will took full effect. Sophia had her inheritance; the estates came to her elder sister Frances, who, in the year of her brother's death, married John Bettesworth, of an ecclesiastical-legal family from Sussex, chancellor of the diocese of London. With the Bettes-worths an odd strain came into the family, such as to qualify them for comparison with the Byrons, with whom they were to become even more closely – in cases, abnormally – linked. We shall come to their story of mutual fixation, cousinly linkage, incest, with the crossing or, rather, doubling of their common genes.

We do not need to follow the careers of outliers of the male line of the Trevanions, curious though some of their stories are. Our theme is the interweaving of this family with that of the Byrons, and it remains to round up the Admiral and Sophia's children. The younger son, George, had made good in the navy after a misadventure characteristic enough of the time. In the borough records at Nottingham we find a bastardy order served upon the Hon. George Byron, by the oath of Mary Goddard, unmarried mother of his child, a girl. He was to pay the church-wardens of St Mary's parish 20s for expenses at the birth and 25s 6d a week for maintenance. This did not prevent him, twenty years later, from *receiving* a small payment a year in lieu of his burgess share, which service abroad prevented him from enjoying. It was fairly regular for the Byrons of Newstead to be made burgesses of Nottingham – George's father had been made one in 1754.

After the Battle of the Saints, Captain George took on board with him the severely wounded young Lord Robert Manners, a captain of great gallantry and promise, who had been in com-mand of the *Resolution*. She had been in the centre of the battle and, in breaking through the enemy line, attracted the fire of nine or ten ships. Lord Robert had his leg shot off besides other wounds. He died on board Byron's frigate, the *Andromache*; Byron reported that Lord Robert was buried at sea with all the honours of war, a hundred leagues from Bermuda. 'If the Duke of Rutland had wanted the body brought home, I would have endeavoured it, but it would have been beaten to pieces in cask.' On Admiral Byron's death, son George wrote to the duke in favour of his mother. Promoted to a command in the East Indies, Captain George died young there, in 1793, at only thirty-five; in the next year his three children, the eldest of whom was to succeed the poet as seventh lord, were granted pensions of £50 a year, which the East India Company was to double to £100.

The daughter who was named after her mother, Sophia, was like her respectable, but remained single. In 1810 she was awarded a pension of £150 a year, since it was represented that she was in a bad state of health, in very low circumstances, and burdened with the charge of several orphan nephews and nieces.

This was in consequence of the frantic extravagance of the two remaining members of the Admiral and Sophia's family, the eldest son Jack, and the youngest daughter Fanny. They were closest to each other, alike in temperament, more than affectionate, indeed Jack was in love with his sister. The Byron–Trevanion inheritance was very evident in them, and this was to be doubled not only in the marriages but the sexual mutuality of their respective children. It was all a matter of genes; but their story is one of the utmost modernity: Jack and Fanny were a pair of aristocratic hippies.

To begin with, 'Mad Jack' Byron was madly handsome, irresistible to any woman, and a superb performer in bed. The marchioness of Carmarthen, whose husband would be the next duke of Leeds and had provided her with three children, fell for Jack and – since, as Baroness Conyers in her own right, she was worth £4,000 a year – he eloped with her. He was well capable of spending that and more besides. Divorced in May 1779, she married him. Oddly enough, in November, Horace Walpole's friend, William Mason – at the request of Lady Holdernesse, her mother – lent her his parsonage house to reside in while the sexy captain was recruiting in Yorkshire. In their brief and hectic married life he gave her two or three children, and then in bearing Augusta, the poet's half-sister, the baroness died, in 1784. Her large income died with her; the gallant captain, wildly extravagant, was unprovided for.

So the following year, at Bath, he made up to a very plain and homely Scots heiress, worth some £23,000, a Gordon lady, and swept her off her feet into church – against the opposition of all her friends and well-wishers – on the unlucky 13 May 1785. They were right, of course, about Mad Jack Byron, who was interested only in her money and could hardly bear her person; it produced extreme unhappiness for the poor woman, but it did produce a child of genius – born, however, 'club-footed', as his father described him. This disability conditioned his genius; the poet grew up with every kind of complex, schizophrenic about his mother, whom at times he could hardly bear (as his father could not), beautiful as his father (whom he tended to idealize: he can hardly have seen him after the age of two), but lame; wild and wilful, with the devil of the Byrons in him, yet with the cultivated distinction and sensibility of his Trevanion grandmother.

The poet's mother was a decent Scots body, virtuous, trying to do her best, but tactless and blundering and fat, constantly dunned for money by her husband – she gave him all that was disposable, till she had very little to keep herself and child. We have seen that the handsome captain skedaddled down to Caerhays in 1786 to escape his creditors; he did not succeed, for in that year he was imprisoned in the king's bench prison for debt. He dunned everybody; he had borrowed from brother George, and never paid back; his sister Fanny, who could not resist him, gave him most of her pin-money. This cannot have contributed to the happiness of her own married life: she was miserable with her husband, Charles Leigh (who became a general). Their son was Colonel George Leigh, who later married his cousin Augusta – against everybody's forebodings, and everybody was right. On her mother's death Augusta had been taken charge of by Lady Holdernesse, and grew up with her grand relations, her half-brother the duke of Leeds and the rest. The poet Byron fell in love with his half-sister (as his father had done with *his* full sister), who was married to her first cousin, Colonel Leigh – they were all three grand-children of Admiral Byron and Sophia Trevanion. The linkages, the temperamental inheritance, doubled – and one can observe the similarities of temperament; the genes would play the devil with them.

Fanny was the only member of the family who kept in touch with the Wicked Lord: she would go down to visit the morose old termagant at Newstead. She had had an untoward experience when young, which perhaps helped to precipitate into her marriage with a man she disliked. In 1770 she was to have been married to a young Captain Halliday, with good prospects. 'The clothes were bought, but he saw Lady Jane [Tollemache] twice at the Richmond Assembly, was captivated, and wrote a letter to Miss Byron to inform her he had changed his mind, and set out for Scotland.' Lady Jane's brother called in Lord Shelburne to help 'towards reconciling and bringing to the most amicable issue everything between Commodore Byron's family and myself'. The young man wrote agreeably:

I confess I have not the least sense of the *injury* so grievously complained of, but rather esteem it in a different light; for what could
have been more *injurious* than to have entered into the most solemn
of all contracts with *one* Lady whilst the *other* has sole possession of
my heart? Whilst I continued to love Miss Byron my behaviour was
irreproachable. Why then has it been less so because, when that love
ceased (which unaccountable effect I can impute to Nothing but the
Caprice of the human heart), I had the *Resolution* to *Declare* it? Miss
Byron has more than once agreed with me (nay, I think all the world
will coincide) that when the Heart shall be alienated from one object
to *Another* it would be both *ungenerous* and *inhuman* not to declare it.

Miss Byron herself was to act in accordance with the principle
in future; meanwhile there was an irate father to propitiate.
'As I never meant an *Injury* to Mr. Byron's Family . . . if I *have*
erred, 'twill be my chief glory to confess my error. I am willing
therefore to submit this Affair to any *Man of Honour* and of *more
Experience* than myself.' Engaging – or, rather, disengaging –
young man! Lord Shelburne was called in, and peace was
made.

Fanny was not, however, happy with the husband she ultimately captured, and set up on her own in their house at Valen-
ciennes. In 1790 Jack, who confessed himself 'mad' that she was
his sister but had no difficulty in confessing his love for her,
joined her in France. He had not seen his wife for some time,
having stripped her of all she could dispose of, though it seems
that she retained a *tendresse* for her demon husband – Jack was
irresistible. His preference for his sister did not preclude him
from scattering his favours among other women, or indeed from
sharing his experiences with her in the telling. 'As for la *Henry*,
who told me that I did so well that she always *spent* twice every
time. I know this will make you laugh, but she is the best piece
I ever—.

We see pretty clearly the terms he was upon with his sister:
'there is no person I love so well as you', 'all I ask is that you
love me as I do you', etc. That there was an element of family
fixation in it we detect from such phrases as, 'the Byrons are
irresistible, as you know'; or in giving an extravagant tip to the
woman opening Fanny's box at the theatre, saying, 'the Byrons
were always so'; or offering to fight a man, '*Vive les Birons*:
we were always so from the time of William the Conqueror.'

To entertain such family pride in their circumstances would seem a work of supererogation, amid the increasing burden of debts, the dunning of money-lenders, creditors, bailiffs, even police. Yet they belonged to the tribe of people who could not mitigate their extravagance: Fanny kept her box at the theatre; they had servants, if unpaid and stealing from them; Fanny had her hairdresser, and when Jack had only a ragged coat to his back a servant stole seventeen pairs of silk stockings from him. Everything with the Byrons was exaggerated, of course, but there can be no doubt of his attachment to Fanny or of his sufferings of mind. He spent his last months feverishly trying to collect the legacy poor old Sophia had left him, though it was already pledged. Then he was spitting blood – he had evidently developed consumption – and he died in 1791, after so mad and riotous a course, at only thirty-four. Such was the poet's father.

The poet's mother tried to be friendly, over his dead body and his memory, with Fanny; but none of the Byrons could ever stand her, poor soul, virtuous, well-meaning, tactless, as she was. When the Wicked Lord's grandson was killed at Calvi in 1794 she realized that now her son was the heir presumptive to the title and estates. She wrote to the old man for help, but received no response: what little he had, over and above the entailed estate, with its mortgages and debts, was for faithful Betty and her illegitimate son. The old man died in 1798; the poet became the sixth lord as a schoolboy.

But what an inheritance!

IX

Newstead and the Poet

I AM NOT WRITING A BIOGRAPHY of the poet Byron – too many of those exist already, and there is an ocean of literature about this fascinating outsize figure. My theme is the family, the dual inheritance, and I must keep to that. However, in every respect this is more important in Byron than even in most men of genius, for he was the most autobiographical and egoistic of writers; his ego, the extraordinary mixture of genes in his inheritance, gave him his force, his eruptive violence and contradictions, the clashing inconsistencies of his character and attitudes, the demons of temperament that drove him on his way, sometimes like a ship without steering gear, though his rational intelligence brought him back on to course again. His ego gave him his inspiration.

No one has understood Byron better than his grandson, Lord Lovelace – his key book, *Astarte*, has been regarded too unperceptively as drawing an unfavourable portrait.* His grandson understood, from the inside, that – for all Byron's profession of radical sympathies, his speech on behalf of the Luddites, etc. – he had no illusions about the people, and was no real radical. For all his romantic rhodomontade he was a realist, and had no more liking for idealogues than Napoleon had – a man for whom Byron, revealingly, had unquestioning admiration. (There was, against earlier romantic leanings, a strong vein of cynicism in both.) Byron was at the opposite pole to his friend Shelley.

* Actually the revised edition, with its re-arrangement and additional material provided by Lady Lovelace, presents a better balance than the original.

His family inheritance, the fact that he was a lord, meant much to Byron – as again it was a considerable element in his *réclame* both at home and abroad. Newstead Abbey meant a great deal to him: it entered into the blood-stream of his imagination and occurs again and again in his poems. One of the many ironies of his life is that it should have been he, of all his line, who sold it, gave up its possession, broke all the ties and brought the story of his family there to an end. All the same, it haunted his imagination; one sees the creative process at work, shaping up the many poems in which the place recurs, boyish and immature in the early verse, improved on in *Childe Harold*, until the evocation of Newstead in *Don Juan* emerges at its best, completely ejaculated and mature.

His genius was very nostalgic – one more paradox that he should have parted with the place that entered into the fibres of his being. Both his mother and his sister Augusta were strongly against his parting with Newstead; for years he himself swore that he never would. Yet he did: he broke not only the link but the whole family chain. Psychologically fascinating – for perhaps there was an inner propulsion to do so? As in so many other respects, he was torn in two.

As an historian, one cannot but grieve at the ending of that long and riveting historical association, yet it is impossible to imagine him, as he earlier fancied, settling there with a wife, rearing a family, seeing to his estates, shooting with the neighbours over the coverts, even keeping them in order, mending his fences: the imagination boggles at the thought! No: the parting with Newstead set him free for the extraordinary, the fantastic European *épopée* by which he is remembered.

Byron had not been brought up at Newstead, and that always makes a difference: he came into it at the age of ten, and never lived there much. Considering that, it is extraordinary how much the place and its associations occupied his mind, and how strongly his memory lours over it today. It had not been expected that the grandson of the Admiral and Sophia Trevanion would inherit, until his cousin was killed at Calvi in 1794. Four years later his great-uncle, the fifth lord, died; when the schoolboy – always sensitive, always mercurial – was told that he was now a lord, he burst into a flood of tears.

That same summer he paid his first visit, with his mother, to Newstead, which immediately gained a hold upon his imagination in spite of – or, more probably, because of – its appalling state of dereliction: it added to its historicity. The monks' hall and refectory were stuffed with hay for the cattle, which were housed in entrance hall and parlour; buildings in the rear-court were roofless, the furniture mostly seized for debt, etc. However, there were the coats of arms, the motto of his ancestors: '*Crede Byron*' ('Believe Byron' – also not without its irony). Here were the old lord's pistols to practise with, and the sword with which he had killed Mr Chaworth. When Mr Chaworth's ultimate heiress was brought over to Newstead, and someone made a joke about their marrying, the schoolboy said: 'What, the Capulets and Montagues intermarry?'

However, as an adolescent he fell in love with Mary, riding over from Newstead to Annesley and sometimes staying there. This story is no part of our theme, except in so far as it throws light upon the youth's temperament. A poet is in love with the idea of being in love – it feeds the imagination. He wrote poems to Mary, as well as the nostalgic 'Hills of Annesley'. She was a few years older, and had the insensibility to say to her maid, 'Do you think that I could ever care for that lame boy?' It is the kind of thing that the wounded and hypersensitive have to take from ordinary fools – but they do not have to put up with it. Nor did the boy of genius. He left the house, not to return.

Mary Chaworth went on to marry the unimpaired fox-hunting ass she was in love with, and was very unhappy with him. He was unfaithful to her; she left him and for a time went off her head. When she recovered, and the lame boy was now famous, she tried to renew relations. Byron brushed her off callously: she had killed that particular nerve in him. (It is like Swift with poor Miss Waring – a great mistake to offend a proud and sensitive man of genius.) But the interesting and subtle thing is that the inner spirit retained the early dream – for Byron has a tender portrait of her, for himself, in a later poem, 'The Dream'. Nor is it less interesting for the historian to speculate on what might have come from the union of those two fated lives, Byron and Chaworth, those neighbouring Nottinghamshire estates, Newstead and Annesley.

From this time also date Byron's youthful poems about Newstead, which at least show how much the place spoke to him:

> Through thy battlements, Newstead, the hollow winds whistle;
>   Thou, the hall of my fathers, art gone to decay:
> In thy once smiling garden, the hemlock and thistle
>   Have choked up the rose which late bloomed in the way...
>
> On Marston with Rupert, 'gainst traitors contending,
>   Four brothers enriched with their blood the bleak field;
> For the rights of a monarch their country defending,
>   Till death their attachment to royalty sealed...
>
> That fame and that memory still will he cherish;
>   He vows that he ne'er will disgrace your renown;
> Like you will he live, or like you will he perish:
>   When decayed, may he mingle his dust with your own!

We must not discount the dedications of adolescence: the tradi-
tions of his fighting stock counted for something in the death
at Missolonghi.

A longer 'Elegy on Newstead Abbey' canters through its history, with not always exact historical knowledge but intense
feeling for it, the tradition and folklore.

> A monarch bade thee from that wild arise,
>   Where Sherwood's outlaws once were wont to prowl...

(He was to become something of an outlaw himself, or at least
considered himself as such in exile.)

> Where now the bats their wavering wings extend
>   Soon as the gloaming spreads her waning shade,
> The choir did oft their mingling vespers blend,
>   Or matin orisons to Mary paid.

In spite of the devastation of the Reformation the image of the
Virgin still presides at the top of the splendid, ruined west front.

> One holy [!] Henry reared the Gothic walls,
>   And bade the pious inmates rest in peace;
> Another Henry the kind gift recalls,
>   And bids devotion's hallowed echoes cease.

Then follows an account of a siege during the Civil War,
which never happened, as we know – the place was simply

looted – all with a good deal of Byronic exaggeration. However, the youth does get right the Civil War episode of Falkland's falling in battle, practically at his ancestor's side. Jolly days succeed Cromwell's usurpation:

> Vassals, within thy hospitable pale,
>   Loudly carousing, bless their lord's return . . .

We may note, in a number of Byron's poems, the recurrence of the word 'vassals': for all his presumed (and assumed) radicalism, he was distinctly feudal. And then the chase – the hereditary occupation of the forest:

> Beneath their coursers' hoofs the valleys shake:
>   What fears, what anxious hopes, attend the chase!
> The dying stag seeks refuge in the Lake;
>   Exulting shouts announce the finished race.

A note in an early edition informs us that it was during his predecessor's reign that the fine lectern was fished up from the lake: it had been thrown there by the monks at the Dissolution, and is now in Southwell Minster.

> Newstead! what saddening change of scene is thine!
>   Thy yawning arch betokens slow decay!
> The last and youngest of a noble line
>   Now holds thy mouldering turrets in his sway.

While the poet was still in his minority Newstead was mostly let, at one time, somewhat improbably, to a couple of maiden ladies. They were followed by a young hunting peer, Lord Grey of Ruthyn. Hobhouse noted marginally that 'an intimacy soon sprung up between him [the youth] and his noble tenant . . . and a circumstance occurred during intimacy which certainly had much effect on his future morals'. Hobhouse was what would today be called 'square', and had not much sympathy with Byron. Byron was, in fact, bisexual; but everything shows that he was active, not passive, and he resented the character, or possibly the direction, of Lord Grey's attentions. To this was added the further humiliation that homely Mrs Byron, 'the puir good woman', fell for the young peer's attractions.

Between tenancies she bustled about doing her best to make parts of the mansion habitable. She struggled hard to bring some order into the place after years of neglect, and with a dilatory agent. A frightful tangle of debt hung round it, which would take a whole study to disentangle; yet four gardeners pottered around, with plenty of weeds to witness to their activity. Servants and tenants alike took advantage of absentee-ism, as usual, to exploit what they could. Mrs Byron struggled, in her Scottish way, thanklessly, only to win unpopularity from everybody. She even approached Fanny to lend her money, driven to distraction as she was by all the claims upon her. The only contribution her son made – extravagant like all the Byrons – was to pay out an annuity to his cousin George's widow, mother of the heir presumptive, who later succeeded him in the title. He went on paying 'Lady' Betty's pension, and insisted on retaining Joe Murray, the ancient butler. Shortly, he recruited a farmer from the estate, Fletcher, as his valet, who remained with him for the rest of his life. I think we may see in these, and similar attachments later, not only the loyal side of his nature, the desire to spin filaments to the past, but his undoubted feudal sense. Later, towards the servant maids in the house and roundabout the estate he certainly exercised his *droits de seigneur*.

On his first visit to Newstead Byron had planted an oak, and nourished the fancy that, as the tree prospered or not, so would it be with him. He was superstitious; it later astonished the 'Princess of Parallelograms', Lady Byron, who fancied herself more rational than she really was, that he would never start anything on a Friday, thought it dangerous to wear black, etc. He regarded her winding a black ribbon round her wedding ring as a bad omen. And it was. Coming back to Newstead, he found his oak neglected and in a sad way:

> I left thee, my Oak, and since that fatal hour
>   A stranger has dwelt in the hall of my sire;
> Till manhood shall crown me, not mine is the power
>   But his, whose neglect may have bade thee expire.

This was another mark against Lord Grey.

Next year, while down at Newstead, his favourite dog, Boats-wain, died – named perhaps to recall the dog that had accom-panied his grandfather on the *Wager*. Byron put up a fine monu-ment to his dog on the consecrated ground of the church and willed originally that he should be buried beside him: today

a popular target for the populace. The inscription tells us what
he thought of them: 'Near this spot are deposited the remains
of one who possessed Beauty without Vanity, Strength without
Insolence, Courage without Ferocity, and all the Virtues of
Man without his Vices. This Praise, which would be unmean-
ing Flattery if inscribed over human ashes, is but a just tribute
to the memory of *Boatswain*, a dog.' The dog died mad. Here
was the cynical turn that was thus early true to Byron – and
the self-pity of a Celt in the lines:

> To mark a friend's remains these stones arise:
> I never knew but one – and here he lies.

Rhetorical exaggeration too: the prosaic Anglo-Saxon
Hobhouse proposed to emend the last two words to 'I lies'.

A primitive atavism made Byron more than usually dependent on the company of animals. He kept at Newstead in these
years a wolf and a bear, besides the more usual birds; in Italy
in later years he trailed about with him a whole menagerie,
dogs, a monkey, a parrot, peacocks, a tame crow, all fighting
and screaming. To this he added the skulls he dug up from
the cloister and kept as ornaments (perhaps inspiration) in his
rooms. One of them he had expensively mounted in silver as
a drinking cup, upon which he inscribed:

> Start not nor deem my spirit fled
> In me behold the only skull
> From which, unlike a living head,
> Whatever flows is never dull.

The poet wished to flog his imagination with these evoca-
tions, and he succeeded in creating half the ghosts and legends
that haunted the place. (What a Celt he was!) When the skull-
cup was first handed round, the door opened and a headless
monk appeared to warn Byron of his early death (of which he
already had a presentiment). Naturally stories proliferated.
The haunted room next to his bedroom was occupied by his
page, young Rushton. Byron was said to have seen the family
ghost, the Black Friar, whose appearance heralded ill to the
Byron in possession, a month before the disaster of his marriage.

> His form you may trace, but not his face,
> 'Tis shadowed by his cowl;

> But his eyes may be seen from the folds between
> And they seem of a parted soul.

Byron came of age in 1809, but before he could take his seat in the House of Lords, where he hoped to cut a figure, he needed to establish the legitimacy of his grandparents' marriage, by speeding a couple of clerks down to Caerhays to take affidavits thereto. He celebrated with a riotous party of his Cambridge friends, before going on the (more than) Grand Tour upon which his heart was set. As he recalled it later: 'We went down to Newstead together, where I had got a famous cellar, and *Monks'* dresses from a masquerade warehouse. We used to sit up late in our friars' dresses, drinking burgundy, claret, champagne, and what not, out of the skull-cup ... and buffooning all round the house in our conventual garments.'

Matthews, shortly to be drowned in the Cam, describes some of the fun and frolics. Running the gauntlet of wolf and bear, 'our average hour of rising was one. It was frequently past two before the breakfast party broke up. Then for the amusements ...there was reading, fencing, single-stick, or shuttle-cock; walking, riding, cricket, sailing on the lake. Between seven and eight we dined, and our evening lasted till one, two, or three in the morning. The evening diversions may be easily conceived.' These were referred to differently in *Childe Harold*, where Newstead is again described:

> Monastic dome! condemned to uses vile!
> Where Superstition once had made her den
> Now Paphian girls were known to sing and smile...

(The Paphian girls were the servant maids, by no means reluctant.)

> The Childe departed from his fathers' hall:
> It was a vast and venerable pile –
> So old, it seems only not to fall,
> Yet strength was pillared in each massy aisle...

> Yet oft times in his maddest mirthful mood
> Strange pangs would flash along Childe Harold's brow,
> As if the memory of some deadly feud
> Or disappointed passion lurked below:

But this none knew, nor haply cared to know;
For his was not that open, artless soul
That feels relief by bidding sorrow flow,
Nor sought he friend to counsel or condole...

Only with his half-sister Augusta could he unfold himself completely and be free: *dimidium animae meae.*

And none did love him – though to hall and bower
He gathered revellers from far and near,
He knew them flatterers of the festal hour,
The heartless parasites of present cheer.

This was hard on his friends, and really untrue to himself. For one of the facets of his character was a genius for friendship. Everyone testified that he had a singular faculty of compelling people to him – the sheer attraction of doubled personality, the spell of genius. But in the midst of it all he was always lonely: there was no one really up to him, or equal to him, with whom he could share fully and freely. This feeling he gives expression to again and again, especially in his self-portrait as the Count Lara. He had too the fatal conviction that no one could ever love him for himself, as he was – only Augusta (who shared his genes).

Amid all the riot of his life Byron was first and foremost a reading and writing man. Wherever he was, at home or abroad, on land or at sea, he was always scribbling poems or his vivid, veracious *désabusé* letters and journals. And he was very well read: his poems give evidence of that; besides this, he was an admirable, independent-minded, candid critic, who needed no instruction from anybody. At this moment, at Newstead, he was reading the criticisms of *English Bards and Scotch Reviewers.* Though he had been attacked – and, like most men of genius, was unnecessarily sensitive about abuse from the third-rate – he was by and large extraordinarily fortunate in the acclaim his work received. Even Jeffery (whom Byron likened to the infamous Judge Jeffreys) became rather too generous in his praise.

Byron had fitted up the rooms at Newstead for habitation in extravagant style: fine French furniture, new wallpapers, resplendent bedsteads with crimson draperies and gilded cornices; black and gold lacquered chairs, rich carpets and cushions; carved mahogany for the dining-room; chintzes and masses of plate, china and napery. It all came to £1,500, and later the Nottingham upholsterer had to put in the bailiffs for the money. One can visualize the richness of the lordly interior, coronets and armorial bearings well in evidence. He had already collected a fine large library there. His bedroom was kept, by the purchaser of the house, reverentially as it was, and we may see it thus today. Lady Byron, who could never get over her obsession for the husband who treated her so badly, paid a secret visit to the place after he had left England for good. She noted that his apartments then were just as he had left them: 'He might have walked in.'

Certainly his ghost inhabits there now.

The poet had his last parting with his mother at Newstead on St George's day – the day we keep as Shakespeare's birth-day – before setting out for the isles of Greece.

Hanson, the agent who had the thankless task of looking after Byron's financial affairs, had been all along in favour of selling Newstead, as the only way of clearing the constantly accumu-lating load of debt. But, from Athens in 1810, Byron wrote to him, 'It is in the power of God, the Devil, and Man, to make me poor and miserable, but neither the *second* nor *third* shall make me sell Newstead, and by the aid of the *first* I will perse-vere in this resolution. My "father's house shall *not* be made a den of thieves". Newstead shall *not* be sold.' His correspon-dence is full of the complications of his financial affairs; New-stead is fielded to and fro, but he insists that he will never sell it. 'If we must, sell Rochdale.'

When he came back to England, he went down gloomily to Newstead for the funeral of his mother. 'Some curse hangs over me and mine. My mother lies a corpse in this house; one of my best friends is drowned in a ditch.' That was the brilliant (and homosexual) Matthews, in the Cam. To Hobhouse: 'In the room where I now write (flanked by the *skulls* you have seen so often) did you and Matthews and myself pass some joyous unprofitable evenings. . . . I have tried reading and box-ing, and swimming, and writing, and rising early and sitting late, and water, and wine, with a number of ineffectual remedies, and here I am, wretched.' He filled up his time with a spate of letter-writing. To another Cambridge friend: 'It is strange that I look on the skulls which stand beside me (I have always had four in my study) without emotion, but I cannot strip the features of those I have known of their fleshly covering, even in idea, without a hideous sensation.'

He drew up his will, to be buried beside Boatswain, leaving £7,000 to Nicolo, one of the two Greeks he had brought back with him: so excessive a sum betokens an emotional attachment. He invited his sister Augusta down: 'I should be glad to see you here, as I think you have never seen the place. Murray is still like a rock, and will probably outlive some six Lords Byron, though in his 75th autumn.' Augusta could not come – too much occupied with the chores of her growing family, and looking after her husband, Colonel Leigh, 'that very helpless gentleman, your Cousin'. Next, 'I would ask George here [this was his cousin, who succeeded him in the title] but I don't know how to amuse him: all my horses were sold when I left England, and I have not had time to replace them. Besides he would be meddling with the wenches.... Dogs, a Keeper and plenty of game with a very large Manor I have – a lake, a boat, house-room and neat wines.'

To Hobhouse, 'I am solitary and sullen.... My sister writes me melancholy letters, things are not going on well there, but mismanagement is the hereditary epidemic of our Brood.' Colonel Leigh had quarrelled with his bread and butter: equerry to the Prince Regent, he had cheated him of part of the sale-money for a horse in his keeping. Byron was expecting to go down to Rochdale,

where something will be decided as to selling or working the collieries. I am Lord of the Manor (a most extensive one) and they want to enclose, which cannot be done without me; but I go there in the worst humour possible and am afraid I shall do or say something not very conciliatory. In short all my affairs are going on as badly as possible, and I have no hopes or plans to better them – as I long ago pledged myself never to sell Newstead, which I mean to hold in defiance of the Devil and Man.

In September, 'My life is as still as the Lake before the Abbey, till the north wind disturbs the one, and Fletcher and my learned Thebans break my pottery, or my tenants or

Mr Hanson ruffle the other.' Now he had got Lucy back from Warwickshire – this was the servant-maid he had made pregnant before going abroad. None of the Byrons could do without sex, and this return had 'plucked up' his spirits. 'Some very bad faces have been warned off the premises; the partridges are plentiful, hares fairish, pheasants not quite so good, and Girls on the Manor —.' His visit to Rochdale was abortive: 'I never went within ken of a coalpit, and am returned with six new acquaintances but little topographical knowledge. However, the concern is more valuable than I expected but plaguy troublesome; it has been surveyed, etc., etc., and will no doubt benefit my heirs.'

Before leaving Newstead Byron received another blow that touched him deeply: the death of the choirboy Edleston, with whom he had been in love at Cambridge: 'one whom I once loved more than I ever loved a living thing, and one who, I believe, loved me to the last.' Byron always said that this particular love had been 'pure'; certainly the boy loved him – and Byron said later that all his life he had been trying to find someone who could love him. I suspect that his wounded egoism was insatiable, for there were plenty of people who loved him. 'Now, though I never should have seen him again (and it is very proper that I should not), I have been more affected than I should care to own elsewhere.' He sat down and added a couple of stanzas to *Childe Harold*, which he was continuing. As always, like the dedicated writer he was, Byron found his real solace in expressing his feelings in writing – which offered release and consolation and proved the only real solvent of inner tensions.

Nostalgically, as always, he went back to Cambridge, where the organ in King's College Chapel brought back memories of that voice. Several times they rose up to shape poems: all the poems supposedly addressed to 'Thyrza' are really about Edleston.

To cheer himself up at Christmas he got some of his Cambridge friends to go down to Newstead with him, as one of them remembered. 'It was winter – dark, dreary weather – the snow upon the ground; and a straggling, gloomy, depressive, partially inhabited place the Abbey was.' In those days of Gothick romances, they all saw it as a Castle of Otranto. Even old Joe Murray began to be 'frightened by dreams and ghosts. It is singular,' thought Byron, 'that he never superstitised for seventy-six years before.' However, the Cambridge friend continued, 'Those rooms which had been fitted up for residence were so comfortably appointed that one soon lost the melancholy feeling of being domiciled in the wing of an extensive ruin.'

Byron had now found a pretty Welsh servant-girl to engage his attention and occupy his bed. This, of course, made Lucy and Bess jealous, and – while his mind was occupied with the proofs of *Childe Harold* – trouble among the women followed him to London. Young Rushton, whom Byron was preparing to succeed Joe Murray, reported Susan's infidelities. Byron replied, 'I am sure *you* would not deceive me, though *she* would. Whatever it is, *you* shall be forgiven.' Susan had written her lord gushing love-letters, while carrying on with other servants. Because Byron was fond of her, this opened the old wound: 'I do not blame her but my own vanity in fancying that such a thing as I am could ever be beloved.'

The real passion of Byron's life was for Augusta. It was during the next year that his love was returned, was consummated and they found in each other blissful, contingent, ominous happiness. They were both orphans of the storm, both *outsiders*, living on the fringes of the family, half-alienated and seeking in each other the security they had never possessed. Augusta was the more stable character, and not wholly the fool she has been made out to be. From early on she had been interested in the 'baby Byron', four years younger, whom she had hardly ever seen. She was born in Paris in 1784, when Mad Jack had been in funds with his first wife and keeping up with the ducal French Birons. The poet said, 'Augusta and I have always loved the memory of our father as much as we loved each other.' No doubt handsome Mad Jack was lovable, as all Byrons were – even Colonel Leigh was lovable; Mrs Byron and Miss Milbanke, who became the poet's wife, not. But one detects in Byron's phrase the desire to draw things together, to return to an ark that had never been.

Brother and sister were all the more happy and at ease when they, somewhat belatedly, found each other. They were extraordinarily alike, not only in appearance but, more important, in temperament and tastes; and one must never forget Byron's own feminine sensibility. When young, Augusta was beautiful, though less strikingly so than he was; she had his fine eyes and profile, dark brown hair, with (in her case) a large, voluptuous, engulfing mouth. They shared the extreme family shyness. Both were 'inflammable' – he once told her as much. Both were highly emotional and intuitive, mercurial in their ups and downs. They possessed the same sense of humour, always a great bond, a love of mimicry and talking nonsense. Lady Byron, who had none, could not bear it – something that excluded her from the Byron freemasonry. She said it prevented him from reflecting seriously on things! It did not. Brother and half-sister were both Byron and Trevanion in equal degree: they had the same blood and sympathies, instinctive and complete; their impulses and feelings corresponded. No one understood this complex, tormented, marvellous man as she did. As he once wrote to her, if they could only have lived together as bachelor brother and sister, they could have lived happily. The impulse, the genes, were too strong for them.

The suggestion to disregard convention came from Byron, but Augusta was not unwilling; and there is no evidence that Colonel Leigh minded. After all, they were all three within the charmed circle of the Byron–Trevanion blood-relationship – as Mrs Byron and Lady Byron were not. Augusta was as much in love. When they exchanged a lock of each other's hair, she wrote (in French): 'To share all your feelings, see only through your eyes, act only by your advice, live only for you: those are my wishes, my intention, and the only destiny that can make me happy.' What surrender could be more complete? Byron wrote on the packet holding her lock: 'La chevelure of the *one* whom I most loved.' Their engrossment in each other was rather like the historic case of Julien and Marguerite de Ravalet, which had such tragic consequences two centuries before.*

In the summer of 1813 Byron and Augusta saw each other both in London and at her home at Newmarket. In January 1814, when they were happily snowed up at Newstead, Byron wrote: 'We never yawn or disagree, and laugh much more than is suitable to so solid a mansion; and the family shyness makes

* v. Tancrède Martel, *Julien et Marguerite de Ravalet, 1582–1603.*

us much more amusing companions to each other than we could be to anyone else.' To Hanson: 'Our coals are excellent, our fire-places large, my cellar full and my head empty; and I have not yet recovered my joy at leaving London.' They stayed for three weeks, blissfully happy. 'Mrs Leigh is with me, and being in the family way renders it doubly necessary to remain till the roads are quite safe.' Augusta was nearly seven months gone with the child that was to be born on 15 April 1814, called by the Byronic name Medora; and it seems likely that she was his child. When his confidante, Lady Melbourne – who herself was no better than she should be – wrote warning him, he wrote back: 'Oh! but it is "worth while", and it is not an *Ape*; and if it is, that must be my fault; however, I will positively reform. You must however allow that it is utterly impossible I can ever be half so well liked elsewhere, and I have been all my life trying to make someone love me, and never got the sort that I pre-ferred before.'

Byron was under the compulsion of genius to express *every-thing*, to speak out and not contain himself; and so far from hav-ing any respect for conventional people's opinions, he wanted to express contempt for them. (They would take their revenge later.) Moreover, he had travelled all over the Mediterranean world, where provincial English sexual prejudices were not regarded or, if so, as a subject of amusement. In this year, 1813, he was writing *The Bride of Abydos*, in which the lovers were originally brother and sister; they were demoted to cousins – authentically enough to Byron–Trevanion relationships. The poem was dedicated to Lord Holland, and at Holland House – that reverberating talking-shop – Byron spoke out openly in favour of incest. (Not until the enlightened Liberalism of Mr Asquith's government of 1906 did it become a crime.) But ordi-nary people took pleasure in being shocked, and censoriousness is always a pleasing indulgence.

More important is the effect on Byron. Augusta was free and easy-going – it was part of her charm – and had no objection to their relationship. Byron was not only a tormented spirit; he sought inspiration in self-torment. He certainly found it: it accounts for the dark passion and colouring of all his work in these hectic years, in *The Bride of Abydos*, *The Corsair* and in *Lara*. He composed *Lara* in 1814, mostly at night in London on his return from innumerable balls and masquerades with which Regency society celebrated the defeat of Napoleon and the ending of the long strain of the war. Society went mad for pleasure and – though conventional appearances received the tribute of the usual humbug – there was little sexual restraint from the regent and the royal dukes downward. Byron sometimes appeared at masquerades as a monk; the *décor* of his poem is Newstead, and Lara is himself. The poem is full of feudality and 'vassals'.

> A hundred scutcheons deck with gloomy grace
> The Laras' last and longest dwelling-place;
> But one is absent from the mouldering file
> That now were welcome in that Gothic pile.

Observe that Lara is rhythmically the same as Byron, and Byron could be substituted for it throughout.

> Through night's long hours would sound his hurried tread
> O'er the dark gallery, where his fathers frowned
> In rude but antique portraiture around:
> They heard, but whispered – *that* must not be known ...

> He turned within his solitary hall,
> And his high shadow shot along the wall:
> There were the painted forms of other times,
> 'Twas all they left of virtues or of crimes,
> Save vague tradition; and the gloomy vaults
> That hid their dust, their foibles and their faults ...

> He wandering mused, and as the moonbeam shone
> Through the dim lattice, o'er the floor of stone,
> And the high fretted roof, and Saints, that there
> O'er Gothic windows knelt in pictured prayer ...

It is all Newstead; but what is more remarkable is that – for all the feverishness and passion of Byron's life at this time, the sudden and dizzy fame enough to turn anyone's head, being the most sought-after figure in society, pursued by women, going about with Augusta, their secret guessed at by not a few – he should have had a singularly *désabusé* appreciation of himself. It is not the least remarkable thing about Byron that he should have this capacity, absorbed egoist as he was, of standing apart from himself and observing what he saw within. Celts are apt to have that disjunction: it is unnerving, and sometimes frightening, to simple uncomplicated Saxons.

> In him inexplicably mixed appeared
> Much to be loved and hated, sought and feared;
> Opinion varying o'er his hidden lot,
> In praise or railing ne'er his name forgot ...
> A hater of his kind? yet some would say
> With them he could seem gay amidst the gay ...
> At times, a heart as not by nature hard ...

Yet he

> steeled itself, as scorning to redeem
> One doubt from others' half-withheld esteem ...

How revealing it is!

> Cut off by some mysterious fate from those
> Whom birth and nature meant not for his foes ...
> He deemed himself marked out for others' hate,
> And mocked at ruin so they shared his fate.
> What cared he for the freedom of the crowd?
> He raised the humble but to bend the proud.

Here is the Swiftian element in Byron – and so much for his supposed 'Radicalism': the radical element in his character was the Celt's pride:

> Cold to the great, contemptuous to the high,
> The humble passed not his unheeding eye ...
> Whate'er his view, his favour more obtains
> With these, the people, than his fellow thanes.

It is obvious that Byron understood his own complex nature perfectly, when hardly anyone else did. Augusta did intuitively, and accepted him for what he was:

> There was in him a vital scorn of all ...
> Till he at last confounded good and ill,
> And half mistook for fate the acts of will:
> Too high for common selfishness, he could
> At times resign his own for others' good,
> But not in pity, not because he ought,

> But in some strange perversity of thought
> That swayed him onward with a secret pride
> To do what few or none would do beside ...

There is his confession, there is the truth; and where Augusta took things as they came, with feminine acceptance, there was that in Byron which could not. He felt guilt – and more: he felt that his fate was fulfilled in guilt, a Lara, a Manfred, a Cain.

> So much he soared beyond, or sunk beneath,
> The men with whom he felt condemned to breathe,
> And longed by good or ill to separate
> Himself from all who shared his mortal state.

It is Swift all over again – of whom it might be said, as Byron more percipiently said of himself:

> His madness was not of the head, but heart.

At this very moment he sent off to Tom Moore, to be set to music, one of his best known and most moving poems, which told the whole truth to anyone of perception:

> I speak not, I trace not, I breathe not thy name,
> There is grief in the sound, there is guilt in the fame:
> But the fear which now burns on my cheek may impart
> The deep thoughts that dwell in that silence of heart.
> Too brief for our passion, too long for our peace.
> Were those hours – can their joy or their bitterness cease?

He did persuade himself to suppress the original opening of *Lara*, which confirms, if it were necessary, the autobiographical character of the poem:

> When she is gone – the loved, the lost – the one
> Whose smile had gladdened though perchance undone ...
> Where sudden mention can almost convulse
> And lightens through the ungovernable pulse ...
> Oh best and dearest, thou whose thrilling name
> My heart adored too deeply to proclaim ...

But he did proclaim it, like a fool, to Lady Melbourne. The golden rule is never to trust any human with such a secret: they are *not* to be trusted. (Swift never gave away Stella's secret: the result is that we do not know to this day whether he married her or not.)

All this while Byron was piling up debts; he handed over £3,000 to Augusta – one understands the significance of that. In London he was living at a frantic rate of extravagance, owing over £800 for tailors' bills alone. In such a tangle, with so many claims and his own incapacity to live within his means – and for all the money his poems were now bringing in – his correspondence is full of the necessity of selling Newstead. He sold the fine library he had accumulated there, and most of the furniture and plate. Newstead and Rochdale were twice offered for sale and withdrawn. Then a rich young Lancashireman, Claughton, offered £125,000 for Newstead, which was too good to be true. He withdrew, so that Byron resumed possession. Lady Melbourne's niece, Miss Milbanke, with whom he was in correspondence, intervened to inquire whether young Claughton was not being taken advantage of. That should have warned him.

It was obvious that he could not live without a woman. Lady Melbourne, who wished him well (and, in spite of her age, had taken advantage of him herself), wanted to see him safely married. So did Augusta, always unselfish and loyal, and with something of the maternal, certainly of family feeling, in her love for him. Earlier, he had insisted that he would never marry, and indeed he never should have done. He had 'a very early horror of matrimony', quite understandably; 'George [i.e. his cousin George Anson Byron] will prove the best of the family and will one day be Lord Byron, for I shall never marry.' Now he was persuaded that, on both counts, marriage was the only way out of the trap. He only fell into a worse one.

He had to marry an eventual heiress and, by a process of elimination, he arrived at Miss Milbanke. Her fortune, however, was prospective and depended on the demise of various relatives; meanwhile, little enough was disposable. Still, she was an heiress and, in order to secure his treasure, he had to engage himself in a marriage settlement of some £60,000. To meet it, Newstead *had* to be sold. Though it has not been noticed, this must have counted for something in the savage score he chalked up against the marriage.

Byron's fatal entanglement with Miss Milbanke is not my subject; but it must be said here that Augusta's intuition told her that Miss Milbanke was not the right person for Byron to marry (if anyone were). Byron's own intuition told him as much, and he hesitated long; eventually, it was Miss Milbanke, fascinated, who closed the trap.

In September he went down to Newstead with Augusta and her children for a last family visit: there they savoured together the inheritance that was doubly strong in them both. Byron was in two minds, meditating flight to Italy and wanting Augusta to accompany him – a step which would have made them outcasts for ever. One day his mother's wedding ring, which she had lost, was dug up in the garden, and he regarded this as an omen. At the same moment Miss Milbanke forced his hand by accepting his tepid proposal outright. He turned deathly pale: 'The stars, I presume, did it'. (On the very day of his wedding – like T. S. Eliot at his first marriage – he knew it was fatal.)

Meanwhile, passively, nervously awaiting his fate, he and Augusta went sadly around the strange home of their ancestors, with all the memories and associations tugging at the heart. In the Devil's Wood – so called because there local folk said the 'Wicked Lord' worshipped his deities, the satyrs he had set up – brother and sister carved their names together, with the date, 20 September 1819. Even when Byron was supposed to be dashing up to his treasure at Seaham, he could not resist turning aside for a last lingering look at Newstead.

We do not need to re-tell the story of Byron's impossible marriage to the last person in the world with whom he could have lived. For Miss Milbanke was another absorbed egoist, of a completely different sort. He said afterwards that he could cope with any human being other than 'a cold-blooded animal like Miss Milbanke'. Where he was all fire and intuition, with a great deal of humour and cynicism, she was all reason and ratiocination, straight-laced and prim, with no sense of humour whatever. What made it worse, her intellectual powers were quite formidable, a thing he did not like in women: it made them conceited, he said – and she, a spoiled child, was very conceited. She was quite a dab at moral analysis, and analysed his failings acutely. Young as she was, she even thought that she could reclaim him, amend him morally – this, to a man of genius, was insupportable. It made it worse that, in a conventional way, she was a 'good' woman; anyone with Byron's view of humanity would prefer a 'bad' one.

It has hardly been appreciated* that Augusta, in a precarious and difficult situation, behaved with loyalty and understanding to both of them. Once Byron had entangled himself beyond redemption she did everything to help Miss Milbanke to understand him, to explain his moodiness, the vagaries of the family temperament. She exerted all the patience and kindness of her easy-going nature. In the last stages of his wife's pregnancy only Augusta's presence could keep the household together – she was peacemaker and mediatrix. Byron felt, quite naturally, that he was trapped – he who didn't even like seeing women eating (a Freudian oddity) – and he behaved like a wild animal.

Frantic (he himself owned that he was not 'in his senses'), he behaved appallingly to both women. He was at the same time driven mad by his impossible financial situation: he was £30,000 in debt, with the sale of Newstead hanging fire, and no money from the Milbankes: his wife's fortune was prospective. While she was having her baby – which turned out a girl, Ada, when it should have been a son to inherit the peerage – there were bailiffs in the house. He was drinking heavily, carrying on with actresses at the theatre, threatening to bring them home, threatening his wife and himself – and all the time writing. (I suspect that it was only by writing that he preserved his sanity.) One can perfectly understand Lady Byron separating from him, though whole libraries of superfluous books have been written to confuse the matter (as with Shakespeare's sonnets). It really needs no explanation.

She suffered a profound shock, and the experience was a further blow to her pride. But she recovered – and entered upon a life-long course of self-justification. From Byron's point of view, the failure of their marriage needed no explanation either; he said that they would have to separate to preserve his sanity. But it was no less a blow to his pride. What added a corrosive to this was that, on every subsequent issue, Lady Byron won, hands down. Financially, she won out. She got her settlement of £60,000 out of the sale of Newstead; eventually she inherited the Milbanke and Wentworth fortunes. Rich, she

* Except by Mr Peter Gunn in *My Dearest Augusta*.

held the purse strings, and we shall see how she made use of them to exert control in the Byron family.

Byron's cousin, George, the seventh lord, sided with Lady Byron in the family dispute: he was rewarded by her with an annuity of £2,000 on his succession. The poet left his personal fortune to Augusta and her children; but this did not operate until Lady Byron's claims were fully met, with the result that Byron's intentions for his sister were largely frustrated: by the time his money came to her it was all eaten up by her creditors and money-lenders. Lady Byron, as disingenuous as she was self-righteous, said nothing about the financial screw she had upon Augusta. She occasionally doled out money as a means of exerting power – all expressed with the best intentions, of course – as we shall see in her attempt to rally to her, and possess, Byron' and Augusta's child, Medora.

Perhaps unknown to herself – for, a clever woman, she was largely unselfaware, a mass of conceit and injured pride, disingenuous and uncandid to a degree – she was really consumed by jealousy of Augusta. She herself loved Byron in her way, but he had found her unlovable. She never could recover from that sentence of exclusion. Obsessed by him, she inserted her fingers wherever she could to touch whatever had belonged to him. It was her life-long obsession; and thus, obscurely, she took her revenge. Psychologically, it is all riveting to observe.

It has not been noted, however, that the person who suffered most, in the event, was Augusta. What Lady Byron did to her was unforgivable. There was a large element of the masculine in Lady Byron's make-up – her ratiocination, her capacity for analysis, her calculation. After her own experience with a man, all her emotional attachments were with women: her close friend, Mrs Villiers; Medora; the dreadful Harriet Beecher Stowe. (Miss Milbanke would have made a good Lesbian academic lady, of an old-fashioned sort.)

Augusta was entirely feminine, soft and yielding, warm and kind-hearted, made for love. Lady Byron extorted a corroboration of her suspicions, a confession, from Augusta, and then held it over her head *in terrorem* for the rest of her life. She was persuaded, herself, that 'my great object, next to the Security of my Child [she had won possession of that one over Byron, too], is therefore the restoration of her [Augusta's] mind to that state which is religiously desirable'. Her object would be attained not by an open break with Augusta but by maintaining this secret control over her. 'The measure which I propose to take appears to me to unite the following advantages – that it will make herself acquainted with my real opinions and feelings, without binding me to avow them publicly; that it will nevertheless suspend this terror over her, to be used as her future dispositions and conduct may render expedient.'

Could cruelty, under the disingenuous guise of what was 'religiously desirable', go further?

I think that it ultimately broke Augusta: from being the gay, light-hearted, amusing woman Byron loved, she became the quivering creature, harassed with anxiety and fear, debts and dependants, whom she has come down to us as being. Exposed as she was in the sensational scandal of the famous poet's separation from his wife, she was rendered still more vulnerable by her appointment in March 1815 as a lady-in-waiting to Queen Charlotte, with an apartment in St James's Palace. Her grand relations, the Leeds and Carlisles, had got that for her as she had her family of children to maintain, and her husband was little help in providing for them.

Byron, with the extremism of his temperament and his challenging attitude towards society and convention, wanted her to join him abroad in exile. 'What a fool I was to marry – and *you* not very wise, my dear: we might have lived so single and so happy, as old maids and bachelors. I shall never find anyone like you, nor you (vain as it may seem) like me. We are just formed to pass our lives together.. ... Had you been a Nun – and I a Monk... no matter: my voice and my heart are ever thine.'

Augusta seriously considered joining him – it was just what Lady Byron's implacable mother wished her to do. But she had her children to consider, and felt she could not go. Lady Byron then put her next step into operation: she made Augusta submit Byron's letters to her for her perusal – and advise as to how to act in regard to them, in the interests of what was 'religiously desirable', of course. To Mrs Villiers: 'She has shown me of her own accord *his* letters to her...they are *absolute love letters.*'

This had the advantage of controlling Augusta's correspondence with her brother. Lady Byron did not wish her to break it off, because it kept her vicariously in touch with Byron, on her own terms. 'I should not advise you for his sake to restrict your correspondence further than by keeping always in view to *rectify* instead of *soothing* or *indulging* his feelings.' The difference between the two women's characters could not be more precisely put. 'And let me also warn you against the levity and nonsense which he likes for the worst reason, because it prevents him from reflecting seriously.' One gasps at her.

Here again she won, for the effect was to impose a control upon Augusta's direct expression of her feelings. The poet's half-sister had always been natural and unforced, now she was forced to conceal and cover up: she became confused. Her surrender to Lady Byron, her giving up her independence to another, her degradation of her love, when she had never felt particularly guilty, the perpetual harping on this string, began the process of deterioration and increasing confusion in her personality, along with the deterioration of her circumstances.

Byron's masculine mind could not understand what had happened, what had caused a change in Augusta: he should have known the deviousness of women, and he had certainly underrated Miss Milbanke. If he had known all, he would have had even more reason to detest her. He reproached Augusta thus: 'it would be much better at once to explain your mysteries than to go on with this absurd obscure hinting mode of writing. What do you mean? What is there known or can be known which you and I do not know much better? And what concealment can you have from me?'

This was the concealment. It does not seem that Byron knew that he owed this change in Augusta to his wife. Lady Byron succeeded in breaking off the correspondence between him and his sister for nine months. It may well be that, though she could never make an impression on Byron's heart, she succeeded in breaking Augusta's.

Byron, of course, was unchanged – and unchangeable from any outside intervention. 'My dearest Augusta – I have always loved you better than any earthly existence, and I always shall, unless I go mad.' But, then, he had the solace that he could transmute his innermost tensions, his passions and despairs, into his writing: there they could be resolved, in his art. In the

exile which was to last to the end of his life he was writing
Manfred, in which the crux of his inner life is again exposed.

> She was like me in lineaments – her eyes,
> Her hair, her features, all, to the very tone
> Even of her voice, they said, were like to mine;
> But softened all, and tempered into beauty...

and

> with them gentler powers than mine,
> Pity, and smiles, and tears – which I had not;
> And tenderness – but that I had for her;
> Humility – and that I never had.
> Her faults were mine – her virtues were her own –
> I loved her, and destroyed her!

When the phantom of Astarte appears to him, we must remember again the habit of poets, conscious or unconscious of
giving their creations names that echo the reality: Astarte
rhythmically echoes Augusta.

> Thou lovedst me
> Too much, as I loved thee; we were not made
> To torture thus each other, though it were
> The deadliest sin to love as we have loved.

In the end Byron cites what is the theme of this book:

> I say 'tis blood – my blood! the pure warm stream
> Which ran in the veins of my fathers, and in ours
> When we were in our youth, and had one heart,
> And loved each other as we should not love,
> And this was shed ...

In this same year, 1817, Newstead was at length sold. From
Venice Byron wrote that 'the sale has been equally unexpected
and agreeable to me, and the price much better than could be
expected considering the times'. The price paid was £94,500,
and the times were those of post-war depression. The purchaser
was a former school-fellow of Byron's at Harrow, who had
served gallantly in the Peninsular War and at Waterloo. Byron
wrote rather grandly to him, 'I should regret to trouble you
with any requests of mine in regard to the preservation of any
signs of my family which may still exist at Newstead, and leave

everything of that kind to your own feelings, present or future, upon the subject.' Wildman politely requested a portrait of the poet, who was already the most famous occupant of the Abbey. Undoubtedly Byron had felt pain on parting with the home of his ancestors, and again it was ironical that he, of all of them, had the most acute and nostalgic appreciation of it. His marriage made the sale financially unavoidable, but the blow was softened by the disgust for his country at the treatment which his defiance of its conventions had brought down upon him. Exile of a kind was his spiritual home; alienation the stand he took up, though its roots were also deep in his personality.

Like Swift or T. E. Lawrence, he was not really English – unlike Shakespeare or Milton.

In his most mature work, *Don Juan*, he has a long, final celebration of Newstead. After the storm and stress of his marriage and the scandal of the separation had subsided, he achieved the balance of a certain worldly cynicism, through which he could distance himself from his environment. Disillusionment sharpened his sight and cleared the ground for his natural wit. Still the family tradition is there: the famous description of the shipwreck in the second canto owes a great deal to that of the *Wager*, even to the rescue of his grandfather's dog:

> Knowing, (dogs have such intellectual noses),
>   No doubt, the vessel was about to sink;
> And Juan caught him up, and ere he stepped
> Off, threw him in, then after him he leaped.

For many of the details, the experiences of the ship-wrecked crew, Byron was indebted to the Admiral's account: Don Juan's

> hardships were comparative
>   To those related in my grand-dad's *Narrative.*

We are given an extended description of Newstead in which the satirical account of a Regency country house-party takes place – one may read it as a complementary piece to Jane Austen's *Northanger Abbey.*

> The mansion's self was vast and venerable,
>   With more of the monastic than has been,
> Elsewhere preserved: the cloisters still were stable,
>   The cells too, and refectory, I ween:

An exquisite small chapel had been able,
  Still unimpaired, to decorate the scene;
The rest had been reformed, replaced, or sunk,
And spoke more of the baron than the monk.

Huge halls, long galleries, spacious chambers, joined
  By no quite lawful marriage of the arts,
Might shock a connoisseur; but, when combined,
  Formed a whole which, irregular in parts,
Yet left a grand impression in the mind,
  At least of those whose eyes are in their hearts...

He describes once more the west front, one of the finest of any
monastic church, and the curious, hallucinatory echo which he
himself had heard, 'once perhaps too much'.

A mighty window, hollow in the centre,
  Shorn of its glass of thousand colourings,
Through which the deepened glories once could enter,
  Streaming from off the sun like seraph's wings,
Now yawns all desolate: now loud, now fainter,
  The gale sweeps through its fretwork, and oft sings
The owl his anthem, where the silenced choir
Lie with their halleluias quenched like fire.

But in the noontide of the moon, and when
  The wind is winged from one point of heaven,
There moans a strange unearthly sound, which then
  Is musical – a dying accent driven
Through the huge arch, which soars and sinks again...

Negotiations for the sale of Rochdale continued for years,
held up by legal proceedings owing to the fifth lord's question-
able leasing of his rights in the collieries. These suits cost the
poet several thousand pounds, though he won them. It was not
until the last year of his life and when he was ready to sail for
Greece that he disposed of the family's Lancashire holding for
£11,225. He was ready to spend all this and more for the cause
for which he gave his life, won a nation's gratitude – and was
forgiven everything.

It is harder for the historian to forgive the breaking of historic
ties. The historian Namier urges the overriding significance of

the land in the holding together of an historic family: once the land has gone, the family loses its centricity, is dispersed, breaks up, is lost.

We shall observe this same process of dispersal and break-up with the Trevanions, when they lost their hold on their lands in Cornwall.

X

Cousins and Lovers

WHAT, MEANWHILE, HAD BEEN HAPPENING to the Byron cousins at Caerhays?

Sophia's elder sister, the senior co-heiress Frances Trevanion, had married in 1747 John Bettesworth, of an old Sussex family. He was, improbably enough, an ecclesiastical lawyer, as his father had been before him. Baptized at St Margaret's, Westminster, in October 1720, Bettesworth went to Christ Church and became a doctor of civil law of the university. Like his father, he held the peculiar of Tarring and Malling in West Sussex, and was chancellor of the diocese of London, 1759–64. Nothing much is known of him: he must have been a dull man.

Frances died in 1762, in her thirty-fifth year, and is buried at Luton, where there is a monument to her in the church. She and her husband must have lived at Luton, for his second wife is buried there too. Frances's son was another John Bettesworth, who lived at Caerhays and had a London house in Nottingham Place. He went to Oxford, matriculating from Queen's College, and made a Welsh marriage, to Frances Tomkyns of Pembrokeshire. He died at Caerhays in 1789, leaving five young children.

The eldest of these, John Trevanion Purnell Bettesworth, born at Caerhays in 1780, assumed the name of Trevanion on coming of age in 1801. A more striking figure is the second son, George Edmund Byron Bettesworth, who was born in 1785, joined the navy as a boy and early won renown. As a lieutenant of eighteen, he was wounded in the capture of the French brig,

Curieux, off Martinique early in 1804; his captain killed, the youth took command of the ship. For his gallantry the government awarded him an honorary sword. In command of his prize, the following year he was again wounded in the capture of a privateer off Barbados. In Trafalgar year, 1805, he brought home from the West Indies Nelson's despatches apprising the government of Villeneuve's escape home to France: this was the preliminary to the final move in the Trafalgar campaign. Bettesworth was immediately given a post – a captain's commission and command of a frigate, the *Crocodile*, at twenty.

His cousin the poet, only a couple of years younger, was thrilled by these exploits, and was writing from Trinity, Cambridge, in October 1807:

I am going to *Sea* for four or five months with my cousin, Captain Bettesworth, who commands the *Tartar*, the finest frigate in the Navy. . . . We are going probably to the Mediterranean, or to the West Indies, or to the Devil; and if there is a possibility of taking me to the Latter, Bettesworth will do it – for he has received four-and-twenty wounds in different places, and at this moment possesses a letter from the late Lord Nelson, stating Bettesworth as the only officer of the Navy who had more wounds than himself.

With such *réclame* the captain was able to command not only a frigate but a grand marriage to a sister of the Whig leader, Earl Grey. At the time of this exploit he was only twenty-two. In the next year he was killed at Bergen, when the *Tartar* was becalmed among the rocks and was attacked by a schooner and five gunboats. This was in May 1808, and he was twenty-three: there is no knowing what he might have achieved if he had lived out his full life. His body was brought back to the Grey family vault at Howick in Northumberland; but there is a life-size statue of him as a hero, the flag beside him, dominating the Trevanion aisle in the little church at Caerhays.

His brother, Major Trevanion, was chief mourner at his funeral. He was serving in the Dragoon Guards; another brother was a captain in the Royal Cornwall Militia, in this warlike time when the county was under constant alert against a French invasion.

Byron was on friendly terms with Trevanion, for this year we find him writing, 'I have been introduced to Julia Byron by Trevanion at the Opera.' This was the sister of his cousin George, who succeeded him.

She is pretty, but I do not admire her – there is too much Byron in her countenance. I hear she is clever, a very great defect in a woman, who becomes conceited in course. [Shades of Miss Milbanke to come!] I have seen my old friend George, who will prove the best of the family, and will one day be Lord B. Pray name my nephew after his uncle, it must be a nephew (I *wont* have a *niece*). I will make him my *heir*, for I shall never marry, unless I am ruined. George will have the title and his *laurels*; my property I can leave to whom I please, and your son shall be the legatee.

This was to Augusta, and such was his intention in 1808.

In the year of his separation from his ghastly wife, 1816, he was writing to Trevanion from Milan, advising him as to the journey and expecting a meeting in Italy. Evidently the Trevanions did not take against him, though the Byrons did.

We arrived here a few days ago after a tedious but undisturbed journey – and, many others having passed before and since, I believe the road may be accounted tolerably safe. Near the frontier – or rather on passing Cesto – it may be as well to take a couple of *gens d'armes*. . . . The Simplon is in very fair order and a most magnificent route it forms – you can also see the Borromean Isles, the road leading along the Lago Maggiore – they are worth the voyage – which is only a few hours. Of the inns here I can only speak from report – *none* very *good* – our own indifferent – the Vetturino brought us to it – and here we shall remain for the fortnight previous to our setting out for Venice. I think you will like Milan – the town is fine and reminds me of Seville, which however is the finer of the two. If you arrive before our departure I hope to see you.

Alas, in the sale of Caerhays and the dispersal of its contents, including the Trevanion family papers, we know no more about Byron's contacts with it. There must have been letters and, clearly, communications with Captain Bettesworth. When Byron was down at Falmouth in June 1809, waiting for the packet-boat to take him to Lisbon, he had not the curiosity, or perhaps the time, to go up the coast to visit the home of his ancestors. He was more interested in the boys in the harbour. He wrote to Matthews, who shared his interest, wishing that 'you were with us in this delectable region, as I do not think Georgia itself can emulate its capabilities or incitements to the *plenum* and *optabile coitum*, the port of Falmouth and parts adjacent. —. We are surrounded by Hyacinths and other flowers of the most fragrant nature, and I have some intention of culling a handsome Bouquet to compare with the exotics we expect to meet in Asia.' In the ancient civilization of the Mediterranean, for which his classical education had prepared him – if for nothing else – he could let himself go. And Matthews was a classical scholar of the first class.

Of Falmouth Byron wrote to Ellice, who married Bettesworth's widow:

The inhabitants both male and female, at least the young ones, are remarkably handsome, and how they came to be so is the marvel, for the place is apparently not favourable to Beauty. ———. The claret is good, and Quakers plentiful, so are herrings salt and fresh. There is a fort called St. Mawes off the harbour [of which an ancestor had been in charge, if he had known], which we were nearly taken up on suspicion of having carried by storm; it is well defended by one able-bodied man of eighty years old, six ancient demi-culverins, that would exceedingly annoy anybody – except an enemy – and parapet walls which would withstand at least half a dozen kicks of any given grenadier in the kingdom of France.

On his last day in harbour he tossed off the breezy verses beginning:

> Huzza! Hodgson, we are going,
> Our embargo's off at last,
> Favourable breezes blowing
> Bend the canvas o'er the mast.
> From aloft the signal's streaming,
> Hark! the farewell gun is fired,
> Women screeching, tars blaspheming,
> Tells us that our time's expired.
>   Here's a rascal
>   Come to task all
> Prying from the Custom-house;
>   Trunks unpacking,
>   Cases cracking,
> Not a corner for a mouse
> Scapes unsearched amid the racket
> Eer we sail on board the Packet.

So much for ancestral Cornwall. Naturally, with his tastes he preferred the Mediterranean.

Until the terrible fuss over the separation from Lady Byron, the public scandal with all the attendant humbug, Byron was on good terms with his cousin George. The gallant captain borrowed £150 from him, in the midst of his marital and financial worries. 'My naval cousin George has just bore down, and his tongue is running nine knots an hour.' When he married in 1816 Byron wrote, 'I wish him as much luck and as little law as possible.' Next year a son and heir, who would be the eighth lord, was born. 'The father is a good man, an excellent officer and has married a very nice little woman – she had a handsome dowry, but he may as well get a ship.' He did, but with the long war over and the long peace setting in, no more exciting task fell to him than to conduct the ashes of the queen of the Sandwich Islands to her Hawaiian resting-place. He was made a lord of the bedchamber to the naval king, William IV, and was a lord-in-waiting to Queen Victoria, 1837–1860. Through the Victorian noonday he automatically progressed in naval rank: rear-admiral 1849, vice-admiral 1857, admiral 1862. Dying in 1868, he was buried at Kirkby Mallory in Leicestershire, not so far away from Newstead.

In 1820 Byron was writing to Augusta of his dislike of George's siding with Lady Byron, to whom he was beholden for support (from Byron's money), and 'I am unacquainted with the others who may be in the line of the title . . . being at feud with most of the Byrons except yourself.' To Augusta he remained ever faithful at heart, whatever his transitory sexual needs and vagaries:

> For thee, my own sweet sister, in thy heart
> I know myself secure, as thou in mine;
> We were and are – I am, even as thou art –
> Beings who ne'er each other can resign;
> It is the same, together or apart –
> From life's commencement to its slow decline
> We are entwined – let death come slow or fast,
> The tie which bound the first endures the last!

In another poem he wrote:

> When fortune changed – and love fled far,
> And hatred's shafts flew thick and fast,

Thou wert the solitary star
　Which rose and set not to the last.

Still may thy spirit dwell on mine,
　And teach it what to brave or brook –
There's more in one soft word of thine
　Than in the world's defied rebuke.

Thou stood'st, as stands a lovely tree,
　That still unbroke, though gently bent,
Still waves with fond fidelity
　Its boughs above a monument.
Devoted in the stormiest hour
　To shed thy weeping leaves o'er me.

But thou and thine shall know no blight,
　Whatever fate on me may fall;
For heaven in sunshine will require
　The kind – and thee the most of all.

Like many of the poet's prophecies this did not come true. Fortunately he never knew the extent of her submission to Lady Byron's psychotically unbending will, and the gradual deterioration and confusion of Augusta's personality under the strain, the ramming home of a sense of guilt which was not natural to her. Nor was the poet justified in his confidence that the *damnosa hereditas* would bring no blight on her children. We shall see how it worked out in the case of the child, Medora, and the infatuation that grew up between her cousin Henry Trevanion and her, in whom the Byron and Trevanion genes were, of course, doubled.

Henry Trevanion was the second son of Byron's cousin and acquaintance, J.T.P.B. Trevanion of Caerhays, and his first wife Charlotte, daughter of Admiral Hosier (presumably of Clementina Churchill's family). Charlotte died in 1810, aged twenty-seven, and is buried at Caerhays. Twenty years later Trevanion married again, in 1830, a young daughter of Sir Francis Burdett, the aristocratic Radical, patron of parliamentary reform. It was Burdett who brought Augusta the news of Byron's death at Missolonghi, and was one of those who turned the funeral procession in London into a demonstration against the government. One sees the political affiliations of the family. At the funeral in Nottingham, when Byron was gathered to his ancestors in the vault at Hucknal Torkard, Henry Trevanion represented his family.

What was Augusta, harassed by money worries, with little or no help from the helpless colonel, herself the chief breadwinner from her exposed job at St James's Palace, to do with all those children? Georgiana was the eldest of them, born in 1808. In 1825, though she was only sixteen, Henry Trevanion, a few years older, came up to London and here was a prospect of marrying off Georgiana happily. Or so Augusta thought, ever sanguine, for all the blows she had received. Moreover, she had fallen for young Henry herself, since meeting him at a family gathering of their relations. No one ever charged Augusta with being frail outside the charmed circle of her Byron–Trevanion flesh and flood. She fell for him as she had for Byron – the genes were too strong for her – and relations followed a similar pattern. After the first careless rapture she was anxious, as she had been with Byron, to see Henry safely married. And she remained loyal to him through all the troubles his sexual temperament brought down upon her and her family.

She wrote enthusiastically to Lady Byron, her mentor and boss of the whole tribe (Byron's successor as seventh lord as well): 'The young man is studying the law and has talent to make the most of his profession – exceedingly clever and in other respects the only person I know *worthy* of Georgey. He was introduced to me by his Father about last July twelvemonth and I've seen much of him since from liking him and finding him so far superior to the *common herd*.' The fathers on both sides were not helpful. Colonel Leigh disapproved; J.T.P.B. Trevanion promised a marriage settlement of £100 a year, but not a farthing of it was paid. Henry had little in the way of means, so everybody fell back on Augusta as usual, who raised £2,000 on her expectations from Byron's eventual legacy (after rich Lady Byron's death). The wedding took place in February 1826 at St James's, Piccadilly, only Augusta and Medora being present of her family to support Georgey and Henry at the altar. (He was more interested in religion than the law.) Lady Byron lent the young couple a house of hers near Canterbury: no one seems to have noticed how appropriate its name was – *Bifrons*. It became still more so in the extraordinary sequel.

In 1827 Trevanion published, with Longman, a book of poems, *The Influence of Apathy*, of which I possess a pretty copy, green and gold, inscribed by Georgey for 'Flossie Trevanion'. Most of the poems were written in adolescence, and they are dominated by the mighty shadow so recently passed from the European scene. Trevanion, too, is haunted by passion and guilt:

> Fly – fly – we must not meet again –
>   Another hour like this will throw
> A careless frenzy o'er my brain –
>   Alas, 'tis half-bewildered now.
> Why stay we here? These moments bring
> To our lost souls a deeper sting;
> Oh, God! why had we not the power
> To shun the death-blast of this hour?

Or –

> Oh! weep not – weep not – let me fly
>   In anger, as when last we parted;
> All – all but this I'll bear – to die
>   Were bliss than thus part broken-hearted.

Some poems cast reflections, as it might be of Newstead:

> Wild, glimmering on the hearth, the blazing pile
> Casts its warm light around the spacious hall;
> And many a ghost to superstition's eye
> The distant shades in such abode would bring;
> On either side the tarnished armour stands,
> On the thick walls, with deep and varied tints,
> Kings, mounted heroes, and brocaded dames,
> In tapestry tell the deeds of other days,
> While, through the crevices the frequent gusts
> Lift the torn cloths and wave their giant forms...

It could be Newstead, but in fact it is the ancient house at Caerhays, which Henry's father was to rebuild – and ruin the family in doing so. For in the background is the sea:

> See yon little bark that's gliding
>   Lightly o'er the slumb'ring wave;
> Summer zephyrs now are riding
>   O'er that blue, unfathomed grave.

> Soon its snow-white sail will shiver
> To the blast that's gathering near...

Several of the poems are about, or written to be set to, music;
one of them is dedicated 'To J . . . T . . . . n, Esq. on his Singing' – Henry's elder brother, John. A volume of songs and a can-
tata by 'the blind organist' of Truro was dedicated to their
mother. Evidently there was something of a cult of music in
the last years of the draughty old house.

The long title-piece has an eloquent tribute to Byron, several
passages of which are marked with approval by a family hand:

> One sad exception – one whose soul hath fled
> Stricken, but not polluted, to the dead;
> The slave of feeling, but too proud to show
> That feeling to a world esteemed a foe;
> Barred from thy native land – compelled to roam –
> Adored of nations – yet without a home:
> No kindred arm thy fevered head to rear,
> No fond attention thy last hour to cheer...

One wonders whether that turbulent spirit did not exert an influence upon its paler shadow; for Henry Trevanion's life was
to follow a similar pattern of passion, guilt and exile. And it
is certainly odd that, amid the innumerable tributes to Byron,
no one has unearthed this moving celebration of him from
within the family.

> A husband, and a father – names with power
> To wound, not calm thee in thy dying hour;
> Such was thy fate – and are there none to mourn,
> Departed spirit, o'er thy hallowed urn?
> Must then thy radiant course like comet glare
> Win the world's gaze, and vanish into air?

There follow further passages the sympathetic pencil has
marked:

> Must barren hearts – the readiest to condemn
> The faults that owed their very birth to them –
> Must those the beings who with icy sneer
> Warped each warm virtue of thy brief career –
> Who spurned the feeling oft too truly shown,
> Because that feeling never was their own? –

The answer Trevanion gave, only three years after Byron's death, was the answer the future would give:

> Forbid it, Greece! While Freedom dare expand
> Her orient standard o'er her native land ...

These lines too are marked by the approving hand. Then Trevanion, a good classical scholar, goes on to rank Byron with the heroes of ancient Greece, citing their names and the roll-call of places where they fell.

> Thy grateful sons shall write for other years
> The name of Byron in a nation's tears.

The title-piece has a moralizing prose-argument prefaced to it, which reads ironically in what was about to happen.

The disposition of Youth to affection; to confidence; to imbibe flattery; to engage unadvisedly in friendships. The result of the abuse of this ingenuousness – suspicion and distrust, art, and indifference to all that previously interested. Suicide considered. The inefficacy of public or private tuition, in the abstract, to avert the evils incident to entering the world; to invalidate the temptations of sin. The tendency of a career of sin to deaden the sensibility of our affections.

And he ended his sermon with 'the incapability of worldly enjoyments to insure happiness. Happiness – tranquillity of mind. Tranquillity of mind attainable only by the means of apathy.'

This vein of religiosity increased his appeal for Augusta who, under the influence of Lady Byron, was becoming more religious herself. This would not have been approved by Byron, who, for all his mother's indoctrination of Calvinism, had the sense to arrive early at the position: 'I do not believe in any revealed religion, because no religion is revealed.' He was not, however, an unbeliever in a *'Great First Cause, least understood; though I conceive He never made anything to be tortured in another life, whatever it may in this. I will neither read pro nor con.'* This was wisdom – a sheer waste of time. Yet Miss Milbanke had the impertinence to think that this man of genius would not reflect seriously: she could teach him!

Henry Trevanion proved himself anything but apathetic in bed, for all his apostrophizing.

Oh! woman! jewelled link of being's chain,
First dream of love, last object of disdain,
Sad is the storm, o'erwhelming is the sea,
Star of the soul! that turns our course from thee:
But all must be forgotten, all must cease
But Apathy, for him who seeks for peace.

True enough for him – yet he could not attain to this blessed consummation. He was very active sexually, and the girls were appallingly pregnable; they seem to have had no idea of birth-control, even of the most elementary kind. Georgey had three girls in quick succession, and herself rather cold, like Lady Byron, came to detest Henry. They quarrelled incessantly. Over Georgey's second confinement Augusta sent Medora down to Bifrons for company; she was then fifteen and soon became pregnant too. The news of approaching scandal reached Lady Byron through her intelligence net, and she provided the money for the three young people to go over to Calais. Here Medora's child was born and left in the charge of the doctor, with whom it apparently died.

Medora returned to live with Augusta in her apartment in St James's Palace. Augusta was frequently absent on duty, while Henry and Medora read the Bible together – he continued to be religious – and the girl found herself pregnant again. Henry poured out his soul to Augusta: 'My dearest Moe [so he called her] – I owe some explanation for the pain I caused you by my wild note. I took laudanum – I promise you not to do so again – would to God that had been all!' A number of well-known people in Regency society took laudanum – the poetess 'L.E.L.' for one, whom Henry knew: he addressed a poem to her.

To Henry, Augusta was all sympathy: 'You know how I have loved and regarded you as my own Child – I can never cease to do so! Show me how I can comfort and support you – confide in me, dearest – too much suffering has been caused by want of confidence. What *might not* have been prevented could I have known, guessed, even *most remotely* suspected – but – I would not breathe a word if I could help it to give *further* pain!' ... To Medora she was less sympathetic: 'You know that I confidently hoped and intended you to be confirmed this Easter. I suppose it is now hopeless – consult your own heart and wishes. I hoped to prepare you myself with the help of reading – but now I feel it would be a great satisfaction to me if some Clergyman were to assist in this.' This was what Byron called the 'Goose' in Augusta; Lady Byron called her 'a moral Idiot'. Actually, Augusta, distracted and confused by the worries of her family and situation, took all the blame home to herself – and who was the better Christian?

Henry had been supposed to be taking a hand in Medora's education – he had indeed; now, in addition to her refusing to be confirmed, all three went down together into the country near Bath, Georgey insisting that Medora should accompany her, she so much disliked being left alone with Henry (and Henry with her). Henry and Medora, with their Byron–Trevanion genes and looks, were obsessed with each other, an utter fixation.

Now Colonel Leigh, usually dilatory, nevertheless took a hand. He went down to Bath and carried Medora back to London; he locked her up in an establishment in Maida Vale where upper-class girls went to have their illegitimate offspring. She was in effect a prisoner, behind bars and locked doors. But Georgey and Henry arranged her escape: they were as anxious to be quit of each other (Georgey was a quiet conventional girl, neither a Byron nor a Trevanion) as Henry and Medora were stuck on each other. These two managed to get abroad to Normandy where their child arrived, but stillborn. Henry was so infatuated with Medora that he wanted a living child by her.

By 1833 the couple had gravitated into Brittany, perhaps atavistically, to the Breton Carhaix. Augusta, who was now keeping Georgey's three children, had doled out what she could for Medora, but lost touch with her in the depths of Brittany, where the girl was ill, after a series of miscarriages. Medora had become a Catholic – Byron was more sympathetic to Catholicism than to any form of Protestantism – and now declared her intention of entering a convent. As usual she found herself pregnant; the abbess was very understanding and got her lodgings outside, where a live child was born, registered as Marie Violette Trevanion.

Henry got at Medora again and prevailed on her to set up in an ancient, tumble-down *château* near Morlaix – it may have reminded him of Caerhays – where they lived as brother and sister and could be taken as such, for they were so like each other. With no idea of money on either side, Byron or Trevanion, they were reduced to poverty; aristocratic delinquents, they never thought of turning their hands to work. Medora, who inherited the scribbling as well as other propensities of both families, afterwards wrote in an autobiography that Henry gave himself up to 'religion and shooting'. She drew a picture of herself as under his domination – unlikely to be true, although there was an ambivalence in their relationship: they exerted a spell on each other, sometimes against their will. But Medora was far too independent not to be responsible for her fate herself. She had the Byron contradiction within her of being under the absolute need to be loved, combined with a strong desire for independence. As for Henry, he was totally incapable of doing without sex.

In these circumstances of poverty, illness and increasing disaccord, they were forced to reveal their whereabouts and – familiar pattern – dun Augusta and Henry's father for money. The latter, convinced that Medora was to blame, sent his brother Bettesworth, Henry's uncle, to bring him home. Henry refused to move. Augusta had been prevailed upon to execute one of her contingent deeds – contingent upon future expectations, Lady Byron's death – for £3,000 for bringing up the child, Marie Trevanion. Medora, forced to ask for help, nothing unwilling, tried to get this legal document out of her mother. This later led to a court case.

Lady Byron, now well alerted, was able to chalk up one more score against Augusta:

Could I have believed that you had a Mother's affection for her, you would not now have had to ask for information. To say nothing of your previous conduct [which she was always saying nothing about] – after she [Medora] had, without any assistance of yours, freed herself from the tyranny of Mr. Trevanion, you left her unprotected and destitute, in a most alarming state of health, exposed to every temptation, and not even beyond his reach!

One can well understand that the former Miss Milbanke, with Mrs Beecher Stowe, would make early patrons of the Women's Rights Movement.

Her malady, the effect of physical and mental suffering combined, can be retarded only by extreme care and by her avoiding all distressing excitement [i.e. sex]. The former I can secure, but not the latter. I would save you, if it is not too late, from adding the guilt of her death to that of her birth.

What a letter! It is obvious that Lady Byron could never forgive Augusta for having had Byron's love, when she could never command it herself.

She now took a surprising, but significant step, fascinating to those who appreciate the inwardness of it. (Where the conventional John Buchan was shocked by the Byron story that loomed large in his wife's Lovelace family, Henry James found it thrilling psychologically.)

Lady Byron now took Medora under her wing. Here was the form her frustrated love for Byron took: she wanted to get her hands on anything that was his. Whether this remarkable woman knew it or not, it took the form of exerting power. Through her moral blackmail she had Augusta in her clutches; now she was in a position to annex Medora. The two Byron daughters, the legitimate one, Ada, now Lady Lovelace, and the unrecognized Medora, got on well with each other; but neither of them could get on for any length of time with Lady Byron. She longed for the love she was unable to inspire, and once told Medora that it would cost her her life if they were to separate. Separation, however, from Lady Byron Medora found as necessary to preserve her sanity as Byron had done.

Characteristically, Lady Byron imposed her conditions, as she had done upon her husband. Medora was to surrender Augusta's deed of appointment to trustees on her child's behalf; she must sign an account of the sums she had received since she had been 'abandoned' (Lady Byron meant, by Augusta); she must return to France. Medora was willing to accept the last two conditions; the first she refused, and it created complicated troubles thenceforward, leading to a breach with her mother. Medora went back to France again as Madame Aubin, a well-known name in Cornwall from the St Aubyns, with whom the Trevanions had been familiar for centuries. (Byron and Shelley had been friendly with the last baronet of St Michael's Mount at Geneva.)

We need hardly pursue the complications of Medora's later

years in France. In her autobiography she depicted herself as being emancipated from the malign spell Henry Trevanion had cast upon her, and she did not go back to him. He went on living in Brittany, she in Paris and then the south of France. In the end a common French soldier fell honourably in love with her, after she had rejected – to Lady Byron's surprise – a dishonourable proposal from a French officer. Medora married the soldier, one Taillefer, though people continued to call her respectfully by the aristocratic name of Madame Aubin. She bore him a son, Elie, in whom one might say Byron's blood flowed up to the threshold of the twentieth century – as that of the ultra-respectable Wordsworth did in the illegitimate line descending from Annette Vallon.

Henry lived on in Brittany on the property he was able to buy from the legacy left him by his father. Georgey made one more effort to live with him there, but after a brief trial gave up. Of his daughters, Ada, the youngest, inherited the family aptitude for versifying. In 1858 she published a volume of verse under her name, undeservedly without notice, for the work is not to be disconsidered and, characteristically, records an unhappy affair of love; the melancholy charm of the verses is not Byronic, but Tennysonian. Oddly enough, Ada was the one to be the ultimate beneficiary of Byron's will, which did no good to Augusta, for Lady Byron outlived her. Ada Trevanion succeeded to £28,000, a substantial fortune in Victorian days; she left half of it to a Trevanion, half to a Leigh, who was also, part Trevanion. Part came from her guilty father.

Georgey too was provided for: when Henry died in 1855, aged only fifty, she inherited his share of what was left of the Trevanion estate. He died in Brittany on Christmas Day, alone, strangely fulfilling his own forecast: 'Tranquillity of mind only attainable by the means of apathy', and the apostrophe to his famous cousin:

> No kindred arm thy fevered head to rear,
> No fond attention thy last hour to cheer;
> Not one to light that moment's awe-ful gloom
> And gild with hope the darkness of the tomb.

By the time of Henry's death the centuries-long Trevanion hold at Caerhays – centuries longer than that of the Byrons at Newstead – had come to an end. Because of the dispersal of the

Trevanion papers it is difficult to make out all that happened there. We know only a little about Henry's father, who was responsible for demolishing the ancient mansion, bringing in Nash to build a romantic Regency castle at such expense that Trevanion could not afford to finish it, while he prejudiced and endangered the whole future of the family – in the long run ruined it – by his folly and extravagance. Just like the Byrons with Newstead; would things have been any better if *they* had inherited Caerhays, Sophia's descendants, instead of her elder sister's? It is highly doubtful.

John Trevanion Purnell Bettesworth was born at Caerhays in 1780, thus seven or eight years senior to his cousin, Byron, whom he knew, as we have seen. As a captain in the Dragoon Guards he assumed the Trevanion name in 1801; in 1804 he was sheriff of Cornwall, and member of Parliament for Penryn in 1807. The election occasioned a great deal of fuss. Sir Christopher Hawkins of Trewithen, a prominent borough-monger, was accustomed to have his say, if not his way, in these parts. He put up for the borough, with a London crony, Mr Swann – the 'black Swann' – and they were returned with a handsome majority. This was hardly surprising, for a posse of voters headed by a clergyman, had offered themselves to Sir Christopher for twenty-four guineas apiece and ten guineas for each of the overseers, and this had been accepted. Trevanion – a virtuous Whig, who merely ruined his family – petitioned against the election; a fuss was made, the wishes of the electors overturned, and Trevanion declared elected.

The Whigs had returned to power briefly; but their rule was a dismal failure, and their record not very virtuous. All the Grenvilles were self-seeking and grasping; the prime minister, Lord Grenville, rushed a bill through Parliament enabling him to hold on to his sinecure, by deputy, as auditor of the exchequer while first lord of the treasury. He admitted his lord chief justice as a member of the Cabinet, which was doubtfully constitutional. So much for Whig reformers! Their great man, Charles James Fox, had died, finding that, after two decades of opposition to Pitt, there was no coming to terms with Napoleon and Pitt had been right after all. Their foreign expeditions were lamentable failures. The Tories returned to carry out Pitt's task of resisting the subjugation of the continent to France.

Trevanion did not seek to return to Parliament; in the following year, 1808, he began the operations on Caerhays in which he was engulfed. In 1822 he had Sir Francis Burdett staying with him, on the latter's popular tour of Devon and Cornwall. Burdett reported to his wife that near Caerhays 'is a singular romantic fishing town and in better times a great smuggling place, and still carries on, under every disadvantage, a considerable Free Trade'. This was Mevagissey, which had enjoyed a prosperous pilchard fishery.

We were in hopes of witnessing the miraculous draught, but it seems the pilchards have left this coast.... Whilst we were admiring from the rock the sea-view and singular appearance of the place, Trevanion said to a man near him he wished to get a pilchard or two for my dinner. The next morning at breakfast the enclosed note was sent – a tolerable sample of Cornish spirit, and hitherto it has appeared everywhere the same.

'John Dabb to J. Trevanion, Esq. Dr Sire, according to your request I have this morning bought a Quarter Hundred of fine pilchards for that worthy gentleman Sir Francis Burdett. Had our seaners [i.e. seiners] been on shore yesterday afteroon they would have given Sir Francis a hearty congratulation.'

Mevagissey has always been rather a radical place.

Eight years after this visit Trevanion, a widower of fifty, married Burdett's second daughter Susanna. Two little daughters of this marriage died in one week, at Burdett's house in St James's Place.

In 1840 Trevanion died at Brussels. Why was he there? Was he taking refuge abroad from creditors, in the usual manner? Or absconding from the confusion he had brought upon the family's affairs, having pulled up and destroyed their roots in Cornwall?

Susanna went on living for many years, and died at her father's country house at Ramsbury in Wiltshire, where there is a Cornish granite monument to her in the churchyard – put up by her sister, the famous Baroness Burdett-Coutts, and her step-grandson, Hugh Charles Trevanion.

The most judicious thing Sir Francis Burdett ever did was to marry the daughter of Thomas Coutts, the rich banker. But Coutts left his vast fortune to the actress he had married, like

an old fool; after his demise she was snapped up by an impec-
unious duke of St Albans, to whom she left £10,000 a year.
Most of the rest she left to Susanna's youngest sister, Angela,
an enormous fortune which this angelic lady spent a long life-
time dispensing in good works, and well earned the title which
the approving Queen Victoria conferred upon her: the Baroness Burdett-Coutts.

The Trevanions staggered unsteadily along under the load
Nash and their extravagance had brought down upon them.
It was said that he tried out an experimental composite material
for a roof to the castle! A large retaining wall needed to be built
to keep the building from slipping down the slope; it gave way,
and had to be rebuilt – like the retaining wall to Balzac's property, which several times gave way and engulfed his money.
A cutting was made through the cliff to give a further prospect
of the sea from the house. It must be owned that the castle,
recognizably Nash, with its juxtaposition of square with round
towers, its round library and double staircase, its terraces and
turrets, is extremely beautiful: all that Regency romance (and
extravagance) could wish. But it could not be finished: it merely
ruined the Trevanions.

The Cornish tradition is that, as a last hope, the Baroness
Burdett-Coutts drove down to see what could be done, and the
young Trevanion set his dog on to bite her footman. The carriage drove away, the Baroness in high dudgeon. With her went
their last hope: the place had to be sold.

And so all the ties were broken which had bound so many Trevanions through the ages to so many places, with the endearing
names, in all that area along Roseland and Fal which they had
dominated. Various farms had been hived off in course of time
to cadet branches and been lost – Tregarthen and Trevoster.
Lands must have been sold, or pledged, to raise Sophia's considerable inheritance out of the estate – perhaps Restronguet,
which they had held since Bosworth. The other gain from that
happy time, Newham on the river near Truro, was sold by
J.T.P.B. Trevanion. In 1803 he sold an annuity of £100 per
annum. In 1808 we learn of a mortgage to Edward Coode of
St Austell of lands near Tregony bridge, Grogoth and Crego
in Cornelly parish, and other properties in Veryan, St Erme

and St Teath on the north coast. In 1824 he raised £15,000
by mortgaging the manor of Caerhays, with lands in seven
parishes, no doubt to meet the sums the castle was costing. Then
the unfinished castle itself was put up for sale, but the first
attempt to sell proved abortive because of the complicated
mortgages upon it. The castle and its demesnes were valued
at only £5,400 – the mortgages must have been heavy; an outside architect, called in, valued it at £10,000. By 1853 charges
on a mortgage of 1843 amounted to £16,620. As with Newstead, the Trevanions were under the necessity to sell, and they
sold everything.

I have a copy of the sale catalogue; to an historian it makes
sad reading. Here are all the places he knows so well, some of
which have recurred in this story.

Lot 1 : the Castle (at present out of repair) is a magnificent structure
built in the florid Gothic style, with spacious apartments, decorated
hall and library, grand diverging staircase, painted windows, groined
ceilings and other embellishments. The parterres and terraced walks
are enclosed within an embattled wall, with turrets and handsome
gateways. The foreground slopes beautifully into a wooded glen,
through which are various undulating paths and drives traversing
pleasure-grounds, deer parks and woodland scenery, now skirting an
expansive sheet of ornamental water [it claimed its victim later], fed
by rivers and streamlets, winding through a most picturesque and
romantic valley, and now leading the way under stately trees and
thicket groves, till abruptly terminated on the summit of a beetling
cliff, whence a splendid prospect is obtained of the English Channel
and different bold promontories.

Never did auctioneer's promotion speak truer. The place was
bought by Michael Williams of Scorrier, of that remarkable
family which was making millions out of mining, while the Trevanions were losing thousands out of incapacity. The castle was
still unfinished; it fell to this fortunate family to complete it
and create in that southward-looking valley the wonderful
gardens which are among the glories of Cornwall.

There follow the lands in those parishes of St Michael Caerhays, Gorran and Veryan, which had for so long upheld the
family: Rescassoe, Trevarrack, Pennare, and Lamledor; fish-
cellars at Gorran Haven, cottages and gardens at Port Holland;
tenements in Veryan, Cuby, Cornelly and Probus parishes.

ery came to the Grenvilles and thence to the Fortescues, making the fortune of the Cornish branch: for the land is solid china
clay. Still more was this the case with the Trevanion half of
Treverbyn – the manor of Treverbyn Trevanion – in the richest
part of the eastern clay district of St Austell. That estate was
bought by a London firm of Gill and Ivimey, and the family
lived off the royalties from it for a century, some of them still
doing so.

As the Trevanions could have done. What fools they were!
Solid china clay – like the Byrons getting rid of Rochdale; solid
coal!

EPILOGUE

Decline and Fall

WE CONCLUDE our story with Namier's theme: when historic families lose their lands they break up and decay, decline and fall. In the case of the Byrons, the descent of the peerage kept a certain continuity going; the Trevanions were lost.

Byron's successor, the seventh lord, had a son and heir, another George Anson Byron. He was briefly a captain of foot, then he married a clergyman's daughter, and died at her home, Thrumpton Hall, Nottinghamshire – not so far from Newstead – in 1870, aged only forty-eight. His father's will had been proved but two years before, at under £30,000; his son's, the eighth lord's, was to be less than £800. His nephew and heir, the ninth lord, became a bankrupt in 1899. His brother, the tenth lord, the Revd. Frederick Ernest Charles, was a clergyman, which must have helped: he held family livings at Langford in Essex, and at Thrumpton, and he married into the peerage, a daughter of Lord Charles Fitzroy. He was succeeded, as eleventh lord, by a farmer and grazier in Western Australia, who, however, kept up the family tradition by serving in the Australian navy in the last war. The family continues.

The Trevanion story is sadder and stranger.

It would seem that J.T.P.B. Trevanion fled from his difficulties, and absconded to Brussels, where he died in 1840. His goods and chattels there, estimated at £100, were granted to a creditor.* This was before the settlement consequent upon the ultimate sale of the estates. His son and heir, John Charles

* Prob/6/217.

Trevanion, had been born at Caerhays in 1804, and may be said to have reinforced his Cornishry by marrying Charlotte Trelawny Brereton, in 1827. Their son, Hugh Charles Trevanion, born in 1829, married a kinswoman of the present queen mother, Lady Frances Bowes-Lyon, sister of the thirteenth earl of Strathmore, raised to the rank of an earl's daughter, for what that was worth, by royal warrant. They had a son, Hugh Arundell Trevanion, who married Florence Eva, the daughter of Sir Daniel Cooper.

I have his father's will, that of Hugh Charles: it makes pathetic reading in its hopeless, nostalgic feeling for Caerhays.* He left bequests to his sister and her family, the Grant Daltons; £100 to his godson, Geoffrey Bowes-Lyon; £200 to his solicitor, Thomas Gill; and £100 to Henry Rockingham Gill, then the lucky lord of the manor of Treverbyn. To the church of St Michael Caerhays he left £10 per annum, for 'keeping in good repair, order and condition for ever, the aisle in the parish church known as the Trevanion aisle; with £5 for the "poor" out of my pure personal estate'. To his wife he left household goods and furniture; stables, carriages and horses; all jewellery, watches, wearing apparel, and two country cottages in Hertfordshire, near the Bowes-Lyon property.

He left in trust £500 a year for his son, Hugh Arundell, after *his* wife's death to go to the sons in tail male, with remainder to the daughters. If these failed, remainder was to go to 'the person in lawful possession of the title of Baron Byron of Rochdale'. All plate, pictures, statues, bronzes, prints, books, manuscripts and musical instruments were to go first to his wife, then to pass as heirlooms. What moneys remained in residue were to go to the purchase of land, 'and it is my wish that my trustees should in exercising this power purchase lands in Cornwall which formerly formed part of Trevanion Estate'. Alas! A final provision was that anyone who became entitled in succession in tail male, 'who shall not then use and bear the surname and arms of Trevanion shall within one year after he is twenty-one take the name of Trevanion or lose his legacy'.

There was evidently already trouble between his son, Hugh Arundell, and his wife, Florence Eva, for they were living apart. This is clear from contingent provisions for their children,

* Will 929, 5 July 1901.

which gave rise to further trouble. The father, Hugh Charles, had lived mostly in London, latterly at 3 Lowndes Square, where he died in 1901.

The son, Hugh Arundell Trevanion, dates his will, in 1917, from The Nook, Buckhurst Road, Bexhill-on-Sea: a descent, surely.* He left £150 each to his two friends, executors; and 'my plate with the crest to my son Cecil Trevanion, together with my gold watch, subject to the use thereof during her life-time by my housekeeper, Hilda Ware'. She is described as 'an old friend of my late wife', and he left her the residue of his property. If there were not enough money to pay for his funeral, a legacy to a servant was to lapse. Evidently not much was left.

There had been three sons of the marriage, we learn from a case brought by the eldest to clarify the position left by his grandfather's will. The chancery judge decided that, after the death of the Bowes-Lyon grandmother, this eldest grandson became the legal holder in tail male and was entitled to posses-sion. This was Hugh Eric Trevanion, born in 1884; he had two brothers, Charles Cecil and Arundell Claude. It is touching to see how these people, divested of their ancient estate, try to keep its memory alive at Caerhays and to revive the family names, Hugh, Charles and Arundell.

Hugh Eric, the heir, died in mysterious circumstances at Hove, on 11 September 1912, aged twenty-eight, and was buried in Norwood cemetery.

The Cornish story about him is borne out by the facts that transpired. It is that in this year he paid a last visit to the home of his ancestors during five centuries. The owner of the castle at the time was John Charles Williams, whom I remember: a benevolent autocrat, who ruled the county for many years as lord lieutenant, a somewhat gnarled and taciturn man who modelled himself upon the duke of Wellington. He must have been surprised to receive a call from the heir of the Trevanions, coming home, so to speak, after the lapse of sixty years. Still more so – himself the model of masculine propriety – when out there stepped from the motor-car filled with the flowers that bloom in the spring, tra-la, a tall, somewhat etiolated youngish man, with high heels and dyed hair.

He was a recognizable victim of mother-complex; he

* Will 1124, 18 June 1918.

detested his mother, with whom he was at cross-purposes, not only over his grandfather's somewhat pompous and complicated will. Nor did his father appear to be enamoured of her; she does not seem to have been a lovable character, and Eric sought love elsewhere.

He found it in a sailor friend, who enjoyed the sainted Victorian names, Albert Edward —; a petty officer on the *Oratava*, plying to Australia. Eric made his acquaintance in 1906, when travelling with his brother Cecil to Ceylon. The officer lent a sympathetic ear to Eric's troubles – sleeplessness, poor health, quarrels with mother; the ship's doctor prescribed drugs for his sleeplessness. Eric kept up a regular correspondence with his new-found friend; and in December 1907 went out, with his youngest brother, to Port Said in the *Asturias* in which his friend was now second officer. There Eric was very ill.

Four years later Eric asked him to come and look after him permanently, for £200 a year, and on a subsequent journey to Egypt offered to settle £10,000 on him. The trip had cost £1,400, while he had given his brother £500 – he had no idea that he was living beyond his means, and had the endemic Trevanion incapacity to live within them. In May 1912 he decided to settle at Hove, with his marine friend for companion; when the latter suggested twin-beds, Eric preferred a large one, since he was nervous sleeping alone. His brother Cecil was married and had a child, to whom Eric as godfather had given £50. He told the gallant Albert Edward, 'You are better off than I am. You had a mother, I had not.' He assured his doctor that he would certainly leave nothing to the family – he was willing to leave it all to the sailor. Not even the pictures? These were family portraits being framed; Eric said – the historian finds this unforgivable – 'I would rather burn them.'

A chauffeur had been engaged in April, to drive Eric down to the West Country – this would have been the occasion when he turned up at Caerhays. On his return to Hove he transferred £7,000 worth of securities to his companion, who banked another £2,600 worth himself: the butler and housekeeper assured his mother that his will left his friend everything. A nurse in the house affirmed that Eric's doctor would take him over for £1,000 a year. She was very hostile to the companion, who never paid her any attention; anyway, in August he told

Eric that he was getting married. (Albert Edward was thirty-five.)

On 11 September Eric died of an overdose of veronal. He had been a drug-addict for a good many years, and was under the doctor's care. He had apparently taken something like three times the average fatal dose. The companion had done all he could and summoned the doctor, who had not seen fit to apply a stomach-pump and empty the stomach. Nor did he think any further proceedings necessary, after the inquest.

This was not good enough for Mrs Trevanion, who agitated for a second inquest, which created enormous interest in the innocent days of 1912, when such events were not of everyday occurrence. At this, everything came out: the young man, 5 ft 11½ inches tall, 'certain signs on the body suggestive of unnatural vice'. He wore a gold wedding-ring on the left hand, upon his arms two bangles, one gold, one brass. M. Auguste Malfaison manicured his nails, and curled, waved and dyed his hair – he objected to a lady doing it. (Those were not the days when it was possible for a man to change his sex, and transform himself from a James to a Jan. Why not Jeanne?) But he also was equipped with vanity-bag, powder-puff, etc. He often wore a silk gown, white satin shoes, and high heels. M. Malfaison, of the delightful name, thought it very wrong of him, as a Roman Catholic, to take veronal.

This was another point in his quarrel with his mother: she was a 'black Prot.', who detested Roman Catholics. So he became a Roman Catholic – she said, only to vex her. He had left home six years before, then addicted only to morphia: putting up with him at home was too great a strain. She had last seen him in July at Harley House, York Gate, when he drove up, leaving his companion in the car. The friend had told her that everything was insured in *his* name, as also were the Trevanion jewels, of which Eric had a good many. 'Why?' she had asked. 'To kick you out if there is any trouble.'

She had done her best to make trouble, locking herself in her son's bedroom after his death, going through his things, all the boxes of drugs. She had taken away a box of cachets. The companion put it to her: 'Does Mrs. Trevanion accuse me of murdering her son?'

The doctor evidently thought not. Eric had taken a half-

bottle of hock to his bedroom on the night of the enormous dose:
this would not have dissolved one-third of the quantity, some
150 grains. In July the boy had taken an overdose of morphine
and suffered a collapse. They all called him 'the boy'; the butler
considered him 'eccentric and nervous, but most *cute*'. The servants agreed that the two companions were on excellent terms,
always went in the car together, never alone, and Eric never
went on foot. This corroborated that the friend's influence was
good in controlling Eric's drinking; he spoke sharply to him
when he drank too much.

The companion had arranged a dignified funeral, thinking
it proper to ask Miss Cooper, of the mother's family, and the
Bishop of London (then Winnington-Ingram). By his own will,
he was proposing to leave £8,400 back to the Trevanion estate,
the rest to Eric's mother. (Did this ever take effect?)

The coroner summed up innocently as to 'the almost insane
infatuation of the boy for his companion', and sagely discerned
a motive for suicide in the intention to marry. An open verdict
was returned.

But the family, the portraits, the jewels, letters and papers
– what has become of them? We learn only that brother Cecil
married and had children; that the Trevanions continue in the
female lines, through Bettesworths and Byrons.

Index